CHRISTMAS
TRADITIONS, LEGENDS, RECIPES FROM AROUND THE WORLD

Making New Traditions
and Renewing the Old

ROBIN REDMON DREYER

authorHOUSE®

AuthorHouse™
1663 Liberty Drive
Bloomington, IN 47403
www.authorhouse.com
Phone: 1 (800) 839-8640

Published by AuthorHouse 08/04/2016

ISBN: 978-1-5246-2121-6 (sc)
ISBN: 978-1-5246-2120-9 (e)

Library of Congress Control Number: 2016912284

Print information available on the last page.

Any people depicted in stock imagery provided by Thinkstock are models, and such images are being used for illustrative purposes only. Certain stock imagery © Thinkstock.

This book is printed on acid-free paper.

INTRODUCTION

Setting family traditions for the holidays are very important to me. I like and want to make each year, just as special as the last, and give my family cherished memories as well as a heritage of where they had originated.

As you will soon see, I have such a love for every aspect of Christmas, that I just didn't know where to stop. The information out there is just endless.

When I talk about Christmas and its celebrations, you will notice, Christmas has never been one day but all month long.

This is always a sentimental time for me from the times as far back as my memory can take me, all the way past the present and into the future. I put up four Christmas trees and I start in January trying to think what I could do to make even greater memories for my family, and I would be lying if I told you it wasn't for me as well. I want to feel this joy all year long.

It's not the giving and getting of gifts (but I have joy with giving) that makes this holiday so memorable, but the coming together with friends and family and sharing the joy of Christ's birth.

I love to see the spirit that takes place in the hearts of man at this time of year and long for it to go all through the year with, love, joy, peace, and charity.

OPENING

The celebration of Christmas is a world wide holiday! However each country creates its own traditions, and celebrates the birth of Christ in its own unique ways. This makes for endlessly creative and diverse manifestations of this one holiday. Here are just a few of the 195 nations traditions, as well as legends, holiday recipes, songs, poems, history and a part of your own heritage.

I would like to encourage you to set traditions for your family as well as your home. Making traditions is making memories. If you have done something more than one year in a row, you are building a tradition.

CHAPTER

Medieval Customs

In England ---- so the story goes ---- Christmas was first observed as a holiday in A.D. 521, During the Middle Ages, Christmas was England's most popular holiday with everyone, from king to beggar, taking part. All who could do so quit work and give themselves entirely to pleasure.

In ancient times, the Northern people worshiped the sun as the giver of life and light. Their festivals in its honor took place near the shortest day of the year when the sun seemed to stand still for twelve days before it began its upward climb, which resulted in spring and the coming of new life to the world.

Fire, Light and Evergreens

Before Christianity was practiced, it was believed that the Northen Europian people would celebrate the winter solstice with fire, light and a lot of joyful celebrating to relieve from the dark cold days and to await their time for spring. The burning of fire was also believed to ward off evil spirits.

Christmas of that time was founded on the birth of Christ, but to gain the exceptance from the pagan followers, traditions from the Christian belief was joined with the pagan belief and therefore the Christians were able to convert.

The tree was an important symbol to every Pagan culture. Evergreens, in ancient Rome were thought to have special powers and were used for decoration, symbolized the promised return of life in the spring and came to symbolize eternal life for Christians. The Vikings hung fur and ash trees with war trophies for good luck.

Ancient tradition: Decoration the home with evergreens. Since pagan times evergreens have been valued for their ability to retain signs of life in the middle of winter, even sometimes producing flowers and berries.

The Druids believed Holly would bring good luck and fertility, also protection from witchcraft. Holly, Ivy and Mistletoe was important to them as well. They also believed that good spirits lived in the holly and Christians thought that the berries were white then turned red from the blood of Jesus.

During this time the yule log was ceremoniously brought into the home on Christmas Eve, and put into the fireplace of the main common room. After decorating with greenery and ribbon, it was lit with the saved end of the previous year chard log, and then burned continuously for the twelve days of Christmas, providing much needed light and warmth.

Advent was observed in Rome during the 6th century. Pope Gregory I (590-604 A.D.) developed most of the Roman Advent Liturgy and shortened the period of observance from 6 to 4 weeks. Sometime after 1000 A.D. Rome excepted the practice of fasting during Advent, which in those times meant, observing amusements such as, travel for recreation, and marital relations, as well as certain foods; no weddings during this period.

The ever-present threat of hunger was the triumphantly overcome with the feast, and into addition to the significant fare such as mincemeat pasties, and wassail and all manner of food would be served at Christmas. The most popular of the main course would be goose, but many other meats would be serve.

In the spacious manor halls, great fires blazed on wide hearths, lighting the walls, high ceilings, and decoration of holiday greenery.

Our custom of caroling most likely came from Medieval England when a chorus of singers, called 'waits', held licenses to sing, day or night, to function sort of as the municipal voice at any and all functions, from the visits of dignitaries to weddings. The were especially busy during Christmastime, at feasts or caroling, telling the story of the nativity in song.

MEDIEVAL CHRISTMAS CAROL
"Holy and the Ivy"

The Holy and the Ivy,
Now they are full well grown
Of all the trees that are in the wood,
The Holly bears the crown.
The Holly bears a blossom,
As white as the Lily flower
And Mary bore sweet Jesus Christ
To be our Sweet Savior.

Recipe: TRADITIONAL MINCE MEAT
'1798'

Other customs developed as part of Christian belief. For example, Mince Pies (so called because they contain shredded or minced meat) were baked in oblong casings to represent Jesus crib, and it was important to add three spices (cinnamon, cloves and nutmeg) for the three gifts given to the Christchild by the Magi. The pies were not very large, and it was thought to be lucky to eat one mince pie each of the twelve days of Christmas (ending with the epiphany, the 6th day of January)

1 1/2 pound beef roast

3/4 teaspoon salt

1 1/2 pound apples, peeled, cored, chopped (3 cups)

8 tablespoons beef suit chopped into small pieces

1 cup apple cider or brandy

1/2 tablespoon mace

1/2 tablespoon cinnamon

1 teaspoon ground cloves

1 teaspoon ground nutmeg

1/2 cup raisins

1/2 cup currents

3 tablespoons chopped candied citron pieces (optional)

Roast or boil meat until just done. Remove meat from the broth and chop into tiny thin pieces. strain meat, then add salt to meat mixing. In a large bowl combine apples, suit, cider, spices and fruit. Mix together well. Then add the beef and cider, raisins and currents, mixing all ingredients well (If you add brandy, let this set in the fridge for about

4 to 6 days to let flavors marry. I like to use half cider and half brandy)
Now you are ready to make your traditional pies.

TRADITIONAL DOUGH

2 cups flour
1 teaspoon salt
2/3 cups lard or animal fat
6 to 8 tablespoon cold water

Put the flour into a medium bowl, add salt and with your hand blend salt into flour. Make a well in the middle of the flour and crumble the fat into the flour. with your hands squeeze fat into the flour until flour resembles pea sized crumbles. Add water gradually and work it into the flour mixture to make a smooth sticky dough. Turn out onto a floured board, and sprinkle flour over top of dough, then start rolling dough out to thickness you desire but not to thin the filling falls through. cut a 6 inch round and put a nice size tablespoon full in center of circle, then fold in half. Dip your finger in water and run it around half of the edge of dough so to help it seal, now crimp the ends.

Place on a greased baking sheet. Bake at 350 degrees until golden brown.

Recipe: WARM SPICED WASSAIL
      Traditional

Wassel comes from the old English words 'waes hael' which means "be well," "be hale," or "good health." A strong, hot drink (usually made of ale, honey, and spices) would be put in a large bowl, and the host would lift it and greet his companions with "waes hael," to which they would reply "drinc hael," which meant drink and be well.

3 - 12 ounce bottles Ale (Anderson Valley Brewing Company's winter Solstice Ale

1 - bottle red wine	(Madeira is more traditional
10 whole cloves	10 whole allspice berries

1 cinnamon stick	thin slice fresh ginger
1/2 teaspoon freshly grated nutmeg	
2 or 3 apples	1/2 cup brown sugar
1/2 cup water	

Chop enough apples to cover bottom of an 8 x 8 baking dish. Sprinkle with brown sugar, pour the half cup water over top of apples. Place in preheated oven at 350 degrees, for about 45 minutes. You want the apples nicely roasted, so they release their juices and create those amazing caramel apple flavors. Don't skip this step-- It adds such amazing flavors and complexity to the finished wassail.

While the apples are roasting, pour ale in a large saucepan on the stove. Add, cloves, cinnamon, ginger, and nutmeg. Add bottle of red wine. Heating over very low flame, when the apples are completely roasted, pour complete contents into ale mixture. Keep wine warm in crock pot or on top of stove.

Recipe of the time: GROGG

10 whole cloves	1 orange cut into fourths
7 cardamon pods, crushed	2 bottles dry red wine
2 sticks cinnamon	1 3/4 cups brandy
1 piece ginger root,	1 3/4 cups vodka
about 1/2 inch.	1/3 cup sugar
2 cups water	
10 whole blanched almonds, cut lengthwise into halves	
1 3/4 cups raisins	
1 cup pitted large prunes	

Tie cloves, cardamon, cinnamon, and ginger root in a cheese cloth bag. Heat spice bag, water, almonds, raisins, prunes and orange quarters in a large heavy kettle; bring to a boil, reduce heat, cover and simmer for 45 minutes. Remove spice bag, orange, and prunes (set aside to eat). Stir in remaining ingredients, cover and heat, until mixture begins to boil. Ladle almond halves and a few raisins into each cup, before filling with hot grogg.

CHAPTER

Germany / Austrian

For the German families, Christmas celebrations and preperations would start December 1st., they would set aside special evenings for baking, making gifts and also making decorations. Gingerbread was a traditional baking event as a family, more so when maling Gingerbread houses.

Children would write letters to leave on the window sill for Santa Claus, which they called Christkind. Sometimes they would decorate thes letters with sprinkled sugar that had been glued on, to give it sparkle.

(Christbaumgeback) is a white dough that can be shaped and baked for tree ornaments.

December 4th is the 'Feast of Saint Barbara', the patron saint of mines. Workers in the gold mines at 'Rouris' celebrate the day with 'Barbara Bread'.

A special gingerbread roll. At night they leave out food for the 'little people'. All over Austria, Barbara branches are cut from pear or cheery trees, brought onto houses and placed into water on December 4th. The indoor warmth creates an artificial spring and the branches come to life.

December 5th, Saint Nickolas Eve - 'Krampus Day' is known as an evil spirit or minor devil almost always clad in frightening fur. Families gather in the square to throw snowballs to chase off this menacing figure.

On December 6th is (Nikolaustag), St. Claus Day. A shoe or boot is left outside the door on December 5th. with hopes the following morning you find presents if you were good -or- unfortunately a rod if you had been bad.

Some homes had more than one tree. It was favored to have a room reserved with a locked door. Before Christmas Eve a tree was brought in and decorated for the children, then on Christmas morning the children were awakened and the door was opened, and the glorious wonder of the spirit of Christmas was spread among the family.

German Christmas Tree - Tannanbaum

Evergreen trees became associated with Christmas on a cold December night when a 16th century German Monk was awed by the sparkling snow covered branches of a small fur tree. He was so taken by the beauty of what he had seen, that when He returned he tied candles to the Christmas tree to show his family, thus the tradition of the Christ Baum or Christ tree was born. Soon this idea spread from Germany and the tradition to decorate evergreens with candles as well as ornaments grew.

Germans are the master decorators. Although trees were used in worship during bible times, before Christ by pagans. It was also recorded as early as 1510 a tree was felled in Latavia, for for a holiday decoration.

Northern Germany, Moravian's made a large four sided pyramid of green brush wood, which dates back to 1722 when refuge was offered to them by a wealthy Lutheran Nobleman. In celebration of that Christmas, the wood frames were built two to three feet tall, set on a table, entwined with evergreens and covered with eatables. Later paper was added to pass on the story of Christmas. Each Child received a verse written in red, green, or black on specially cutout paper. Gilded fruit and nuts also adorned the Moravian pyramid.

Germany's religious reformer Martin Luther (1483-1546) is often credited with starting the Christmas tree custom the first appearance of the tree was recorded in Germany many years after Luther died. It was in 1605 in Strousbourg, in Alsace, then in Germany. It was chronicled ("At Christmas they set up Christmas trees in their rooms.....") but it is possible the custom dates back to 1550. By the 19th century this custom spread across most of Germany and the German Royal brought the Christmas tree to England. The Dutches or Orleans, from Mecklenburg brought it to Paris. Emigrants from Germany and the Dutch brought the customs to America.

They lit the tree with candles with special candle holders that were clipped to the branches of the tree, and were made from medal. These candles represented light. The evergreen tree represented eternal life.

In North Germany the house wives will polish up a seven branch candlestick called the 'Star of Seven'. she carefully puts this treasured ornament (which may be a heirloom) passed down from many generations, on a table or over the fireplace. The family will gather around it on Christmas Eve and light the candles, then just before the clock strikes twelve midnight, they and their neighbors will proudly carry the blazing stars along the snowy paths, over icy fields, through woods blanketed with frost and Ice to their church. As the stars of seven flicker brightly, the parents with their sons and daughters, dressed in their very best clothing, kneeling, praying, then singing traditional hymns, welcoming the Christchild once again into their lives.

Boys would dress up as kings and carry a star dangling from a string, walking around the village singing carols.

They also lay out advent wreaths of holly with four red candles in the center. They light one candle each Sunday, and the last on Christmas Eve. Children would count down the days until Christmas by using a daily advent calendar, they would open one window each day, and found a Christmas picture inside.

1847 was the first fruit and nut ornaments made of glass in Germany. The Christmas pickle ornament was not made in Germany and started many decades later in America. No known information was found on it except in the U.S.

Traditional recipes:

LEBKUCHEN
German Honey Bars

2 3/4 cups all purpose flour	1/2 cup honey
2 teaspoons ground cinnamon	1/2 cup dark molasses
1 teaspoon baking powder	3/4 cup brown sugar
1/2 teaspoon baking soda	3 tablespoons butter, melted
1/2 teaspoon salt	1 large egg
1/2 teaspoon ground cardamon	1/2 cup chopped toasted almonds
1/2 teaspoon ground ginger	glaze (recipe follows)

Preheat oven to 350 degrees. Grease a 15 x 10 jelly roll pan; set aside.

Place flour, cinnamon, baking powder, soda, salt, cardamon and ginger in a medium bowl; stir to combine.

Combine honey and molasses in a medium sauce pan, bring to boil over medium heat, remove from heat; cool 10 minutes, stir in brown sugar, butter and eggs.

Place brown sugar mixture into a large bowl; gradually add flour mixture, beat at low speed until dough forms. With a spoon, stir in almonds, (dough will be slightly sticky). Spread evenly into a prepared pan. Bake 20 to 22 minutes or until golden brown. Remove pan to a wire rack; cool completely.

Prepare glaze:

1 1/4 cups powder sugar
1 teaspoon grated lemon peel
3 tablespoons fresh lemon juice

Stir together until smooth. Spread over cooled bar cookie. Let stand until set, about 30 minutes. Cut into 2 x 1 inch bars. Store in a dry air tight container, at room temperature. Will freeze up to 3 months.

Makes 6 dozen bars

AUSTRIAN CREAM COOKIES

2 eggs
1 cup sugar
1 cup whipping cream
3 3/4 cups flour
3 teaspoon baking powder
1 teaspoon salt
creamy icing

Beat eggs until light, add sugar gradually; blend in cream.

Mix flour, baking powder and salt into separate bowl. Gradually stir together and chill one hour. Heat oven to 375 degrees. Roll dough out 1/4 inch to 3/8 inch thick on floured board. Cut in 2 inch squares. With knife make two 1/2 inch indention on each side of each square. Place on lightly greased baking sheet. Bake 10 to 13 minutes, cool, and frost irregularly with colored icing.

Makes 4 dozen cookies

DARK PFEFFERNUSSE

(Traditional German Molasses Christmas Cookies)

1/2 cup shortening	3 1/2 cups flour
3/4 cup brown sugar (packed)	1/2 teaspoon baking soda
1 egg	1/4 teaspoon salt
1/2 cup molasses	1/2 teaspoon cloves
mixture of 3 drops anise oil,	1/2 teaspoon cinnamon
and 1 tablespoon	

Heat oven to 350 degrees. Mix shortening, sugar, egg, molasses and anise mixture. Measure flour and the rest of the dry ingredients together. Then add gradually to molasses mixture. Mixing together with hands, kneed dough until right consistency for molding. If dough seems to soft, refrigerate until firm. Mold the balls 3/4 inch diameter, place on greased baking sheet. Bake about 12 minutes or until golden brown on bottom. Cookies harden on standing.

Store in air tight container with a slice of apple to mellow them.

Makes 8 dozen cookies

LIGHT PFEFFEERNUSSE

Traditional German Christmas cookie

3 eggs	1 teaspoon cinnamon
1 cup sugar	1/8 teaspoon cloves
3 cups flour	1/4 cup almonds, blanched and ground
1/4 teaspoon baking powder	1/2 cup chopped candied lemon or
1/4 teaspoon salt orange peel,	(4 ounce package)
1/8 teaspoon white pepper	

Heat oven to 350 degrees.

Beat eggs and sugar until frothy. Measure flour, baking powder, salt, white pepper, cinnamon, and cloves into a medium bowl. Gradually add to egg mixture.

Add almonds and peel, mix thoroughly with hands. Roll dough 1/4 inch thick on lightly floured board, cut into 1 inch rounds. Place on lightly greased baking sheet. Cover with towel or place in a cupboard; leave overnight to dry. For a softer cookie do not dry, bake immediately after cutting.

Bake 20 minutes or until golden brown.

Makes 12 dozen 1 inch rounds

You can make these 2 to 3 weeks before Christmas, then mellow with a slice of apple.

NURNBURGER

German City of Toys

1 cup honey	1 teaspoon cinnamon
3/4 cup brown sugar, packed	1/4 teaspoon cloves
1 egg	1/2 teaspoon allspice
1 tablespoon lemon juice	1/2 teaspoon nutmeg
1 teaspoon lemon rind grated	1/3 cup chopped citron
2 3/4 cups flour	1/3 cup chopped nuts
1/2 teaspoon soda	icing glaze

Bake at 350 degrees

Bring honey to boil in heavy sauce pan. Cool thoroughly. Stir in sugar, egg, lemon juice and rind. In a separate bowl combine flour, soda, cinnamon, cloves, allspice, nutmeg, gently mix well. Gradually add to sugar mixture, mixing well. Add citron and nuts. Chill dough overnight.

Roll out chilled dough 1/4 inch thick on a lightly floured board. Cut 2 inch rounds. Place on greased baking sheet. With fingers round up cookies a bit to warm the center. Press in a blanched almond halves like peddles of a daisy, then place a piece of citron in the center. Bake 10 to 12 minutes or until just set. Immediately brush with glaze. Remove from baking sheet, cool and store until mellow.

Makes 6 dozen cookies

LOVE LETTER COOKIES

An Old German Cookie

2 cups all purpose flour	2 teaspoons finely grated lemon rind
1/2 cup sugar	finely grated rind of 1 orange
1 teaspoon salt	1/2 cup sour cream
1 cup butter,	room temperature

Heat oven to 350 degrees.

Measure Flour into sifter, sifting into a large bowl. Blend flour, sugar and salt. Cut in softened butter and rinds until mixture resembles coarse meal. Blend sour cream in evenly. Gather dough into firm ball. Divide in half. Roll on well floured pastry board to 1/8th inch thickness. Cut into 2 x 3 inch pieces.

Fold ends to center, overlapping slightly; seal with a tiny piece of candied cherry, place on ungreased baking sheet. Brush top with water and sprinkle with sugar. Bake 6 to 8 minutes.

Makes 4 dozen cookies

GERMAN SPICE COOKIE

3/4 cup sugar	1 teaspoon cinnamon
3/4 cup honey	1/8 teaspoon allspice

2 eggs	1 cup chopped almonds
3 1/2 cups all purpose flour	3/4 cup chopped candied orange peel
1 teaspoon baking powder	Egg White Icing

Heat oven to 400 degrees.

Mix sugar, honey and eggs thoroughly. Blend flour, baking powder, cinnamon, allspice, into a large bowl, gently mixing. Stir into sugar mixture. Mix in almonds and orange peel. Roll dough 1/4 inch thick on lightly floured board; cut into fancy shapes. Place on lightly greased baking sheet, leaving 1/2 inch between cookies, bake 10 to 12 minutes. While cookies are still hot brush with icing. store cookies in covered container for 1 week to mellow.

Makes 4 dozen cookies

EGG WHITE ICING

1 cup confectioners sugar
2 egg whites
1 teaspoon lemon juice

Start beating egg whites, when frothy start adding sugar gradually, then add the lemon juice halfway between sugar, then whip for 5 minutes.

SPRINGERLE COOKIES

Springerlers are among Germany's most famous Christmas cookie. These Anise flavored pictures, are made by imprinting rolled out dough with a special rolling pin or wooden mold, Because of the shaping technique, the cookies are made one day and baked the next.

2 eggs
1 cup sugar
2 1/2 cups flour
anise seed

Heat oven to 325 degrees.

Beat eggs and sugar together thoroughly. Stir in flour until dough is well blended and very stiff. Refrigerate the dough for 3 to 4 hours. Roll out dough to 1/8th inch thick on lightly floured board. Press well floured Springerle board or rolling pin down firmly on dough to emboss the design. Cut out the little squares; let dry on lightly floured board sprinkled with anise seed for at least 10 hours at room temperature. Bake for 12 to 15 minutes

Makes about 8 dozens

LEBKUCHEN

Traditional Christmas cookie,
from the Black Forest Region of Germany

This is another type of gingerbread cookie, is often given to Children on St. Nickolas Day, December 6th, the day for gift giving in many European countries.

In Germany, as in many European countries, Children celebrate Saint Nickolas Day, December 6th, by putting their shoes outside for S. Nickolas to fill.

Bakeries and home kitchens are full of sweets such as these honey cookies.

Lebkuchen are traditionally rolled out cookies but the shaping has been simplifies.

1/2 cup honey	1 teaspoon cinnamon
1/2 cup molasses	1 teaspoon cloves
3/4 cup brown sugar, packed	1 teaspoon allspice
1 egg	1 teaspoon nutmeg
1 tablespoon lemon juice	1/3 cup citron, cut up
1 teaspoon grated lemon rind	1/3 cup chopped nuts
2 3/4 cups all purpose flour	
1/2 teaspoon soda	

Bake at 400 degrees.

Mix honey and molasses; bring to a boil. cool thoroughly. Stir in sugar and egg, lemon juice and rind. Stir together the dry ingredients, blend into sugar mixture. Mix in citron and nuts. Chill overnight.

Roll small amounts of dough at a time, keeping the rest of dough chilled. Roll out dough 1/4 inch thick on a lightly floured board; cut into rectangles 2 1/2 x 1 1/2, and place 1 inch apart on a greased cookie sheet, bake 10 to 12 minutes or until no impression is left when touched gently in the center of cookie.

Brush icing over cookies immediately. Quickly remove from baking sheet cool and store in air tight container with a cut orange or slice of apple to mellow.

Makes 6 dozen cookies

GERMAN CHRISTMAS STOLLEN

Every year in Germany, the local bakeries produce the most magnificent bread. This Weihnachtsstollen (Christmas Bread) dates back to 1500's in Germany when it was first made with oil because during the Advent season they were not permitted to eat butter. This oil based dough was hard and tough. and not as good as when made with butter.

Today the most popular and historic Stollen comes from Dresden and is baked and sold at the Dresden Christmas Market, this tradition has been going on since the 1500's, and draws thousands of people to the market at Advent.

Traditional Stollen is baked in a long bell shaped pan or is baked free form in an oval-shaped loaf.

Nearly every German home serves a version of stollen at Christmastime.

3 cups raisins	1 cup granulated sugar
1 cup heaping candied oranges	2 teaspoons salt
3/4 cup white rum	4 large eggs, lightly beaten
9 cups all-purpose flour, divided	1 teaspoon almond extract

4 packages active dry yeast

1 grated and dried peel of an orange

2 cups milk

1 grated and dried peel of a lemon

1 cup unsalted butter

TOPPING

1/2 cup unsalted butter, melted

2 to 3 cups granulated sugar

1 cup confectioners sugar

In a large bowl combine raisins, candied orange and rum. Soak overnight.

Grate the orange and lemon, place the grated peel on a baking sheet and dry at 255 degree oven for 5 minutes; set aside until ready to use.

In the bowl of your stand mixer, mix together 3 cups of flour and yeast.

In a medium sauce pan, heat milk, butter, sugar and salt; the butter must be melted and the mixture warm. Remove from heat and let cool 5 minutes. Once this is cooled yet still warm, add this to the flour and yeast mixture. Mix on low speed using your paddle beaters until well combined.

Scrape sides of the bowl, add the beaten eggs, almond extract, and grated peels and mix on medium speed for 30 seconds.

scrape sides of bowl again, and mix on high again for 3 minutes.

By hand stir in the raisins and orange soaked in rum.

Now using dough hook to your mixer, add 5 cups flour and turn mixer on medium speed for 3 to 4 minutes. Pat dough into a large ball.

Oil a large bowl, place dough ball into the bowl and flip the dough over to cover well with oil. Cover bowl with plastic wrap and set in a warm, moist place for 90 minutes or double in size.

When dough has risen, punch down with fist.

Remove the dough from bowl and divide into 8 equal pieces.

Cover with a towel and let rise 10 minutes.

Shape each piece into an oval shape loaf, then place on parchment lined baking sheet.

Once all the dough is on the baking sheet, cover with cloth and let rise for 25 minutes, or doubled in size.

Preheat oven to 350 degrees.

Bake dough 30 minutes on top rack of oven. Turn dough around 180 degree angle and bake 5 more minutes to brown evenly. Check the bottoms of the loaves so they don't burn.

Remove done loaves form oven and cool completely on a wire rack.

After completely cooled, place 2 to 3 cups of granulated sugar in an oblong dish.

Brush 1/2 cup melted butter over the 8 loaves.

Now place each loaf into dish of granulated sugar and scoop over loaf to be sure it is coated well.

Dust a generous amount of confectioners sugar over the tops of each loaf.

Wrap with plastic wrap or place in plastic bag.

(The Stollen will stay fresh 2 to 3 days, but after that it will become dry).

CHAPTER

Switzerland or Swiss - German

Switzerland is made up of four cultural traditions:
Swiss-German - Tree
French - Tree
Italian - No Tree
Romanian - Tree

Many holiday traditions here, reflect those countries.

Gifts may be given on Christmas Eve or New Years Day, and they are brought by Christ Kindl or Saint Nicholas or even Father Christmas with his Wife Lucy.

Both the manger and the Christmas tree hold sway.

Carols drift on the air in four languages.

Switzerland has maintained its careful neutrality by absorbing the best of all nations.

In the tinkling of a silver bell, heralds the arrival of Christ Kindl - a white clad angel with a face veil held in place by a jeweled crown. The tree candles are lit as she enters each house and hands out presents, from the basket held by her Child helper.

The week before Christmas, the Children dress up and visit each home bearing a gift for each home. Bell ringing has become a tradition and each village competes with the next, when calling people to midnight mass. After the service, families join together to share huge doughnuts called (Ringli) and hot chocolate.

The (Chlausjagen) Festival or Feast of Saint Nicholas is celebrated at dusk on December 6th, with a procession of (lifeltrager) Illuminated lanterns in the shape of a bishops mitre on their heads.

The Swiss wait for the Christchild called Christ Kindl, to arrive with gifts for all in his reindeer - drawn sleigh.

RIPPLI

Loin Ribs / Smoked Pork Loin

1 tablespoon Butter

.22 pound bacon

2 onions, chopped

.66 pounds cabbage, cut into strips

1 garlic, pressed

.44 pound celery, cut into pieces

.55 pounds carrots, cut into slices

4 tomatoes, peeled and cut into slices

1.10 pound potatoes, cut into slices

pepper

1/2 teaspoon dried -or-1 teaspoon

fresh thyme

1.76 pounds smoked loin ribs from pork

3.4 ounces white wine

1/4 teaspoon soup powder (instant soup)

Heat butter in frying pan.

Add bacon, onion, garlic and caramelize.

Add cabbage, celery, carrots, and potatoes, cover and steam until vegetables are tender.

Season with pepper and thyme.

Place ribs in with vegetables.

Add white wine and soup mix, cook on low heat for about 1 hour.

Add tomatoes and cook 10 more minutes.

Feeds 4

BRUNSLI

Swiss Brownie Christmas Treat

5 ounces granulated sugar	2 tablespoons powdered cocoa
1 pinch salt	2 tablespoons flour
9 ounces ground almond	2 fresh egg whites
1/4 teaspoon ground cinnamon	3.5 ounces bitter baking chocolate
1 pinch ground cloves	2 teaspoons Kirsch brandy

Mix sugar, salt, almond, cinnamon, cloves, cocoa and flour in a bowl.

Add egg whites, stir until ingredients are evenly distributed.

Cut bitter chocolate into really small pieces, pour hot water over the bitter chocolate, let rest about 5 minutes.

Then pour off all the water but about 1/2 tablespoon.

Stir until smooth, and immediately add melted chocolate and Kirsch brandy.

Knead to a soft dough.

Roll out dough on a flat, floured surface of confectioners sugar. Roll out to about 1/4 inch thick.

Cut out different shapes and place on parchment lined baking sheet.

Let rest for about 5 to 6 hours or overnight in a dry place.

Preheat oven to 480 degrees.

Bake for about 4 to 6 minutes, in center of oven.

Let cool completely before serving.

Makes 50 cookies

ZIMTSTERNE

Cinnamon Cookies

3 fresh egg whites	1/2 tablespoon cinnamon
1 pinch salt	1/2 tablespoon lemon juice
9 ounces confectioners sugar	12 ounces ground almonds

Beat egg whites and salt in a bowl, with electric beater and whip until egg whites are stiff.

Add confectioners sugar a little at a time until well blended. Put 0.4 cups aside for frosting.

Add cinnamon, lemon juice and almonds, and mix into a soft dough.

Roll out dough on flat surface lightly covered with confectioners sugar.

Roll out about 1/4 inch thick.

Cut out stars or other shapes and place them on parchment lined baking sheet.

Let them rest for 5 to 6 hours, or overnight in a dry place.

Carefully brush cookie with reserved frosting.

Bake for about 3 to 5 minutes at 480 degrees on middle rack of your oven.

Let cool completely before serving.

DREIKONIGSKUCHEN

Epiphanies Cake - Breakfast

The tradition to this cake/bread is that each person takes a piece of cake. The person that has the token bean in it, will be king or queen for the day. All others have to fulfill a wish for the King/Queen of that day. This would be a lot of fun.

26.5 ounce white flour

1 ounce yeast

2.6 ounce plus 2 tablespoons sugar   5 tablespoons warm water

1/2 teaspoon salt

2 eggs

Zest of one lemon

7 ounces raisins

3.5 to 5 ounce butter

1 token dried bean

1.25 to 1.5 cups milk

Mix flour, sugar, salt and zest in a bowl.

Melt butter and add cold milk.

Dissolve yeast in water and add 2 teaspoons sugar.

Stir in eggs and flour mixture.

Knead to a soft dough.

Add raisins and the token, and knead evenly through the dough.

Tear dough apart into 6 to 8 pieces. (remember you will be forming this into a wreath shaped bread).

You will want one fist size to go in the center, with wreath pieces around it.

Arrange the smaller pieces around the center piece.

Place cake on a well buttered form. Let rise in a warm place until doubled in size.

Before baking, brush top of dough with beaten yoke of 1 egg.

Preheat oven at 440 degrees, and bake for 40 to 50 minutes.

Let completely cool.

Make a paper crown to set on top of the bread

RINGLI

Christmas Doughnuts

1 package active dry yeast
1/4 cup warm water (105 to 115 degree)

2 eggs

1 cup whipping cream

1 teaspoon vanilla

1/3 cup sugar

3 1/2 cup flour

3 teaspoon baking powder

1 teaspoon salt

1/4 teaspoon ground cinnamon

1/4 teaspoon ground nutmeg

vegetable oil

Dissolve yeast in warm water in a large bowl. Beat eggs, whipping cream, vanilla, and sugar until light and fluffy, stir in yeast, then the remaining ingredients (except oil), until dough is soft and easy to handle.

Heat oil, (2 to 3 inches) in a deep-fat fryer or heavy saucepan to 375 degrees.

Roll dough 1/3 inch thick, on a well floured surface. Cut with a floured doughnut cutter, or cookie cutters of a tree, bell or stars. Slide dough into hot oil with a wide spatula, fry until golden brown, about 2 minutes on each side. Remove from oil. Drain on paper towel.

Serve plain, sugared, or frosted. Makes 2 dozen

CHAPTER

Christmas trees (Yolka), were banned by the communist regime and were replaced by 'New Years' trees. Yolka comes from the word, which refers to fur trees.

Peter the Great, after he visited Europe during the 1700's introduced the custom of decorating Christmas trees. Legend is, the 11th century Prince Vladimir, traveled to Constantinople to be baptized, and returned with stories of miracles preformed by Saint Nicholas of Myra. Since then the feast of Saint Nicholas (December 6th) was observed.

Most Christian Russians belong to the Eastern Orthodox Church, and it is customary to fast until after the first Church service on January 6th, Christmas Eve. The church in Russia still uses the Julian calendar, therefore their Christmas celebration is 13 days behind the Georgian calendar that Western churches use.

On Christmas Eve a traditional meal called: "THE HOLY SUPPER" is served. Dinner begins when the first evening star appears in the sky. The family gathers around the table to honor the Christ Child. A white table cloth is symbolic of Christ's swaddling cloths covers the table. Hay is brought forth as a reminder of the cave where Jesus was born. A tall white candle is placed in the center of the table, symbolic of Jesus being "The Light of the World". A large white loaf of Lenten bread (Pagach), symbolic of Christ, the bread of life, is placed next to the candle.

The legend of Grandfather Frost (D'yed Morez), the Russian equivalent of Santa Clause, arose in the major cities. It is still said that Grandfather Frost lives deep in the woods of southern Russia and came to town in a sleigh. Grandfather Frost had a reputation for bringing gifts to good children and forgetting those who were naughty. He could be both jolly and cold hearted. During the Christmas season, he would roam the streets, hanging out toys to well behaved children, and overlook those who behaved badly.

Grandfather Frost dresses in red robes, trimmed in white fur, his beard is snow white and bushy and long. Sometimes his outfit made him look more like a wizard than a Santa Claus known in Europe, that put gifts under the Christmas Tree did. However he did not come down the chimney (houses in Russian cities had no fireplace). He did make house calls. Some children open their gifts Christmas Eve, but others were told that Grandfather Frost wouldn't come until they were fast asleep, and they would find their gifts under the tree Christmas morning.

Advent was a time of fasting, so on Christmas Eve they would celebrate with a twelve course meal, each course was in honor of each Apostle. Each meal began with the Lords Prayer, said by the head of the house. Gifts were usually opened after the dinner.

On Christmas Day the Family would attend Church services

Some of the things they may have in their multi-course meal would be: New potatoes with parsley and butter, kidney beans with shredded potatoes, garlic and pepper salt, fresh fruit and nuts, fresh figs, apricots, oranges and dates eaten throughout the meal. Holiday traditions: Russian Christmas foods, champagne, Bellini and caviar. It's a Christmas celebration in grand style at the turn of the century.

PAGAHC

Lenten Bread

Usually served at meatless meals as for Lent and/or Advent and beautiful Christmas Eve supper, known as velija. It is a flat bread with a potato or cabbage filling and makes an excellent vegetarian entree'.

* Dough:

1 cup water plus 1/4 cup lukewarm water
4 1/2 teaspoons plus 1 1/2 teaspoons sugar
1 teaspoon salt

2 1/2 tablespoons canola oil (or butter if not fasting)
1 package active dry yeast
3 cups all purpose flour

* Potato Filling:

2 cups diced potato, cooked and mashed
salt to taste
1/2 cup grated cheddar cheese, (if not fasting)

* Cabbage Filling:

1/2 pound cabbage, cored and chopped
salt to taste
1-2 teaspoons canola oil (or butter if not fasting)

In a medium saucepan, bring 1 cup water, 4 1/2 teaspoon sugar, and oil to a boil. Remove from heat and cool to lukewarm. dissolve yeast and 1 1/2 teaspoons sugar in 1/4 cup lukewarm water and set aside.

Place flour in a bowl of a stand mixer or regular bowl and add sugar wate mixture. Mix until well incorporated.

Knead dough until smooth, about 7 minutes, by machine and at least 10 minutes by hand. Transfer to a greased bowl. Cover and let rise until double.

Punch down dough, and turn out on a floured surface and divide into two portions. cover with greased plastic and let rest for 15 minutes.

On a parchment - lined baking sheet, roll one portion of dough into a 9 x 13 rectangle or a 12 inch circle. Spread eather potato filling or cabbage filling onto dough to within about 1/2 inch of the edge.

Roll the second portion of dough on a lightly floured surface, place dough on top of filling topped dough, and seal edges together. Prick top with fork to let steam escape. cover with greased plastic wrap, for about 30 minutes. Heat oven to 375 degrees, bake about 30 minutes, or until golden brown on top and bottom. Cool on wire rack.

* Potato Filling:

Season mashed potatoes with salt. If it is not a day of fasting add cheese to hot mashed potatoes and mix well. Allow potatoes to cool before placing on dough.

* Cabbage Filling:

Saute' cabbage in oil or butter and season to taste. Allow to cool before placing on dough. Then you just follow the dough placing instructions.

KUTYA

1 pound wheat berries	1 cup raisins (optional)
1 pound walnuts in the shell	1/2 cup poppy seeds
2 cups granulated sugar	1/2 cup dried apricots (chopped)
1 vanilla bean, grated	confectioners sugar
peel of one lemon grated	

Shell the walnuts. soak the wheat overnight, cover with water, about 1 inch above the grain. Put the pot of wheat on the stove to boil for 2 to 3 hours on a very low simmer, there should be enough water to keep the wheat from burning.

Be sure to keep the heat on low and watch very carefully. Add water if necessary. Pour off water. Rinse with cold water. Pour off all liquid.

Pour wheat berries out on a lint less towel and dry for 2 hours. Place the wheat berries in a food processor and grind them. Remove the berries to a bowl and then grind the walnuts in the food processor. Mix the ground walnuts with the ground wheat. Add 2 cups granulated sugar, lemon peel, vanilla bean and the optional ingredients. Mound in a dish and sprinkle with confectioners sugar.

Serves 6

Recipe: HONEY CAKES with CREAM CHEESE FILLING and CHERRY COMPOTE

3 1/2 cups rye flower

2 1/2 teaspoons baking powder

1/3 cup sugar

pinch salt

1/2 teaspoon ground cloves

1/2 teaspoon ground cinnamon

1/4 teaspoon cardamon

1 1/2 cups vegetable oil

8 eggs

1/2 cup warm water

3/4 cup plus 2 tablespoons honey

powdered sugar for dusting

SYRUP

3/4 cup dark rum

3/4 cup simple syrup (equal amounts sugar and water, simmer until sugar dissolves

1/2 cup orange juice

1/4 cup fresh lemon juice

1 teaspoon vanilla

CREAM CHEESE FILLING

1 pound cream cheese

1/2 cup butter

1 teaspoon honey

1 cup plus 2 tablespoons sugar

1 orange zest

CHERRY COMPOTE

1 pound dried cherries

1 cinnamon stick

1 tablespoon sugar

water to cover

Preheat oven to 300 degrees.

Sift together flour and baking powder in a medium bowl. In another bowl combine sugar, salt, cloves, cinnamon, and cardamon in a mixing bowl. In a separate bowl whisk oil, egg, and water together, then add to sugar mixture.

Add Honey then gradually stir in sifted flour, soda mixture, then mix on high speed of mixer for 5 minutes. Spray 12 mini bunt pans with non-stick spray. Pour batter into molds, bake for 16 minutes. Test with a toothpick for doneness. Remove cakes from molds. while warm....

Brush with syrup, and allow to cool

For syrup, combine all ingredients in a sauce pan, and bring to a boil. Remove from heat and set aside.

To make Cream Cheese Filling you will ad all ingredients together and blend with mixer until nice and fluffy. (be sure all is room temperature)

Plating: Put filling into a pastry bag, and pipe 3 teaspoons of filling into center of each cake.

Spoon Cherries and some syrup around the cake, then sprinkle with confectioners sugar.

To make the Cherry Compote you will want to combine cherries, sugar and cinnamon in saucepan with enough water to cover. Heat to near boil. Remove from heat and stir. Cherries should be coated with the syrup liquid. Drain to set aside.

SIBERIAN PELMENI

1 pound veal neck, cut into cubes	4 ounces white Pullman loaf--
1 pound beef shoulder, cut into cubes	(crust removed, and soaked in)
1 large onion, sliced and caramelized	1 cup heavy cream
1/2 cup chopped dill	1 egg
salt and freshly ground pepper	
	80 won-ton wrappers

In a large bowl, combine meat cubes, onions, dill, soaked bread, anion, egg, salt and pepper and let it set 2 hours in refrigerator, so flavors can marry.

Then

Grind mixture through a meat grinder two times using a medium die. Mixture should be finely pureed and sticky. Cut rounds out of the won-ton wrappers.

Fill each wrapper with a half a teaspoon of this mixture. Fold over and make tortellini shape. Pull sides inward. Place in saucepan of boiling water and boil 3 minutes. Serve in deep dish plate.

3 cups thinly sliced mushrooms	3 tablespoons fresh dill, chopped
3 tablespoons cooked or pickled beets diced	
18 mint leaves coursly chopped	3 quarts beef or chicken consomme'/bouillon, hot

Divide mushrooms slices, diced beats, mint leaves, and dill in between 8 dishes. Add 10 Pelmeni and pour consomme' over each.

LENTEN PIROGI

2 pounds potatoes, cooked and drained	salt and pepper
(save water from cooked potatoes)	2 cups flour (sifted)
2 onions, chopped	1/2 teaspoon salt
1 stick butter	1/4 cup potato water

FILLING

Cook potatoes in simmering water until soft. Put cooked potatoes through a ricer. Saute' onion in butter to caramelize, add half the onions to the riced potatoes and season with salt and pepper.

For the PIROGI, sift flour and salt into a bowl. Add vegetable oil and enough water to make a soft dough, and mix until the dough no longer sticks to the hands. Cover dough and let rest for 5 minutes. Roll out dough on a floured surface, to 1/4 inch thickness. Cut dough into small squares, and place a dollop of potato mixture in the center of each square. Fold dough over to form a triangle and pinch edges to seal. Place in boiling water and boil for 10 minutes.

When they are all cooked and drained, serve with remaining sauteed onions over the top.

BOBALKI

2 cups flour, sifted
1/2 teaspoon salt
1/4 cup water or broth
vegetable oil

Sift flour and salt into a bowl. Add some vegetable oil and broth to make a soft dough, and mix until dough is no longer sticking to the hands. cover dough with plastic wrap and let rest about 5 minutes.

Roll out dough into 3 inch long pieces. Place them into boiling water and boil for 10 minutes.

You can eat them any way you like......

MUSHROOM SOUP

2 cups dried mushrooms 1 teaspoon salt
8 cups cold water 2 tablespoons chopped onion
1 clove of garlic 1 tablespoon butter

Break dried mushrooms into small pieces and rinse thoroughly with cold water and remove dirt granules. Cover mushrooms with 8 cups of water, add salt and garlic. Cover and simmer for 2 hours or more until mushrooms are tender. Add more salt to taste. When soup is done, saute' onion in butter and when onions are tender add to soup, (they can be a little scorched for a different taste).

Simmer just a little bit more.

Traditionally served Christmas Eve at Holy Supper.

STURGEON KULEBIAKA

2 pounds of clean sturgeon fillet, cut into 6 portions (5 1/4 ounce each)
salt and freshly ground pepper
3 hard-boiled eggs, peeled sliced 1/4 inch thick
1/2 cup white cabbage, thinly sliced and blanched
1/2 cup cooked Basmati rice
2/3 cup cream mushrooms Duxelle (recipe follows)
1/2 cup loosely packed, picked fines herbs
6 pieces puffed pastry 6 x 4 inches 1 per portion
egg wash for pastry

Preheat oven to 350 degrees

Season fish portion with salt and pepper. Place half an egg slice in the middle of a 2 x 4 inch piece of puff pastry then blanched cabbage. Top with Basmati, rice, mix with mushroom Duxelle, fines herbs and last, the fish. Make sure each layer is even.

Moisten the edges of the puff pastry with a bit of egg wash, and bake for 15 minutes.

1 bunch asparagus, peeled, blanched and cut on the bias, 1 1/2 inches long
1 clove garlic mashed
salt and freshly ground pepper
1/4 cup minced chervil
1 1/2 ounce golden Osetra caviar

Heat asparagus in butter, with mashed garlic clove. Season lightly with satl and pepper, and add chervil. Place the asparagus in the middle of the plate without the butter. Cut the fish portion in half, and place on top of asparagus, so that the cut side shows. Remove the garlic clove from the reserved butter and add into the caviar. Mix the caviar carefully and spoon evenly to sauce each plate.

CREAMED MUSHROOM DUXELLE :

1/8 pound butter

1 onion, minced

1 1/4 pound mushrooms minced

1/4 kilo frozen Porcine pieces,

(they come in kilo bags) thawed

1/4 cup vermouth

1/2 cup sour cream

1/2 cup Bechamel sauce

1/4 cup minced chives

pinch nutmeg

1/2 teaspoon ground fennel seed

salt and freshly ground black pepper

Melt butter in saucepan, add minced onions and saute' until translucent, add mushrooms and porcine and cook until liquid has evaporated. Add vermouth and slowly simmer until evaporated. Add sour cream, bechamel, chives and spices.

BUERRE FONDUE

1 cup water 1/4 butter
1 shallot, thinly sliced squeezed lemon juice
pinch salt

Bring water to boil, with shallot and salt. Simmer until shallot is tender.

Whisk in butter and lemon juice.

CHOCOLATE NESSELRODE CAKE

2 cups flour

2 cups sugar

1 teaspoon baking soda

1 teaspoon salt

1/2 teaspoon baking powder

3/4 cup water

3/4 cup buttermilk

1/2 cup shortening

2 eggs

1 teaspoon vanilla

4 ounce melted unsweetened

chocolate, (cooled)

Nesselrode Filling

coco fluff

Nesselrode filling: 1 cup whipping cream, 1/4 cup confectioners sugar 2 tablespoons cocoa in a chilled bowl, beat until stiff.
Substitution for Nesselrode: 1/4 cup finely cut up candied fruit and 1 teaspoon rum flavoring.

Coco Fluff: (chocolate fluffy frosting)

Preheat oven to 350 degrees

Grease and flour three 8 inch round layer pans. Beat sugar, shortening, eggs vanilla, with electric mixer. When creamy add cooled chocolate, soda, salt, powder, and buttermilk. Continue beating. alternate adding flour and water until all is well blended. Scraping bowl with each addition. Pour evenly into prepared pans. Bake until a wooden pick inserted in center of cake comes out clean. Cool on wire racks. Fill layers and Ice top with Nesselrode filling.

Ice side of cake with coco fluff. Refrigerate.

RUSSIAN TEA MIX

3 cups sugar	1 teaspoon cloves
2 cups orange flavored instant breakfast drink	1 teaspoon cinnamon
1 cup instant tea	

In medium bowl, combine all ingredients, mixing well. Store in a tightly covered container.

*For each serving, place 2 rounded tablespoon fulls of mix into a cup; fill with 1 cup boiling water and stir well.

Makes 6 cups of mix

Makes 32, 1 cup servings

MORAVIAN GINGER COOKIES

Moravian ginger cookies are a crisp, spicy, paper-thin. The Moravian who founded Bethlehem, Pennsylvania USA, in 1741, brought this cookie recipe with them. It originated from the Pennsylvania Dutch.

1/3 cup molasses	1/2 teaspoon salt
1/4 cup shortening	1/4 teaspoon soda
2 tablespoons brown sugar	1/4 teaspoon baking powder
1 1/4 cups all purpose flour	
1/4 teaspoon each of-- cinnamon, ginger, cloves,	
dash each nutmeg, and allspice	

Mix molasses, shortening, and sugar thoroughly, measuring flour, baking powder, salt, soda and spices and stir together. With hands blend the flour mixture into the molasses mixture until well blended.

Cover; chill about 4 hours.(A thorough chilling is needed to hold dough together).

Heat oven to 350 degrees. Roll dough paper thin, a little at a time, cut into desired shapes; place on a ungreased cookie sheet, Bake 8 minutes, or until lightly brown.

If desired, when cool, frost with easy creamy icing.

Makes about 5 dozen

SCANDINAVIAN JULEKAGE

The Scandinavian's most popular coffee-cake.

1 package active dry yeast	2 tablespoons shortening
1 1/4 cup warm water (105 degrees)	1/2 cup raisins
3/4 cup Lukewarm milk (scalded, cooled)	1/3 cup cut-up citron

1/2 cup sugar	3 1/4 to 3 3/4 cups
1/2 teaspoon salt	all-purpose flour
1/2 teaspoon ground cardamon	egg yolk glaze
1 egg	

Dissolve yeast in warm water in a large bowl. Beat in milk, sugar, salt, cardamon, egg, shortening, raisins, citron, and 1 1/2 cups flour. Beat until smooth. Stir in enough remaining flour to make dough easy to handle.

Turn dough out onto a flour covered surface, knead dough until smooth and elastic, about 5 minutes. Place dough into an oiled bowl, turning dough to coat with the oil. Cover and let rise in a warm place until doubled in size, about 1 1/2 hours. Punch dough down; shape into a round loaf. Place dough in a greased round layer pan 9 x 1 1/2 inch round. Cover and let rise for about 45 minutes to double in size.

Preheat oven to 350 degrees, brush dough with egg yolk glaze. Bake until golden brown, about 30 to 40 minutes.

CHAPTER

France

In France, Christmas is called Noel. This comes from the French phrase 'Les Bonn's Mouvelles', which means the 'good news' and refers to the gospel. In Southern France, some people burn a yule log in their homes, from Christmas Eve until New Years Day. This comes from an ancient tradition in which farmers harvest. Along time ago part of the log was used to make the wedge for the plough as good luck for the coming harvest. Although the tradition of the yule log has faded, the French like to make the yule log shaped cake, called 'Buche de nol' which means 'Christmas Log'. The cake among other foods in great abundance is served at the grand feast of the season which is called 'Le Reveillon' which is a very late supper held after Midnight Mass, held on Christmas Eve. The menu of the meal veries.

In Alsace, goose is the main course. In Burgundy, it is turkey with chestnuts, and the Parisians feast upon Oysters and 'Pot De fole gras. LeRevellion' may consist of Poultry, ham, salads, cakes, fruits and wine.

The French families used to have a Three Kings Cake, with a bean hidden in it. Whom ever had the bean in their slice, was made king for the day, or queen for the day.

The children would go out looking for the kings taking hay for the camels.

Another name for this day is the 'Twelfth Day'. It is the last of the 12 days of Christmas, which use to be one long holiday. It was the last night of the feast of fools, before the 'Lord of Misrule' had to give up his crown and become themselves once again.

In the morning they also find that sweets, fruits, nuts and small toys.

The French also typically do not set up Christmas trees in their homes, instead focusing their attention on elaborate nativity scenes called crA-ches. These scenes often include little figures called santons or ('little Saints'), in addition to Joseph, the Virgin Mary, the Christchild, Magi and shepherds, the craftsman also produce figures in the form of local dignitaries and characters. The molds have been past down from generation to generation, since the 17th century.

In France it is a time for the whole family to come together at Christmas time to holiday and worship. On the eve of Christmas, beautifully lit churches and cathedrals, ring out Christmas carols with the bells.

Once dinner is over and the family retires to bed, they leave a fire burning and a food and drink on the table in case the Virgin Mary visits. On Christmas Eve, children leave their shoes of wooden clogs called 'sabots' at the hearth for the Christchild or Pere Noel to fill. In the North of France, children are given gifts on December 6th, which is Saint Nicholas Day. In the morning they also find sweets, fruits, nuts, and small toys.

FRENCH ROAST GOOSE

1 1/2 gallon cold water	salt and pepper to taste
1 cup kosher salt	1 apple peeled and quartered
1/2 cup brown sugar	1 onion peeled and quartered
2 bay leaves	1 orange quartered
1 teaspoon black peppercorn	

1 (10-12 pound) young goose, fully thawed or fresh

Add 1 1/2 gallon water to large stock pot, large enough to fit goose and brine mixture. Add salt, Brown sugar, bay leaf, and peppercorns to water in stock pot.

Stir until salt and brown sugar is dissolved. Unwrap goose and clean cavity well. Rinse and trim any excess fat on the neck and the tail end of the goose, and place into the brine so that it is completely submerged. Cover and refrigerate overnight, or up to 24 hours.

Remove the goose from the brine and pat dry inside and out, with paper towel. Sprinkle goose cavity generously with salt and pepper. Put the apple, onion, orange and lemon; into the goose cavity, and place the goose brest side up in a large roasting pan with rack to keep the goose at least 1 inch off the bottom.

With a small sharp knife or a sharp needle, prick the goose skin all over, especially where you can see or feel fat under the surface, be careful NOT to piece the flesh, only the skin and fat. This will allow the fat to drain during the cooking process and make for a crisper skin. Salt and pepper goose to taste and add 2 cups of water to bottom of the pan.

Roast at 350 degree for 2 1/4 to 3 hours, until it reaches an internal temperature of 170 degree. Remove from oven and cover with aluminum foil, let rest at least 25 minutes before carving.

ROAST TURKEY with CHESTNUT STUFFING

1 pound fresh chestnuts	1/2 cup fresh leaf parsley
1/2 cup (1 stick) butter	finely chopped
1 turkey gizzard	kosher salt
1 large onion, chopped	freshly ground pepper
4 celery stalk, chopped	1 large egg, lightly beaten
1 loaf day old white bread,	1/2 cup (1 stick) butter,
cut into cubes	room temperature
1 tablespoon fresh sage, finely	14 pound turkey, room temp.
chopped	
1 tablespoon fresh thyme leaves	fresh sage leaves
4 1/2 cups home-made turkey	3 tablespoons all-purpose
stock	
flour	

Preheat oven to 400 degrees. Using a small pairing knife, cut an X into the flat part of each chestnut. lay the chestnuts on a baking sheet, flat side up; pour 1/4 cup water over top of chestnuts and bake 20 minutes. Take the chestnuts out of the oven, and while hot, wrap them in a clean towel. Roll them around to crack their skins. Peel the chestnuts while warm, chop them.

Melt butter in large pan, then add the turkey liver, and saute' 2 to 3 minutes, until just cooked. Remove from pan and set aside.

Add the chopped onion and celery and saute' for 3 to 4 minutes until tender, add the bread cubes, sage and thyme and saute' for 5 to 7 minutes to lightly toast the bread.

Stir in 1/2 cup turkey stock, then the parsley. Season to taste with salt and pepper. Transfer to a large bowel, finely chop turkey gizzard, and add it to the stuffing, then add egg and toss to combine.

If you plan on cooking the stuffing separately, season the turkey cavity with kosher salt.

Blend 1 tablespoon kosher salt and 1 teaspoon freshly ground pepper into the softened butter. Using your fingers, carefully work the butter under the skin, and down the length of the turkey Brest, so its spread 3 to 4 sage leaves evenly spaced over turkey on brest both sides.

If your stuffing the bird, do so now. (don't stuff ahead of time). Truss the turkey or you can easily tie the drumsticks together, and set the turkey on the rack, in roasting pan. Season the outside of the bird with kosher salt and pepper. Roast for 1 hour, occasionally basting 2 more hours. (if your turkey is larger than 14 pounds, lower the temperature to 350 degrees.

If you are baking the stuffing separately, transfer the stuffing into a separate buttered baking dish and cover with foil. Bake 40 minutes at 375 degrees, then remove foil and bake 20 more minutes.

After 2 1/2 hours, begin checking the turkeys internal temperature with an instant read thermometer inserted into the turkeys thigh without hitting the bone. When it reaches 155 degrees take the turkey out of the oven. Transfer to carving board and let it rest 30 minutes. (the turkey will continue to cook and reach 165 degrees).

Pour the drippings into a large measuring cup. let the fat rise to the surface, skim fat keep 3 tablespoons and discard the rest. Return to the roasting pan and add fat, sprinkle flour over the fat and heat on stove over medium heat, stirring 2 minutes. Whisk in the turkey stock and drippings, bring to boil. Reduce the heat and boil until thick. Whisking continually.

Remove stuffing from turkey cavity, carve the turkey and serve.

OYSTER FRITTERS

Vegetable oil	2 teaspoons baking powder
2 eggs slightly beaten	1/2 teaspoon salt
1 cup milk	1 1/2 cups oysters,
2 cups (10 ounce) flour	drain and chopped

Heat about 1 to 2 inches of oil in deep heavy pan to about 365 degree.

Whisk the egg and milk together in a small bowl.

Combine the flour, baking powder, and salt in another bowl and blend well. Add the egg and milk mixture and blend with a spoon until smooth.

Stir the chopped oysters into the batter, drop by spoonfuls into hot fat.

A cookie scoop works well to keep them small and round.

Cook in batches, turning to brown both sides. Drain on paper towel.

Serves: 4 to 6

WILD BLACKBERRY WINE

4 pounds blackberries
2 1/4 pound granulated sugar
1/2 teaspoon pectic enzymes
1/2 teaspoon acid blend
1 camp-den tablet, crushed
7 pints water
1 package wine yeast and nutrient

Thoroughly wash the berries, place them in a nylon jelly bag. Crush them and strain the juice through the bag and into the primary fermented.

Be sure to press as much juice as possible, leaving the solids fairly dry. Tie the jelly bag tightly and insert it into the fermenter along with the sugar, pectic enzymes, acid blend, camp den and 7 pints of water. Stir until the sugar is dissolved, cover and and allow to rest for 24 hours.

Sprinkle the wine yeast and nutrient over it to sit, stirring once daily for 5 days. Strain the solids and rack into a dark 3 gallon secondary fermentor. Add additional water to make up the volume, and apply an air lock. Rack the wine in 3 weeks, and again in 2 months.

Bottle. For the best flavor, allow a year for the wine to mature before enjoying it.

Make 3 gallons

BUCHE DE NOEL

In France, after the midnight-Mass on Christmas Eve, families have an elegant supper and traditionally prepare Buche de Noel a beautiful log cake.

3 eggs	1/4 teaspoon salt
1 cup sugar	1 cup whipping cream
1/3 cup water	2 tablespoon sugar
1 teaspoon vanilla	1 1/2 teaspoons powdered
3/4 cup flour	instant coffee
1 teaspoon baking powder	cocoa frosting
	gumdrop holly

Heat oven to 375 degree, line jellyroll pan, 15 1/2 x 10 1/2 x 1 inch with aluminum foil or waxed paper, greased. Beat eggs in small mixer bowl on high speed until very thick and lemon colored, about 5 minutes. Pour eggs into large mixing bowl; gradually beat in 1 cup sugar. Beat in vanilla water and vanilla on low speed. Gradually add flour, baking powder and salt, beating just until batter is smooth. Pour into pan, spreading batter to corners. Bake until wooden pick inserted in center comes out clean. Loosen cake from edges from pan; invert on towel. generously sprinkled with powdered sugar, remove foil; trim stiff edges of cake if necessary. while hot, roll cake and towel from narrow end. cool on wire rack at least 30 minutes. Beat whipping cream, 2 tablespoon sugar, and the coffee, in chilled bowl until stiff. Unroll cake, remove towel, spread whip cream over cake, roll up and frost with cocoa frosting. decorate with gumdrop holly.

SOUFFLE' DE NOE'L

6 egg yolks	1 ounce gelatin
1/3 cup sugar	2 tablespoon cold water
juice of 3 lemons	1 cup heavy cream, whipped
grated rind of 2 lemons	until stiff
	with dash salt and dash ginger

Put egg yolks and sugar in sauce pan, on the lowest flame, beat with a whisk until light and creamy. Do not let mixture boil. Remove from the fire and stir in the lemon juice and rind, and allow the mixture to cool.

Soak the gelatin in the cold water for 5 minutes. Set over a very low flame and stir till dissolved. Strain it through a fine sieve into the cold egg yolk mixture. Fold in the whipped cream mixture. Pour into a crystal bowl and chill until set, Garnish with whipped cream, candied fruit and citron.

FRENCH HONEY-FILLED BISCUITS

Cookie

1 cup flour	2 egg yolks
1/4 cup sugar	1 cup finely chopped candied
1 teaspoon salt	fruits
1/3 cup butter	honey
	confectioners sugar

Measure flour into mixing bowl - make a well in center of the flour. put in sugar, butter, sat and egg yolks. work the ingredients in center into a smooth paste; work in flour until well blended, mix in fruits. Wrap in wax paper.

Chill 2 hours

Heat oven to 350 degrees.

Roll dough 1/8th inch thick on lightly floured surface; cut into 2 inch fluted rounds. Bake on ungreased baking sheet 8 to 10 minutes, or until, tinged with brown. cool. Put together sandwich fashion, with honey as filling; Sprinkle tops with confectioners sugar.

Makes 2 dozen double cookies

FRENCH GATEAU BON BON

2/3 cup soft butter	2 cups flour
1 cup sugar	1/2 teaspoon baking powder
1 egg	1/2 teaspoon salt
1 package cream cheese softened	1/8 teaspoon soda
1/2 teaspoon lemon juice	orange marmalade
1 teaspoon finely grated lemon rind	easy creamy icing

Mix the first 6 ingredients until light and fluffy. Blend dry ingredients, add to butter mixture. Mix well, then chill.

Heat oven to 350 degrees.

Using 1/4 dough at a time, (keeping remaining dough refrigerated until ready to roll out) roll 1/8 th inch thick on lightly floured surface. Cut 1 inch rounds.

Place half the rounds on parchment lined cookie sheet. Put 1/4 teaspoon marmalade in center of each round. (For larger bon bons cut each round 1 1/2 inches and add 1/2 teaspoon marmalade in center) Cover with remaining halves of rounds, seal edges with floured fingers.

Bake 8 to 10 minutes, until edges are slightly browned When cool, frost with tinted icing.

Makes 7 dozen 1 inch bon bons

PARISIAN ORANGE COOKIES

2 tablespoons grated orange rind	1 tablespoons sherry flavoring
1/2 cup water	1 1/4 cup flour
1/4 cup sugar	1 tablespoons baking powder
1/2 cup butter	1/2 teaspoon salt
1 cup sugar	

Heat oven to 375 degrees.

Blend orange rind to water and 1/4 cup sugar in a sauce pan. Boil gently over medium heat, 10 to 15 minutes, until mixture is a thin syrup consistency. Add enough water to make 1/4 cup syrup. Cream butter, 1 cup sugar, and flavoring until fluffy. Measure dry ingredients and stir syrup then dry ingredients into creamed mixture; mix thoroughly. Roll in 1 inch balls. Place 2 inches apart on lightly greased baking sheet. Flatten with bottom of greased glass dipped in sugar. Bake about 8 minutes.

Makes 4 1/2 dozen cookies

CHAPTER

Italy

The most important part of the Christmas celebration is the nativity and the telling of the Christmas story. It was believed in Italy '1223' Saint Francis made the story known. The families would attend midnight mass on Christmas Eve. The Nativity was found as far back as '1025'. Their tradition was to wait to pit the baby in the crib the evening of December 25th. Another loved traditions is to go caroling and playing music on traditional horn candlelight procession called 'The Parade of Light' are conducted and are followed by 'The Feast of Saint Lucia'.

In 1582 Italy had a great famine, and a miracle was performed by Saint Lucia, she brought a boats full of grain to the starving people.

The tradition of exchanging gifts veries from region to region, and could be done on Christmas Eve or Christmas Day.

Presents are left under the Christmas tree, by Santa Clause (called Bobbo Natale) or according to older tradition by baby Jesus himself. In some regions children receive gifts earlier on Saint Lucius Day or during Epiphany, on January 6th.

December 26th is Saint Stephen Day and is also a public Holiday in Italy. Great celebrating will go on through January 6th. which is the time all decorations are taken down.

On Christmas Eve no meat is eaten. Often a light seafood meal "The Feast of the Seven Fishes" is eaten and then people go to Midnight Mass service. After. After Mass, the usually celebrate with hot chocolate and a slice of Italian Christmas Cake. Common types of fish eaten were Baccala, (salted cod)

clams, calamari, Sardines, eel. Then follows the typical Italian Christmas sweets such as 'Pandora, Panettone, Torrone, Panforte, Struffoli, Caggionetti, Monte Bianco, or others depending on the regions cuisine.

Christmas on the 25th of Dec. is celebrated with a lunch that consist of a meat dish, cheese and local sweets.

STRUFFOLI

Honey Drenched Christmas Fritter

3 1/2 cups flour

6 eggs plus 1 egg yolk

1 lemon, zested and juiced plus

1 lemon, zested

1 orange, zested

1/2 teaspoon salt

1 tablespoon lime-cello

4 cups canola oil for

frying

2 cups honey

confectioners sugar for dusting

In a mixing bowl, place flour, eggs, yolk, zest of 1 lemon, orange zest, salt, and lime-cello, mix well to form a firm dough, 8 to 10 minutes. Place in refrigerator and allow to rest 30 minutes.

Remove from the refrigerator and cut golf ball size pieces of dough from the main batch. Roll each ball into a 1/2 inch thick dowel rope. Cut each dowel rope into 1/2 inch pieces. Roll each piece into a ball, and continue until finished with all dough.

In a 12 to 14 inch pa with at least 3 inch sides, heat the oil to 375 degrees. Drop enough balls in to cover about half the surface of frying oil, and fry until dark golden brown. They will puff up while cooking, with a slotted spoon roll often to brown evenly. As they finish, remove them to a paper towel to drain.

When all the Struffoli are finished cooking, heat the honey, lemon juice, and zest together in a wide 6 to 8 quart saucepan until quite warm, about 150 degrees and substantially thinner, add Struffoli to honey and stir gently to coat. Remove from heat and cool 5 minutes in the pan, stirring regularly.

Pour out into the form of a pyramid, or a ring mold. Sprinkle with confectioners sugar and serve.

Serves: 10

TORRONE

Italian Cookie

2 2/3 cups sugar

2/3 cup light corn syrup

1/2 cup water

2 egg whites, room temperature

2 teaspoons vanilla

1 teaspoon orange extract

1/2 cup diced candy fruit, plus additional for topping

1 cup sliced almonds

Combine sugar and corn syrup and water in a saucepan. Cook over medium heat until candy thermometer temperature reaches 269 degrees.

Meanwhile, with an electric mixer, beat egg whites to form stiff peeks. When sugar reaches 260 degrees, slowly pour into egg whites in a fine stream, while still using mixer whip together evenly. Add extracts and beat on medium speed for 13 minutes. Now fold in candied fruit into the mixture; mix for another 2 minutes, then fold in 1/2 cup almonds. Pour mixture into a 9 inch square baking dish, sprayed with nonstick baking spray, then dust with flour.

Top with remaining almonds and candied fruit. Let set overnight and then cut into serving pieces.

Makes 12 to 16 nougats

PANETTONE

Italian Christmas Bread

To prepare marinated fruit:

1/3 cup golden raisins

1/3 cup chopped dried apricots

1/3 cup dried chopped tart cherries

1/4 cup triple sec (orange flavor liqueur) or orange juice

Combine all ingredients in a small bowl, let set for 1 hour. Drain fruit in a sieve over a bowl. reserve fruit and 2 teaspoons of liqueur separately.

Dough

1 package dry yeast (about 2 1/4 teaspoons)	6 tablespoons melted butter
1/4 teaspoons granulated sugar	1/4 cup milk
1/4 cup warm water (100 to 110 degrees)	1/4 cup granulated sugar
3 3/4 cup all-purpose flour; divided	1/2 teaspoon salt
	1 large egg
	1 large egg yolk
	2 tablespoon pine nuts

To prepare dough, dissolve yeast and 1/4 teaspoon granulated sugar in warm water in a small bowl, let stand 5 minutes. Lightly spoon flour into a dry measuring cup, level with a knife. Combine 1/2 cup flour, butter, milk, salt, egg, and egg yolk, (1/2 cup flour through egg yolk) in a large bowl. Beat at medium speed with a mixer 1 minute or until smooth. Add yeast mixture and 1/2 cup flour. Beat 1 minute, and stir in marinated fruit, 2 1/2 cups flour, and pine nuts. turn dough out onto a lightly floured surface. Knead until smooth and elastic (about 8 minutes). Add enough remaining flour, 1 tablespoon at a time to prevent dough from sticking to hands.

Place dough in a large bowl coated with butter turning to coat top of dough.

Cover and let rise in a warm place (85 degrees) free from drafts, about 1 1/2 hours. Dough will not double in size. (press 2 fingers into dough, if indention remain, the dough has risen enough).

Punch dough down; let rise 5 minutes. Divide dough in half. Shape each half into a ball, let rise 1 hour.

Preheat oven to 375 degrees.

Uncover dough. Place coffee cans in bottom rack of oven, bake at 375 for 30 minutes. or until brown and loaf sounds hallow when tapped. Remove bread from cans, and cool on wire rack. Combine reserved 2 teaspoon of liqueur and one teaspoon butter, brush over loaves. Sprinkle evenly with Turbinado sugar.

PIZZELLE

An Italian Tradition

2 sticks (1 cup) butter 1 1/2 cups granulated sugar
6 large eggs 4 teaspoons baking powder
3 1/2 cups unbleached flour 2 teaspoons anise seed

Melt butter and let cool, add remaining ingredients and mix thoroughly. Heat pazzelle iron and brush lightly with oil. When iron is hot, drop a teaspoon full on each iron circle, just a tad off center. Remember when you close the lid it pushes the batter forward. (cookies take 10 to 15 seconds to cook) open the lid and let cool on a rack, or add a filling and roll up before cooling on rack.

Makes 50 cookies

PANDORA DI VERONA

Golden Cake

yeast mixture:
1/4 cup warm water
1 tablespoon active dry yeast
1 tablespoon sugar
1 egg yolk
1/2 cup all-purpose flour

In a small bowl, add all ingredients and blend well. Cover with a damp towel (lint free) let rise in a warm place. 2 hours or until doubled in bulk.

cake:

5 cups all-purpose flour	1/2 cup water
8 egg yolks, plus 1 egg	1 lemon zest
3/4 cup sugar	2 cup confectioners sugar
3 tablespoon unsalted butter, melted	1/2 cup water

On a clean work surface mound 3 of the remaining cups of flour and make a well in the center. In a bowl beat 4 egg yolks, 1/2 cup sugar, the butter and 1/2 cup water. Add the yeast combination from above and mix well. Pour the entire mixture into the flour well gradually, mix the flour mixture into the liquids to form a sticky dough. Knead the dough for 5 to 10 minutes or use the dough hook attachment on the electric mixer. The dough should remain some what tacky, unlike bread dough.

Grease or oil large bowl and add the dough turning to coat all sides. Cover with plastic wrap, and let rise in a warm place for 2 hours.

Punch down the dough and add remaining flour, egg yolks and 1/2 cups water, egg, sugar and lemon zest and knead until blended, then knead an additional 10 minutes, on a floured work surface. Place in a greased bowl and cover with plastic wrap then let rise for additional 2 hours.

Butter and flour 2 pandoro molds or 2 coffee cans. Punch dough down and divide into 2 parts, roll each piece into a ball. Place each ball in each mold, let rise for 1 1/2 hours.

Preheat oven to 375 degrees.

Bake for 35 minutes or until pick inserted in center comes out clean. Let rest 10 minutes and let rest 10 minutes, then unmold. Let cool completely.

In a small bowl combine confectioners sugar and water, stir well. (I like to add a drop of flavoring like vanilla, or almond, or butternut.) Drizzle Pandoro and serve in wedges.

Makes: 2 cakes, serves 14 to 16 people

BOLOGNESE

Pronounced: boh-luhn-yeyz. This is more than just a meat sauce. the traditional recipe has changed through the years but is still one of the most versatile sauce in the kitchen. It derives from the Northern Italian City of Bologna.

2 tablespoons butter

1 tablespoon olive oil

4 ounce pancetta, chopped

1 large onion, chopped (1 cup)

2 medium carrots, chopped (1 cup)

stems of 1 head fennel, chopped (1 cup)

2 pounds ground beef

1 pound ground pork

2 cups dry white or red wine

1 1/2 cups whole milk

1/8 teaspoon ground nutmeg

1 28 ounce can whole tomatoes undrained and cut up

1 Parmesan cheese rind (1 to 2 in.)

In a 4 quart Dutch oven heat butter and olive oil over medium-high heat. Add pancetta. Cook and stir until just starting to brown, about 8 minutes. Reduce heat to medium, add onion, cook and stir until translucent, about 5 minutes. Add carrots and fennel. Cook 2 minutes more.

Add beef and pork to dutch oven. Season with 1/2 teaspoon kosher salt and 1/2 teaspoon black pepper. Using a fork, break up meat, (you want to retain some larger pieces for texture). Cook until browned. Add wine. Using a wooden spoon, scrape up brown bits from the bottom of pan. Simmer, uncovered, until wine has evaporated.

Add milk and nutmeg to dutch oven. Simmer, uncovered, until milk has evaporated, stirring frequently. Add tomatoes, stir to combine. When tomatoes just start to bubble, reduce heat to low; add Parmesan rind. Simmer, uncovered 2 1/2 to 3 hours, stirring occasionally. As sauce cooks liquid will evaporate and the sauce will start to look dry. Add 1/2 cup water at a time (2 to 3 cups total), continuing to simmer until liquid evaporates.

Makes 12 servings

ANISE BISCOTTI

1 cup sugar

1/2 cup butter, softened

2 teaspoon anise seed ground

2 teaspoon lemon peel grated

2 eggs

3 1/2 cups all-purpose flour

1 teaspoon baking powder

1/2 teaspoon salt

Preheat oven to 350 degrees.

In a large bowl with electric mixer, beat sugar, butter, anise seed, lemon peel, and eggs.

In a separate bowl stir together, flour, baking powder and salt.

Gradually add flour mixture to the creamed mixture and this will form a type of dough.

On ungreased cookie sheet, divide dough in half and shape each half in a rectangle shaped loaf.

Bake 20 minutes or until pick inserted in center comes out clean.

Cool on baking sheet 15 minutes.

Cut crosswise into slices, turn them cut side down on baking sheet. Bake for 15 minutes more.

Remove from baking sheet to wire rack to let cool completely.

Serves 4

CHAPTER

Ireland

Ireland is in western Europe. Christmas is the largest celebration of the year. The celebration starts on December 8th with many families putting up their decorations and Christmas Trees. According to Christian tradition, the immaculate conception was on this date. Their traditions are mostly the same as the western countries. Not only do the celebrate Christmas for the relgous aspect but they give this time to prayer remembering those who died and decorate the graves with wreaths.

Their greeting is 'Merry Christmas to You' (Nodlaig Nait Cugat)

Christmas Day and Saint Stephen Day are both public holidays.

A candle is lit and set in the window to welcome Mary and Joseph

Traditionally, Santa Clause, (Daddy of Christmas) in Ireland is 'Father of Christmas' also is called Santy, or Santa, he brings presents to children, which are opened Christmas Morning. It is traditional to leave minced pies and a bottle of Guinness, along with a carrot for Rudolf. In recent years they have Americanized the tradition to milk and cookies.

On Christmas Eve fish is traditionally eaten. For Christmas Day their choices may be turkey, goose, ham or the traditional spiced beef. They truely enjoy their rich desserts, such as yule log cake, minced pies and not to be outdone, the Christmas Pudding.

Mincemeat

5 quarts apples chopped	1 quart brandy
3 quarts shredded beef	1 cup vinegar
3 quarts sugar	1 tablespoon black pepper
2 quarts raisins	1 tablespoon salt

1 quart suet or butter	2 tablespoons cinnamon
1 quart fruit juice or cider	2 teaspoons pumpkin pie spice
1 quart molasses juice of	3 lemons

Put everything into the stew-pot at once and cook until apples are done.

Best done with Jonathan apples. Can be processed in jars, a quart will make a nice pie.

IRISH CHRISTMAS BAKED HAM

No Christmas is ever complete without baked ham.

Baked stuffed hams are believed to have originated in the Catswold, centuries ago with ham stuffed with apricots based on a medieval dish from Oxfordshire. The American style, glaze crusted, is definitely preferable to the original British flour and water crust, as it adds sweetness and flavor to the ham.

6 pound piece of gammon boned and loosely rolled (gammon is raw cured bacon leg, cut, and only called ham when it is cooked).

1/2 pint red wine
2 bay leaves
1/2 pound fresh apricots or dried and soaked in cold water whole cloves
3 tablespoons demerara sugar

Put gammon into a large basin and add wine and bay leaves. Cover and leave to marinate for at least 6 hours, turning the gammon from time to time.

Heat oven to 350 degrees.

Wash and dry if using fresh apricots, cut them in two and remove stones. If using dried apricots, soak and pat dry and cut in two. Remove gammon from marinade and put to one side. Put the wine, bay leaves and apricots into saucepan and simmer until apricots are soft and have absorbed the wine, about 15 minutes. Remove bay leaves and let apricots cool slightly.

Dry gammon thoroughly. Stuff as many of the apricots into the opening of the gammon.

Wrap gammon with double layer of foil and make a slit in the top to let the steam escape. Place wrapped gammon in baking tin and roast in oven 2 hours.

Remove gammon from oven and raise temperature to 425 degrees. Unwrap foil and leave the gammon to cool slightly. Using a sharp knife, remove the skin on the gammon, leaving a layer of covering fat to more than 1/8 inch, lightly slash the fat diagonally 3/4 inch apart in both directions to form a diamond pattern and stud the center of each diamond with whole clove.

Spread sugar firmly over gammon uncovered into a roasting tin. Bake in hot oven for 15 minutes, or until the sugar has melted and turned a golden brown.

IRISH POTATO SOUP

Irish potato soup is a traditional favorite that never goes out of style. Enjoy its goodness anytime.

2 tablespoons butter	2 cups plus 3 tablespoons
1 small onion, chopped	water, divided
1 celery stalk, chopped	1 teaspoon Worcestershire
2 (10-1/2 ounce) can condensed	sauce
chicken broth	1/4 teaspoon dried thyme
6 potatoes, peeled and diced	1/4 teaspoon black pepper
	2 tablespoons cornstarch

In a stock pot, melt butter over medium heat, and saute' onion and celery 3 to 4 minute, or until tender.

Add potato, broth, 2 cups water, Worcestershire sauce thyme and pepper; mix well. Bring to a boil over medium high heat, then reduce heat to low and simmer 35 minutes.

In a small bowl combine 3 tablespoons water and corn starch, stir, then stir into soap and cook until thicken.

IRISH DUBLIN CODDLE

A Traditional Irish Dish,

This is a comfort food in the highest degree; a stew like dish made of salty bacon and pork sausage and potatoes.

2 tablespoons vegetable oil	2 carrots, peeled and finely
2 medium onion, thinly sliced	sliced
4 ounce piece salty back bacon	8 ounce white potatoes finely
weight after rind removed	sliced
6 fat traditional pork sausages	salt and pepper
	2 cups rich beef or chicken stock

Heat oven to 425 degrees.

In a large frying pan, heat the oil, add onions and cook over medium heat for about 4 minutes. Cut the bacon pieces into 1/2 inch cubes. Add onions and bacon and stir well, cut the sausages in half and add to bacon.

Raise heat, constantly stirring, cook until sausage starts to brown, taking care not to burn onions.

I heat proof casserole, place layer of onion, bacon and sausage mixture followed by the layer of sliced potato and sliced carrots. Season with salt and pepper. Then repeat.

Carefully pour over stock. Cover with a lid or double layered foil. Place in center of oven and cook for 45 minutes.

Take a peek to make sure coddle is not drying out, if necessary, (If needed top with a little bit of water, but don't flood the stew).

Lower the heat to 350 degrees, and cook for 30 minutes more, until bubbling and potatoes are thoroughly cooked.

Remove from oven and let rest 10 minutes before serving.

* Coddle is excellent served with 'Irish Soda Bread' and butter, to soak up the lovely juices in the dish, as is the Irish way.

IRISH SODA BREAD

4 cups flour

1/4 cup sugar

1 teaspoon baking powder

1 teaspoon baking soda

1 teaspoon salt

1/4 cup butter

3 to 4 tablespoons caraway seed

2 cups raisins

1 1/3 cup buttermilk

2 eggs

milk

Heat oven to 375 degrees.

Combine flour, sugar, salt, baking powder, baking soda. Cut in butter, until mixture resembles coarse meal. Stir in caraway seeds and raisins. Combine buttermilk and eggs, stir into dry mixture until moistened. Turn out onto a floured surface and knead lightly until smooth. Shape dough into a ball, and place on a 7 inch round loaf pan, cut a 4 inch cross about 1/4 inch deep, on top of dough ball. Brush top of loaf with milk.

Bake loaf for about 1 hour or until golden brown.

EASY CHRISTMAS PUDDING

1 cup ready to eat prunes, chopped

2 cups raisins

2 cups currents

1 cup Demerara sugar

1 cup suet

1 cup fresh white bread crumb

2 cups sultanas

1 lemon, grated rind, and juice

1/2 chopped almonds

1 cup cooking apples, peeled cored and grated

1 medium carrot, peeled and grated

1 cup plain flour

1/2 teaspoon ground cinnamon

1/2 teaspoon ground coriander

1/2 teaspoon ground nutmeg

3 eggs

5 fluid ounces Guiness beer

1 tablespoon black treacle

1 fluid ounce Irish Whiskey

In a large bowl mix dry ingredients. Mix the egg, Guiness, whiskey, treacle together and stir into the mixture, cover and let set overnight in a cool place. Butter three 20 ounce of pudding bowls, put a circle of grease proof paper in the base. Pack mixture in the bowls and smooth the tops. Leave about 1 inch space to the top.

Cut a layer of grease proof paper into a 12 inch circle, cover each pudding with the paper and tie with string around the edge, tie another string across the top of the pudding, so it is easy for you to lift in and out of the pan.

Place bowls in a heavy based sauce pan (placing an upturned plate on the bottom of the pot, first to rise the pudding bowls off bottom of the pot). Pour boiling water around the edge, until it comes up to 2/3 way up the sides of the bowls. Cover with a lid and simmer for three hours. Top up the pot to starting level each hour.

Lift out the puddings after 3 hours and let them cool, put on a new piece of parchment, cover, and then cover tightly with foil.

Store in a cool place until Christmas. The puddings will keep for up to six months.

To serve: Cut into portion size and heat. In microwave, on full power, two minutes until piping is hot. Heat 2 tablespoons brandy in small saucepan, set alight and carefully pour over pudding. Serve with Brandy Custard cream.

CHRISTMAS BRANDY SAUCE

Always use the same liquor in the sauce as you did in the pudding, to get the best marriage of flavors. You can also make this up two days in advance. Refrigerate, then reheat as you need it.

2 ounces butter
2 ounces plain flour
1 pint milk
2 ounces caster sugar, fine
5 tablespoons brandy or cognac or dark rum

In a nonstick saucepan over medium heat, gently melt the butter. Once melted, stir in flour, stir quickly to create a thick smooth paste. Cook for one minute taking care not to burn.

Using a hand whisk, slowly add the milk, stirring vigorously, continue whisking until thick smooth sauce is formed, this will take 3 to 5 minutes. Take care not to have the heat too high, or the base of the sauce will burn.

Once sauce is formed, add the sugar and whisk a little more until the sugar is completely dissolved. Lower the heat and gently cook for 5 minutes, stirring from time to time.

Finely add the liquor, whisk into the smooth sauce, the sauce can then be cooled and kept covered in the refrigerator for a few days.

On Christmas day, simply reheat on the stove top or the microwave. Add a tiny drop of liquor to liven up the flavor.

once you flame your pudding, serve.

DO NOT SERVE THIS DESERT TO CHILDREN! For them you can use a plain butter custard for children.

-OR-

Recipe:

CHRISTMAS PUDDING BUTTER SAUCE

4 ounces soft unsalted butter
8 ounces confectioners sugar
3 - 5 tablespoons brandy or cognac (for children just use vanilla or flavoring)

Place the soft butter into a large bowl. Beat with electric hand whisk until light and creamy.

Add confectioners sugar and beat until all sugar is incorporated.

Add liquor to taste (or flavorings). Adding to much liquor will cause the custard to curd, if this happens then simply add more confectioners sugar, until mixture binds back together.

Spoon butter into a serving dish, cover and store in refrigerator until required.

The butter can be stored up to 5 days.

Serves 6

IRISH BLACKBERRY CRUMBLE CAKE

1 cup blackberries	1 teaspoon salt
1/2 cup brown sugar	1 teaspoon baking powder
1 1/2 cup white sugar	1 1/2 teaspoon cinnamon
1/2 cup cooking oats	1/2 teaspoon nutmeg
1 cup all-purpose flour	3/4 cup milk
	1/4 cup butter, cut into small pieces

Preheat oven to 350 degrees.

Mix 1/2 cup sugar, cinnamon, nutmeg and mix well, toss the blackberries in and set aside for 20 minutes.

Mix brown sugar and oats together and set aside.

Mix 1 cup of sugar with flour, salt and baking powder together.

Add milk to flour, sugar mixture. Stir in and blend well.

Butter a 9 x 11 baking dish. Pour batter into prepared dish.

Place berry mixture on top of batter, top with sugar oat mixture.

Bake for 30 to 45 minutes, until golden brown and berries are bubbly.

ROAST GOOSE

1 (9 to 11 pound) goose
salt, pepper, paprika

Trim excess fat off goose, rub cavity of goose gently with salt. Fasten neck skin of goose to back with skewers. Fold wings across back with tips touching.

Tie drumsticks to tail. Prick skin all over with a fork. Place goose breast side up on rack in shallow roasting pan. Roast uncovered in a 350 degree oven until done. 3 to 3 1/2 hours.

Remove excess fat from pan occasionally.

1 hour and 15 minutes before goose is done you can put vegetables around goose, brush potatoes with fat and sprinkle with salt and pepper and paprika. If necessary, place tent of foil over goose to prevent excessive browning. Goose is done when drumstick meat feels very tender.

Let meat stand for 15 minutes for easier carving.

GIBLET GRAVY

Gizzard, heart, neck and liver
1/2 teaspoon salt
1/4 teaspoon pepper
1/2 cup drippings
1/2 cup all-purpose flour

Cover organs with water, sprinkle with salt and pepper. Heat to boil, then reduce heat, simmer until gizzard is fork tender. 1 1/2 hours. Add the liver the last 5 to 10 minutes of cooking, drain; reserve broth for gravy. Cut up giblets, and refrigerate broth and giblets until ready to use.

Pour drippings from pan of roasted goose into a bowl. Return 1/2 drippings to pan; stir in 1/2 cup all-purpose flour, cook over low heat stirring constantly.

until mixture is smooth and bubbly; remove from heat. add enough water to reserved broth to measure 4 cups, stir into flour mixture, heat to boiling. Stirring constantly. Boil and stir 1 minute. Stir in giblets and sprinkle with salt and pepper. Heat until giblets are hot.

Makes 4 cups gravy

ROAST POTATOES - BACON AND CHEESE

3 pounds medium size potatoes
6 slices bacon halved length-ways and then cut cross-wise into 1/2 inch pieces.
2 tablespoons olive oil
1/2 cup grated parmigiono-reggiano cheese
2 garlic cloves, finely chopped
1/4 cup finely chopped flat-leafed parsley

Preheat oven to 425 degree.

Generously cover potatoes with cold in a 4 quart pot and 1 tablespoon salt.

Bring to a boil, then simmer until potatoes are tender when pierced with fork. (about 12 minutes. Drain. Cool potatoes to warm, peel and slice length-wise.

Cook bacon in a 12 heavy skillet, over medium heat, stirring until cooked through, but still flexible. Drain on paper towel, reserving grease in skillet.

Brush bottom of 15 x 10 inch baking pan with oil and half the reserved bacon fat. Sprinkle potatoes with 1/2 teaspoon salt and 1/2 teaspoon pepper, and arrange, cut sides down in baking pan. Bake until undersides are golden brown, 30 to 35 minutes.

Reduce oven temperature to 375 degree.

Turn potatoes over and sprinkle with cheese, bacon and garlic, and drizzle with remaining bacon fat. Bake until cheese is melted, about 15 minutes. Sprinkle with parsley then serve.

POTATO CANDY

1 small potato boiled
1 pat butter
1/2 teaspoon vanilla
1 pound confectioners sugar
peanut butter

Mash potato with fork. Add butter and vanilla. Gradually add confectioners sugar until it becomes stiff enough to roll out. Roll out thin and spread peanut butter over top. Roll up and refrigerate it. When it becomes hard cur into sliced and eat.

CHAPTER

Greece

Greece is in Southern Europe. Citizens of Greece often spend Christmas presenting small gifts to hospitals and orphanages. The custom of giving gifts to family members is unusually in this country.

The city of Thessaloniki draws many tourists each Christmas with their giant lighted tree and ship display. In public sights throughout Greece their are lighted and decorated boats symbolizing the Greek merchant fleet. The Christmas trees are decorated with gifts on Christmas Eve which remains on the tree until New Years Day (Saint Basil's Day) then they are opened. The children believe that St. Basil gives the gifts to them. It is believed that St. Basil makes his visits to the home by way of boat. Families hang a small wooden bowl on a small cross with a sprig of basil. once per day, a family member dips the cross and basil into Holy Water, then sprinkles it throughout the home in order to keep the KILLANTZAROI (evil goblins) away.

The Christmas season begins with 40 days of fasting. The week before Christmas, Greek families begin baking, one of the most popular of the baked goods is 'Christ's Bread' (Christopsomo), a sweet bread made into large loaves of various shapes. An ornament made of the father's profession is baked into the crust. The bread is served with honey, dried fruits and nuts. A coin was baked into a sponge cake (vasilopete) on Saint Basil's Day (New Years Day), the cake is broken into small pieces, the first piece is set aside for St. Basil; the second is for Christ, The third piece is given to the animals. The fourth piece symbolizes material possessions. The remainder of the loaf would be divided between the family members, before those pieces are eaten, each member dips his piece in wine, and invokes St. Basil. The family member who finds the coin in their bread will have prosperity and good fortune in the coming year.

The coin is used to buy a candle that is light in the Church, on Christmas Day.

After the dinner the family lifts the table three times for good luck.

CHRISTOPSOMO

Greek Christmas Bread
'Christ's Bread'

This traditional bread goes back thousands of years.

5 cups & 1/4 cup flour	1/2 teaspoon vanilla (substitute
(plus more for surface)	for Mastic, grown only in
1 packet yeast (1/4 oz. or 7 gm.)	Greece, may order on-line)
1/4 cup warm water	3 eggs, 1 used for egg wash
1/2 teaspoon sugar	1/2 cups (1 stick) butter, melted
1/4 teaspoon salt	1/2 teaspoon lemon zest
1/4 cup olive oil	1/2 cup almonds, slivered
1 tablespoon brandy	1/2 teaspoon orange zest
3/4 cup warm milk	1/4 cup raisins

In a large bowl add: yeast, water, sugar, salt, oil, brandy, milk, vanilla, 2 eggs, butter, lemon and orange zest - mix well.

Next add: 1 cup flour and mix well. Continue to add flour one cup at a time. Mixing well after each addition.

After all flour is added mix in almonds and raisins.

knead dough about 10 minutes on a well floured surface. Dough should be elastic and not sticky. Add more flour as needed or more water if too dry.

Place dough in oiled bowl and turn it over making sure dough is well oiled. Cover bowl. Allow to raise til double, about one hour.

Remove dough from bowl and knead for 30 seconds on floured surface.

Break into equal parts. Place on baking sheet lined with parchment paper.

Shape each dough piece into a circle.

Break off small piece of each dough to make your own design if desired.

Set and let raise another 30 minutes.

Using the remaining egg to create an egg wash. Break egg in bowl, add a splash of water and mix well. Brush egg was over bread.

Place in preheated oven of 350 degrees, for 40 minutes or until golden brown.

Remove from oven and let cool. Serve.

Makes 2 loaves

KATAIFI

Greek Pastry and Cheese Roll

4 tablespoons butter	7 ounce feta cheese, crumbled
(plus extra to grease pan)	1 1/2 cups Gruyere cheese or
4 eggs	Kaseri, grated
Fresh cracked black pepper	11 ounce pastry Kataifi
1 pinch salt	4 tablespoons vegetable oil

Preheat oven to 350 degrees.

Butter an oven proof dish.

Beat eggs with salt and pepper, stir in cheese, set filling aside until ready to use.

Tease out the Kataifi pastry into 20 to 25 long strand sections. Keep pastry covered with a damp cloth to prevent drying out.

Take one section of Kataifi and pat it down gently. Place about one tablespoon of cheese mixture at one end of pastry and roll up, and then place in baking dish. Continue until cheese mixture is rolled up and the baking dish is full.

Heat oil and butter together, and pour about one tablespoon over each roll. At this point you can wrap and put in freezer or place in refrigerator for 24 hours.

One hour before baking, beat together milk, cream and remaining two eggs. Season with pepper. Pour over cheese rolls in baking dish; let set for one hour or until liquid is absorbed.

Bake in oven for 35 to 45 minutes. You want it golden brown and the egg cooked. Serve immediately with a lemon, to be squeezed on top before eating.

SPANAKOPITA

Greek Spinach Pie

2 (10 - 12 oz.) bag spinach cellophane package	1/2 teaspoon ground pepper
1 onion finely chopped	2 to 3 tablespoon oil, for greasing pan
1 bunch scallions, washed and trimmed	2 3/4 cup flour, all purpose
of roots and brushed tops, finely sliced	2 teaspoon baking powder
1 leek small, trimmed, washed, finely diced	1/4 teaspoon salt
4 to 5 tablespoons oil	1 egg
7 to 10 sprigs each, dill, parsley, finely chopped	2 tablespoon oil
12 to 14 ounces feta cheese (goat)	1 cup cool to warm water
1/4 cup Parmesan cheese and / or Romano cheese grated	2 cups extra flour, for kneading and rolling

* HOW TO MAKE SPINACH FILLING

Prepare the spinach, then cook in a large pot,(without water). Set over high heat until wilted, drain and rinse with cold water. To cool down spinach, squeeze spinach in palm of your hand to remove excess water, then chop up bundles of spinach and set aside.

In a large non stick pot, saute' onion, scallions and leeks with 4 to 5 tablespoons oil, set over medium heat for about 7 to 10 minutes or until wilted, add the prepared spinach dill and parsley, continue sauteing for 2 to 4 minutes; transfer to large mixing bowl and allow mixture to cool slightly. In a medium size bowl, break apart feta cheese into half inch chunks, add Parmesan or Romano cheese, eggs and pepper; stir to combine well. Add this mixture to the spinach and mix well. Trying to keep feta cheese in tact; set bowl aside.

HOW TO MAKE DOUGH

In a medium size bowl, combine flour, baking powder and salt; then make a well, add the egg, oil and water, then stir to break up egg, using a whisk, start bringing in the wall of flour and mix well; when things start to get sticky, continue mixing with your hands, forming the dough into a ball; dough will be sticky at this point.

Dust your work surface with 1/4 cup extra flour to keep things from sticking.

Place dough in the center of work surface, then press down on dough, pushing it across and away from you, using the palm of your hand. Lift and fold the flap of dough over, to the top of dough. Rotate dough a quarter turn, in one direction (left or right) and then press down again in the same manor. Repeat kneading the dough for about 5 minutes, sprinkling extra flour to prevent sticking; rotate the dough in the same direction insures proper kneading.

NOTE: At this point, preheat oven to 425 degrees and adjust oven racks to center of oven, grease baking pan and set aside.

ROLLING, ASSEMBLING AND BAKING THE SPINACH PIE:

Dust rolling pin with some of the extra flour. Take a little more than half the dough and roll it out into a rectangle, large enough to fit the bottom of the sides of the pan. It's easier to allow your dough to slightly stick to your work surface; this will help to hold out the rubber like dough. The flaps of the dough should go up the sides of the pan and slightly hang over the sides of the edge. If by chance you made a tear or hole in the dough, dust your fingers with some flour, and pinch the hole together to seal it. Transfer the rolled out dough into the greased pan.

Roll out the other part of dough, in the same manor, about 3/4 of an inch larger than the bottom layer. After you have rolled it out, leave it on the work surface to relax as you fill the pan with filling; the dough will shrink a bit, so you might have to roll it out just before placing on top of pie.

Transfer and evenly spread filling into prepared pan. Bring sides of the bottom dough over the filling, then brush the sides with a little bit of water; don't worry if the flaps are not equal in size, and don't bother washing pastry brush, use it as it is.

Place top of dough over the top of pie filling, and tuck its edges down between the sides of the pan and pie, using the pastry brush, stretch the dough if needed, to bring it down between the sides of the pan and the pie. Brush the pie with a little bit of oil to evenly coat the dough. Score the top of the dough into 24 to 32 squares, by placing the blade of the knife into, but not through the dough, since this might tear the dough, and don't cut all the way through to the bottom of the pie; the filling may ooze out during the baking.

Then score a criss-cross pattern into the squares in the same manor.

Bake pie in preheated oven for 30 to 35 minutes, or until top is golden brown. With small browned areas and bubbles; the top crust should also be browned; rotate pan halfway through the baking time. Allow the pie to cool in the pan for 10 to 20 minutes, then cut through pie to make squares; transfer and lay squares onto a serving platter, in a single layer to prevent the squares from becoming soggy. Then serve.

BAKLAVA

1 cup unsalted butter
1/2 (16 ounce) package phyllo dough
2 cups chopped pecans

1 1/2 tablespoons whole cloves
1 1/2 cups water
1/3 cup white sugar
1 cinnamon stick
1 cup honey
Preheat oven to 350 degrees.

Melt butter over low heat, pour 2 teaspoons butter in the bottom of a 9 x 13 baking dish. Layer 3 sheets of phyllo dough in the bottom of pan. Trim dough to fit. Sprinkle 2 tablespoons of pecans over phyllo dough, layer 3 more sheets of dough, brush generously with melted butter, sprinkle with 2 tablespoons pecans. Continue dough * butter * pecan layers until pan is 3/4 full.

With a sharp knife score the phyllo dough to form diamonds. Press clove at each end of diamond, pour remaining butter over the dough.

Bake 45 to 50 minutes until golden brown.

Meanwhile, combine the sugar, water and cinnamon stick in a medium saucepan, bring to a boil, stirring constantly. Simmer 10 minutes.

Add honey and simmer 2 minutes longer, remove from heat and discard cinnamon stick. Pour honey mixture over hot baklava. Let cool on wire rack.

Cut into diamonds.

LEG OF LAMB WITH RUBY GLAZE

1 boned,(5 to 7 pound) rolled and tied leg of lamb
1 package (12 ounce) fresh or frozen cranberries
1 cup sugar
1 cup port wine
1 to 2 teaspoon grated fresh ginger

Place lamb on rack in shallow roasting pan. Roast, uncovered, at 325 degrees for 30 minutes.

Meanwhile, combine cranberries, sugar and wine in medium saucepan. Bring to a boil over high heat. Stirring to dissolve sugar.

Reduce Heat; simmer uncovered, until cranberries pop, about 5 minutes. Remove from heat. Stir in ginger.

Spoon enough cranberry glaze over lamb to coat evenly; reserve remaining glaze. Continue roasting lamb for 2 to 3 hours (approximately 25 to 30 minutes per pound). or until meat thermometer inserted in thickest part registers 155 degrees (medium).

Baste lamb occasionally with glaze during roasting.

Let stand 10 minutes before carving.

Serve with remaining glaze, warm or chilled.

HOLIDAY ROAST WITH GRAVY

1 (4 1/2 to 5 pound) eye of round roast 1 (15 ounce) can tomato sauce
2 tablespoons minced garlic 1/2 cup dry red wine
1 tablespoon plus 1 1/2 teaspoon 1 large onion, chopped
chopped fresh rosemary 2 tablespoon Greek seasoning
2 teaspoon pepper 3 tablespoons flour
2 teaspoons dried oregano 1 cup beef broth
3 tablespoons vegetable oil, divided

Cut 12 (1 inch deep) slits in top and bottom of roast.

Stir together garlic, rosemary, pepper, oregano and 1 tablespoon vegetable oil,

to form a paste. Rub mixture into slits, cover and chill at least 8 hours or up to 12 hours. let roast stand at room temperature 30 minutes.

Brown roast on all sides in remaining oil in a heavy duty roasting pan.

Stir together tomato sauce and red wine, onion and Greek seasoning, and pour over roast in roasting-pan.

Bake, covered, at 325 degrees, for 1 hour and 35 minutes or until a meat thermometer registers 135 degrees. remove roast, reserve sauce in roasting pan, keep roast warm.

Whisk together flour and beef broth until smooth. Whisk into sauce mixture in roasting pan. Cook mixture, whisking frequently over medium heat 15 to 20 minutes or until thickened.

Serve gravy with roast.

AIOLI

Winter Crudities with Walnut Garlic Dip

1 (12 ounce) russet potato, peeled, quartered
3/4 cup walnuts, toasted
2/3 cup extra virgin olive oil
1/3 cup lemon juice
2 tablespoons cold water
1/3 cup finely chopped fresh parsley

3 garlic cloves
1 tablespoon chopped fresh
oregano

Assorted raw vegetables (such as carrots, radishes, red and green bell peppers, celery, ect....)

Cook potato in medium saucepan through boiling salted water, until potato is tender, about 15 minutes.

Drain.

Cool completely.

Blend meats, cup oil, lemon juice, garlic, and oregano in processor, about 1/3 smooth.

Add potato, 1/3 cup oil, 2 tblsp. water. Using pulse or on and off switch, process just until blended, and mixture is creamy. DO NOT OVER PROCESS!! or mixture will become sticky.

Transfer mixture to a medium bowl. Mix in parsley and season with salt and pepper. (can be prepared a day in advance). Cover and refrigerate.

Serve with vegetables.

SESAME SEED COOKIES

A holiday cookie from the Sparta region of Greece.

1 cup butter	4 cups flour
1 3/4 cups sugar	2 teaspoons baking powder
2 eggs	1/2 teaspoon salt
2/3 cup toasted toasted sesame seed	1/4 cup water

Mix butter, sugar, and eggs until fluffy.

Stir in 1/3 cup sesame seeds.

Mix together dry ingredients. Add alternately with water to sugar mixture.

Chill dough until stiff enough to roll, 1 to 2 hours.

Preheat oven to 350 degrees.

Roll dough on a lightly floured surface into a 1/8 inch thick rectangle.

Cut dough into strips 2 1/2 inch x 3/4 inch.

Press the entire side of each strip into dish containing sesame seeds.

Loop one end over the other, making a bow-knot effect.

Place on lightly greased baking sheet, or parchment lined.

Bake 8 to 10 minutes, or until lightly browned.

Makes 9 dozen cookie

KOURABIEDES

Greek Christmas Cookie

1/2 cup butter	2 cups all-purpose flour
1/3 cup granulated sugar	1 teaspoon baking powder
2 eggs whole cloves	
1/2 teaspoon brandy flavoring	confectioners sugar

1 teaspoon vanilla

Preheat oven to 350 degrees.

Mix, butter, 1/3 cup sugar, eggs, and flavorings until creamy.

In a separate bowl, mix together flour, baking powder, and gradually add to the creamed mixture. Mixing well.

Shape into balls, about 3/4 inch in diameter or in cylindrical shapes formed in 2 inch half moons. Place cookies on parchment lined baking sheet.

Bake 10 to 12 minutes or until cookies are set., but not browned.

Let stand 2 minutes, before removing from baking sheet.

When cool, dust with confectioners sugar.

**Place a whole clove in center of each cookie before baking.

Makes 8 dozen cookies

CHAPTER

Sweden / Scandanavia

Traditional Christmas greeting for the Swedish is 'Glad Jul'.

Since the 1700's, the evergreen tree has been a part their holiday tradition, introduced to Sweden from Germany, it wasn't until then that the majority of the country adopted this custom. The tree was usually gotten a few days before Christmas Eve and decorated, and will stay up until January 13th, St. Kunt's Day.

The decorations that adorn the Swedish trees would be hand made baskets, that were woven and sometimes made from straw; these baskets were sometimes filled with candy, to be eaten on January 13th 'Saint Knut's Day'

The straw ornaments (Juldocka) are hand made figures that represent children and animals and date back to a time when the only material for ornaments was straw.

The wooden heart symbolizes the belief that everyone is lovable at Christmastime.

The tissue and cardboard ornaments (Julgrans Keramellar) contains small gifts inside. They are made especially for the children.

Other decorations included candles, apples, Swedish flags, small gnomes wearing small red caps. The houses may be filled with red tulips and smell like 'Pepparkaker', which is a heart, star, or goat shaped gingerbread biscuit.

1880 was when the commercial ornaments became available.

The Advent tradition is observed in Sweden on the four Sundays before Christmas. Each Sunday a new candle is lit, with a special reading and placed in a special candle holder.

Candle lit processions to the church, feature Scandinavian Christmas's, where, in the home, It is always the mother who lights the candles on Christmas Eve.

Christmas begins with the Saint Lucia ceremony. Before dawn on the morning of December 13th, the youngest daughter from each family, puts on a white robe, with a red sash; she wears a crown of evergreens, with tall lighted candles attached to it. She wakes the parents and serves them coffee and 'Lucia Buns'. The other children accompany her. The boys dressed as star-boys, in long white shirts and pointed hats.

The custom goes back to Lucia, a Christian virgin martyred for her beliefs, at Syracuse in the 4th century. The St. Lucia ceremony is fairly recent, but represents the traditional Thanksgiving for the return of the SUN.

Often she is followed by a Star-boy who wear pointed hats and carry star wands.

Christmas will continue through December 13th and ends on January 15th (St. Knut's Day) the day after Christmas. From the 13th on, there is the baking of cookies, dreads, cakes and the preparation of ham which is served at the Christmas buffet. The exchanging of gifts are usually done on Christmas eve, December 24th.

In some Scandinavian homes a bowl of rice porridge is placed in the attic for the Christmas Elves.

After Christmas Eve dinner, a friend or family member dresses up as (Jultomten) or 'Tomte', a gnome figure, unlike Santa Claus, is suppose to live under the floor boards of the house or barn and rides a straw goat. Tomte watches over the family and the livestock. The make-believe Tomte has a white beard and dresses in red robes, and distributes gifts from his sack. Many gifts are given with a tag that has a funny rhyme that hints at the contents. Tomte knocks on the door of your home carrying a sack of gifts.

The Swedish eat lyc - treated cod fish and welcome the Christmas Elves and the julbok, which id the Christmas goat, who is responsible for distributing the presents.

Swedish, Julafton Christmas Eve dinner, may be a smorgasbord, or buffet with 'julskinka' or Christmas ham, pickled pigs feet, lut fish, or dried cod fish. many different types of sweets. 'Risgryngrot' a special rice porridge with an almond hidden in the batch. Whoever finds the almond will marry in the coming year.

Mulled wine is a favorite for the Scandinavians. This is made with red wine, raisins, mulling spices, and is served warm or hot; it is traditionally drank during the winter.

SWEDISH RICE PORRIDGE

Hearty, cultural favorite / Sweedish American pioneers would make over a period of an entire day.

1 large apple, honey crisp, gala, fuji, ect....
1 cup uncooked rice (minute white rice)
1 cup water
3 inch cinnamon stick
3 cups milk
3 tablespoons sugar
1/3 cup raisins
1 teaspoons vanilla
honey to drizzle

Cook rice in a big saucepan according to package instructions, adding in a cinnamon stick while cooking rice.

As the rice cooks, peel, core, chop the apple into very small pieces and set aside.

Pour the milk into the saucepan, and stir. Cook until the milk begins to simmer. (If you warm up the milk, before adding it, this dish will cook faster).

As the milk simmers, add the apple, sugar, raisins, stir to combine.

Cover the saucepan and simmer 25 minutes. As it cooks, it will thicken up, so stir it once or twice.

Remove saucepan from the heat, stir in vanilla.

Remove and discard cinnamon stick.

Serve Swedish Rice Porridge with a drizzle of honey or with cream.

Refrigerate leftovers.

JULSKINKA - CHRISTMAS HAM

Traditional Swedish Christmas Ham

"God Jul" - Merry Christmas, and

"Julbord" - Christmas Buffet

Ham in Sweden is salt-cured and unsmoked. Fresh ham is often served cold but warm is exceptable.

1 (7 to 9 pound) fresh (unsmoked) salt cured ham
2 large egg yolks
1 tablespoons brown sugar
6 tablespoons grainy mustard (Swedish if you can get it)
6 tablespoons finely crumbled gingersnap or breadcrumbs

Heat oven to 350 degrees.

Place oven rack in the upper third of the oven. Rinse ham and remove any excess salt and pat dry. place pork rind side up in a heavy roasting pan, put in the oven and roast until the internal temperature reads 160 degrees (about 4 1/2 hours) remove from oven and increase heat to 450 degree.

Carefully carve rind off of ham. (In Scandinavia, this crispy, delicious, heart - attack - inducing cracklings are often served as a side dish). Whisk together the egg yolks, brown sugar and mustard, and spread evenly over the entire surface of the ham.

Sprinkle with the crumbled ginger snaps or bread crumbs over ham until totally covered.

Return ham to oven and cook for an additional 15 to 20 minutes or until golden brown.

Remove from oven and cover loosely with aluminum foal and let it rest 15 minutes. Carve and serve warm or cool completely and serve it cold.

SAINT LUCIA CROWN

Bread

1/16 to 1/8 teaspoon crushed saffron	4 1/2 to 5 cups all-purpose flour
1/2 cup (scolded) luke-warm milk	1/2 cup cut-up citron
2 packages active dry yeast	1/4 cup chopped blanched almonds
1/2 cup warm water	1 tablespoon grated lemon peel
1/2 cup sugar	powder sugar glaze
1 teaspoon salt	candied cherries
2 eggs beaten	
1/4 cup softened butter	

Stir Saffron into milk, dissolve yeast in warm water in a large bowl.

Stir in saffron-milk, sugar, salt, eggs, butter and 2 1/2 cups flour, and beat until smooth.

Stir in the citron, almonds, lemon peel, and enough remaining flour to make dough easy to handle.

Turn dough onto a lightly floured surface; knead util smooth and elastic, about 10 minutes.

Place in a greased bowl; turn dough once, greased side up, let rise until double, about 1 1/2 hours. (dough is ready when pressed in center holds imprint) it is time to punch it down.

Punch down dough and cut off 1/3 of the dough for the top of the braid and reserve. Divide the remaining dough into three equal parts; roll each part into 25 inch strips and on a greased cookie sheet.

Braid strips together, then shape into a circle like a wreath and pinch the ends together to seal.

Divide reserved dough into three equal parts. roll each part into 16 inch strips. Place close together on another greased cookie sheet. Braid strips and form into a circle and pinch ends together to seal.

Cover both braids and let rise until doubled in size. (about 45 minutes)

Preheat oven to 375 degrees.

Bake until golden drown, 20 to 25 minutes,

When cool make holes for 5 candles in the small braid.

Drizzle both braids with powdered sugar glaze, garnish with cherries and insert the candles.

Place small braid onto large braid.

POWDERED SUGAR GLAZE

1 cup confectioners sugar
3 to 4 teaspoons water
Mix together until the consistency desired for your glaze.

LEFSE

Potato cake
Bread

Originally baked on top of the stove, this thin Scandinavian flat bread was a simple household staple. Now, a Christmas delicacy, it is served warm or at room temperature with butter or a cinnamon sugar mixture, or preserves.

3 cups fluffy mashed potatoes
3/4 cup to 1 cup flour

Heat electric skillet to high setting.

'Do not grease skillet'.

Add the potatoes and flour working with hands until soft dough forms, and it is of rolling consistency. (avoid adding too much flour).

Form dough into a roll 10 inches long, and about 2 inches in diameter.

Cut roll into 1/2 inch slices.

Cover in plastic wrap while rolling out each Lefse.

On a well floured pastry cloth roll out one slice paper thin.

Transfer to the heated griddle using a long spatula.

cook until brown spots appear on bottom surface, about one minute.

Flip to other side and bake for about 30 to 45 seconds.

Place between cloth towels to keep from drying out.

Cool completely. Store in refrigerator in a sealed plastic container.

Serve with jam, butter, sprinkle white sugar, cinnamon or brown sugar, then fold or roll up to serve.

Robin Redmon Dreyer

FATTIGMANDS BAKKELS

Scandinavian Fried Cookie

3 egg yolks	1 tablespoon rum flavoring
1 whole egg	1 teaspoon vanilla
1/2 teaspoon salt	1 cup flour
1/4 cup confectioners sugar	

Heat deep fat (at least 2 inch deep) to 375 degrees.

Beat together egg yolks, whole egg, and salt together until very stiff, about 10 minutes.

Blend in confectioners sugar and flavorings thoroughly.

Measure and add flour all at once, mixing well.

knead dough on a well floured board, until surface is blistered in appearance, about 7 minutes.

Divide dough in half; roll each half very thin.

With pastry wheel or knife, cut dough into 4 x 2 diamonds.

Make 1 inch slit in center of each; draw a long point of a diamond through slit and curl back in opposite direction.

Fry until delicately browned in deep hot fat, about 1/2 minute. Turn quickly and brown on other side.

Drain on absorbent paper towel, and sprinkle with confectioners sugar, just before serving.

Makes 2 to 3 dozen

KRUMKAKE

Scandinavian Delicacy

4 eggs 1 teaspoon vanilla
1 cup sugar 3/4 cup flour

1/2 cup butter, melted 2 teaspoons corn starch
5 tablespoons cream

Heat Krumkake iron over small electric or plain gas surface unit (6 inch) on medium heat.

Beat eggs and sugar together, thoroughly; add butter, cream and add vanilla.

Measure flour and cornstarch; stir into egg mixture. Beat until smooth.

Test iron with a few drops of water; if they "jump" iron is correct temperature.

Drop batter (about 1/2 tablespoon for 6 inch iron, more for larger iron).

on unreleased iron; close gently - do not squeeze.

Bake on each side about 15 second, or until light, golden brown.

(Do not be alarmed if first few are dark; iron cools slightly while in use).

Remove with a knife, immediately roll on wooden roller.

Make 6 to 7 dozen 4 inch. Krumake

JULEKAGE

coffee cake

1 package active dry yeast	2 tablespoons shortening
1/4 cup water	1/2 cup raisins
3/4 cup luke-warm milk	1/3 cup cut up citron
(scalded then cooled)	3 1/4 to 3 3/4 cup flour
1/2 cup sugar	
1/2 teaspoon salt	Egg yolk glaze
1/2 teaspoon ground cardamon	
1 egg	

Dissolve yeast in warm water in a large bowl, beat in milk, sugar, salt, cardamon, egg, shortening, raisins, citron and 1 1/2 cup flour. Beat until smooth, stir in enough remaining flour to make dough easier to handle/

Turn dough onto lightly floured surface; knead until smooth and elastic, about 5 minutes.

Place dough in a greased bowl; flip over once, cover, and let rise in a warm place until doubled in size (about 1 1/2 hours).

Punch down dough, shape into a large round loaf.

Place in a greased 9 inch round layer pan.

Cover and let rise until doubled, about 45 minutes.

Heat oven to 350 degrees.

Brush dough with egg yolk glaze - 1 egg yolk and 2 tablespoons water.

Bake 30 to 40 minutes, until golden brown.

PEPPARKAKOR

Frosted Cookies

Frosted Pepparkakor are sometimes served on Saint Lucia's Day, December 13, when early in the morning when the oldest daughter awakens her family by bringing cookies along with the traditional saffron buns and steaming hot coffee.

These crisp and fragrant Swedish ginger cookies are often hung on a tree made of wooden dowels, which is also decorated with apples and topped with a sheaf of wheat.

Some traditional Swedish shapes for the cookies are pigs, horses, roosters, hearts, and gingerbread boys. These cookies are hung on the wooden dowels.

1 1/2 cup sugar	2 teaspoons baking soda
1 cup softened butter	1/2 teaspoon salt
3 tablespoons molasses	2 teaspoons cinnamon
1 egg	1 1/2 teaspoon ginger

2 tablespoons milk

3 1/4 cups flour

1/2 teaspoon cardamon

1/2 teaspoons cloves

FROSTING

3/4 cups water

1 envelope unflavored gelatin

3/4 cup granulated sugar

3/4 cup confectioners sugar

1 teaspoon baking powder

1 teaspoon vanilla

In a large bowl mix sugar, butter and molasses until light and fluffy.

Add egg and 2 tablespoons milk, blending well.

Blend flour, baking soda, salt, cinnamon, ginger, cardamon, and cloves; mixing well to form a smooth dough.

Cover with plastic wrap and refrigerate for one hour for easier handling.

Heat oven to 350 degrees.

On a floured surface, roll 1/3 of dough at a time; to 1/8th of an inch thickness. Cut with floured 2 1/2 inch cookie cutter. Place one inch apart on an ungreased cookie sheet.

Bake 9 to 11 minutes until set.

While cooling on cookie racks, mix icing.

In a saucepan combine water and gelatin and let stand five minutes.

Stir in sugar, bringing to a boil and reduce heat. Simmer 10 minutes.

Stir in powder sugar, beat until foamy. Stir in baking powder and vanilla.

Beat at highest speed until thick, about 10 minutes.

Spread frosting on the cooled cookie.

Let cookies set several hours to set.

SANDBAKELSER

Swedish Cookies

1/3 cup blanched almonds   3/4 cup sugar
4 unblanched almonds 1 egg white
3/4 cup butter 1 3/4 cups flour

Put blanched almonds through a nut grinder twice to make a real fine grind.

(1 teaspoon vanilla 1 teaspoon almond flavoring may be substituted for almonds)

Mix in butter, sugar and egg white thoroughly.

Measure flour and add to the creamed mixture, and chill.

Heat oven to 350 degrees

Press dough into tin molds, tiny fluted forms, to form thin coating.

Place on ungreased cookie sheet,

Bake 12 to 15 minutes, turn out.

Makes 3 1/2 dozen cookies

GLOGG

Swedish Mulled Wine

Gloog, (pronounced gloog) is an infused wine who's name means 'glow'. It is a combination of red wine, port, or brandy. This is always served warm. It is incredibly popular during the Christmas season, and makes for a warming drink, whenever the temperature turns chilly.

The legends go, that King Gustav I, Vasa of Sweden, loved a warm drink from German wine, sugar and spices. His drink was better named "GLODGAG VIN"; means 'glowing-hot wine', a name which was then shortened to 'glogg' in the later 1800's.

Many traditional Swedish recipes call for 'Agavit', a vodka flavored with caraway seed or dill seed. Brandy is commonly found as an alternative.

1/2 cup sugar

1/2 cup water

1 750 ml. bottle dry red wine (Cabernet)

1 750 ml. bottle port wine

1 cup brandy

1 cup raisins

1 cup blanched almonds *(white) NO SKINS, MAKES IT BITTER

peel of 1/2 of orange

2 peeled slices of ginger

10 cardamon pods, crushed

2 cinnamon sticks

8 whole cloves

Heat sugar and water in a large saucepan, until it has dissolved.

Add liquor, raisins, and almonds.

Tie spices and peel in a spice bag or tea-ball; place into the saucepan.

Heat mixture over medium heat until it begins to steam, (DO NOT BOIL)!

30 to 40 minutes.

Taste and add more sugar if you desire it sweet. Dissolving 1/2 cup sugar to 1/4 cup water at a time, so as not to over do.

When the mixture is warm, remove spices and serve immediately, making sure to float some raisins and almonds in each glass.

Alternately, remove the almonds and raisins and place glogg into jars, and can be placed in the refrigerator for 1 to 2 weeks, so can be made ahead.

CHAPTER

Holland / Netherlands

The greeting for the holiday is: "Vrolijk Kerstfeest" which means: Merry Christmas.

The Dutch have two Christmas's, the first is 'Eerste Kerstdog' December 25th. The second Christmas is 'Tweede Kerstdog' December 26th.

Saint Nicholas or 'Sinterklaas' as he is called in the Netherlands, arrives in Amsterdam aboard his ship the 'Spanje' (is Dutch for Spain) as throngs of children gather in the harbor to greet him.

Sinterklaas arrives well before his feast day, December 6th. Mid-November finds his steamer chugging through the canals of north Holland, South Holland and the other provinces of the Netherlands. Also aboard the ship is the saints faithful servant 'Zwarte Piet' or 'Black Pete', some people say Zwarte Peit is dark-skinned from climbing down chimneys to deliver Sinterklaas gift, others say he is a moor, a decedent from the people from Northwestern Africa, who conquered Spain in the 700's. The Saints famous horse is white, and the name is Amerigo. They are said to have traveled all the way from Spain to prepare for Saint Nicholas Eve, called 'Sinterklaas-Avond.

Traditionally Amsterdam always hosted the saints official entrance into the country. He continues to pop through late in the day, December 5th. Pete electrifies the celebration even more. Throngs of people gather to greet the famous visitors, waving flags, shouting, and singing a traditional song:

"Look there is the steamer from far away lands.

It brings us St. Nicholas, he's waving his hands.

His horse is a prancing on deck, up and down.

The banners are waving in village and town."

The steamer docks amid booming guns and ringing church bells and cheering voices, young and old.

To the Dutch, St. Nicholas Day is the time of the greatest rivalry in the Christmas season. St. Nicholas comes on the last Saturday of November, by steamer. As he comes into port from Amsterdam, all businesses and traffic stops as the people pour out to greet him. He disembarks with his servant Black Peter and riding his white horse. He is dressed in traditional Bishops robes, while Black Peter wears Spanish attire. They are greeted by the Mayor, and lead a great parade through the streets to the Royal Palace, here all the Royal children are waiting and must give account to their behavior over the past year, just as all Dutch children must do. After the Princes and Princesses have proven their worth, the parade continues to a major hotel, where St. Nicholas will set up his headquarters for the season.

December 5th. is St. Nicholas Eve is when presents are exchanged. The presents are called "surprises" because they are disguised as much as possible to make the final discovery more delightful. A small gift may be wrapped in a large box, or hidden inside a vegetable or sunk in a pudding. A large gift may lurk in the cellar with clues to its location. All surprises must be accompanied by a poem, verse or clue. On Christmas as itself, there are no presents. There are Church Services both Christmas Eve and morning, and a big Dinner in the evening.

The Christmas tree is the center of the home celebration, which consists of carols and story-telling in the afternoon. December 26th is also a holiday, called second Christmas Day, and is a time to relax and probably go out to eat.

The people of the Twente in East of Holland, hold a special Advent ceremony in which special horns are blown to chase away evil spirits and to announce the birth of Christ. The horns are hand made out of one-year-old saplings and are three to four feet long. They are made from hollow elder tree branches and blown at every farm in the neighborhood. Blown over wells, they sound a deep tone, similar to a foghorn.

Anytime during the Christmas season, Dutch families enjoy Christmas stories. Reading, aloud, by candle light of the Christmas tree, is a time honored tradition. A favorite legend is that of 'The Three Skaters'. The Christmas story ends and bedtime is near.

Christmas morning many families go to worship and wish everyone a 'Merry Christmas' as they meet. Hearts are filled with good will and thanksgiving as families return home for Koffietafel late Christmas morning. This meal is not breakfast, which took place before going to Church, it is rather an elaborate brunch. The meal is called 'Coffee Table', because coffee is usually served.

Koffietafel may include such extravagant foods as smoked salmon, or pate', kerstkrans, bitterballen, or cocktail meatballs, and zoute bolletjes, and 'salted bullets'. A bowl of groentensoep, Dutch vegetable soup or erwtensoep, a famous Dutch pea soup, sometimes served with little fried meatballs. The fish course may be mossel-rijst schotel an Indonesian style casserole once a Dutch colony. Mussels over a cream style rice. The drink of the season is coffee or Dutch gin.

DUTCH SPECULAAS

Saint Nicholas Cookies

This is a 16th century Dutch cookie. They were traditionally made in wooden molds carved by the bakers themselves. The molds were carved out of fruit wood or nut wood, carving these molds were once a bakers art. It required much skill, The depth of each carving had to be the same all over for a cookie to be browned all over. Today many bakers use machines with metal molds molds.

1 cup soft butter	2 teaspoon cinnamon
1 teaspoon vanilla	1 teaspoon nutmeg
1 cup granulated sugar	1 teaspoon ground cloves
1 1/4 cups dark brown sugar (packed)	1/2 teaspoon ginger
2 large eggs, beaten	1/2 teaspoon anise seed
3 1/2 cups all-purpose flour	1/8 teaspoon salt
2 teaspoons baking soda	

Combine butter, vanilla, brown sugar, granulated sugar, beat util light and fluffy. Add beaten egg and blend well.
Sift the flour and all remaining ingredients together, then beat into the creamed mixture a little at a time.

At this point you may do several thing:

Form cookies by rolling small pieces of dough into balls and baking on an ungreased cookie sheet for 10-15 minutes. Baking at 350 degree oven.

OR-

Divide dough into 2 equal rolls about 2 1/2 inches in diameter, wrap well and chill for several hours or overnight. After chilling, ether cut the rolls into 1/8-inch to 1/4 inch slices; place on a greased cookie sheets 1/2 inch apart,

OR-

Roll the cooled dough out to 1/8 to 1/4 inch thickness and use cookie cutters.

Bake at 350 degrees for 10 to 15 minutes.

Makes about 60 cookies

HOLLANDS OLIEHOLLEN

Apple-raisin doughnut

A line of people forms at outdoor stands on New Years Eve to sample freshly made oliehollen, ounchy doughnuts. The entire nation shuts down to celebrate the New Year.

1 cup milk	3 cups all-purpose flour
1 tablespoon sugar	2 cups chopped, tart apples
1 tablespoon unsalted butter	3/4 cup dried currents or raisins
1/2 teaspoon salt	oil for deep frying
1 package dry yeast	confectioners sugar
1/2 cup very warm water	
1 egg	

Heat milk, sugar, butter and salt, just until warm. dissolve yeast in warm water. Then add milk mixture, egg and 1 1/2 cups flour, beat until smooth.

Stir in apples and currents and add the rest of flour to form a soft dough.

Cover and let rise in a warm place, until double in size, about 1 hour.

Drop by spoonfuls a few at a time, into hot oil, that has been heated to 375 degrees. Fry until golden brown, about 5 minutes.

Drain on paper towel, and roll in confectioners sugar.

Makes about 30 fritters
SNEEUWBALLEN
(Snowballs)

The end of the year is highly celebrated in Holland as it is in so many other countries, enjoying this doughnut type pastry filled with raisins, candied fruit, and filled with whipped cream and dusted with powdered sugar.

It is one of many recipes celebrated, in the using of these traditional celebrations of the new year.

1/2 cup water	2 large eggs
1/4 cup unsalted butter	2 tablespoons dried currents
1/8 teaspoon salt	or raisins
1/4 teaspoon sugar	2 tablespoons dried candied
1 1/2 cups all-purpose flour	fruits or peels
	oil for frying

Combine water, butter, salt, and sugar in a small deep saucepan, and bring to a boil. Boil gently until the ingredients have melted. Remove from heat. Add the flour all at once and mix rapidly, with a wooden spoon, to a smooth paste.

Add eggs one at a time, beating thoroughly after each addition. Add currents or raisins, and candied fruit.

Heat oil to 375 degrees, and with a metal spoon that could be used i the hot oil, drop the dough into the oil by spoonfuls. Fry 5-8 minutes or until puffy and a golden brown.

Drain on paper towels, and dust with confectioners sugar.

Yields: 8 large or 16 small snowballs
BANKETLETTER
(Almond Filled Pastry)

The Confectioners in the Netherlands rank among the finest in Europe, and are perhaps the greatest lovers of sweets. In early November, irresistible Saint Nicholas goodies begin to appear in bakery shop windows, and in every home, the cooks armed with beloved family recipes and special seasonal ingredients, set themselves at the oven to preform some of that Christmas magic.

Dough:

1 cup very cold unsalted butter (no substitutes)
2 cups all-purpose flour
1/2 cup cold sour cream
1 large beaten egg yolk

Cut butter into small pieces and add to flour, using a pastry blender, or two knives, cut the butter into flour until the butter is the size of peas. Mix sour cream with the egg yolk and blend into flour and butter mixture with a fork, just until the dough forms a ball.

Divide dough into two peaces, wrap well, and refrigerate for several hours or days if desired. Allow dough to become room temperature before making cookies.

Filling:

1- 8 ounce almond paste, or (make your own)
1/4 pound blanched almonds
1/2 cup granulated sugar
1 large egg beaten

Grind the almonds and mix with the sugar. Add the egg and using a wooden spoon or your hands, work until smooth. The almond paste will keep for several weeks if wrapped well and refrigerated.

Roll dough out to 1/8 inch thick and cut dough into strips 3 1/2 to 4 inches wide.

work almond paste into little round sticks, about the length and diameter of your finger. Lay these almond paste sticks either end to end for a long cookie that may be formed into a wreath or crosswise to roll the dough around each stick individually. For sticks, cut the dough, place a dab of water at each end and tuck under. Begin again with the next 'stick'. Sticks may also be formed into initials by making slits where parts of letters may join, and dampening with a little water.

Place cookie initials, or wreath seams side down on cookie sheet, and brush with one egg that has been beaten with teaspoon of water.

Bake at 400 degrees for 20-25 minutes or until golden brown, cool on rack.

Makes about 20 cookies

APPELILAPPEN

(Apple Fritters)

Traditional favorites grace a Dutch table laden with the first Christmas Day feast. The meal is abundant with atmosphere. The custom is for the youngest to the oldest person present, was to read the account of the nativity from the Bible.

Fritter Batter:

1 cup all-purpose flour
1/2 cup salt
1 tablespoon corn oil
1/2 cup water or milk

2 egg whites, stiffly beaten
oil for deep frying
confectioners sugar

Sift flour and salt into a bowl. Make a well in center and add oil and water or milk, beating until smooth. Allow to rest for 45 minutes to an hour.

Fold in beaten egg whites with a rubber spatula.

Apples:

4 to 5 tart apples 1 tablespoon cinnamon
1 cup light brown sugar, firmly packed 1 teaspoon nutmeg

Core and peel apples, slice into 1/4-inch to 1/2-inch rings.

Coat with sugar that has been mixed with cinnamon and nutmeg.

Heat cooking oil to 375 degrees. Dip coated apple slices into fritter batter, and fry in hot oil. Turn several times, until both sides are golden brown.

Drain on paper towels and sift with confectioners sugar.

Makes 4 to 6 servings

PEPERNOTEN

(spicy Cookie Ball)

At traditional Christmas dinners enjoying coffee and light deserts after the main meal then they enjoy more coffee and cookies and chocolate next. Chocolate bells and wreaths are common, plain or topped with nuts, chopped or sugary sprinkles.

2 cups all-purpose flour	1 1/4 cup dark brown sugar,
1/2 teaspoons baking powder	firmly packed
1/4 teaspoon cinnamon	2 large eggs
1/4 teaspoon nutmeg	1 tablespoon diced candied
1/4 teaspoon ground anise seed	orange peel
1/4 teaspoon ground cloves	

Sift flour, baking powder, and spices. Add remaining ingredients and combine until mixture forms a dough.

With floured hands, form the dough into about 60 1/2 inch balls and place on greased cookie sheet, bake at 350 degree for 15 to 20 minutes, or until they are light brown.

Store in air tight container. Makes about 60 balls

BESSENSAPPUDDING

(Current Pudding)

As the table is cleared and coffee is served, everyone still has room for a light desert. One of those delicate deserts might be Bessensappudding, a wonderfully delicate, yet tart current pudding desert.

4 eggs, separated
1 cup crushed current juice (you can use 1 cup frozen concentrated cranberry cocktail juice, omitting all or part of the sugar).
1/2 cup brown sugar, firmly packed
1 envelope unflavored gelatin, softened in:
1/4 cup water

Stir yolks (and sugar) till thick and foamy. Add juice and heat mixture on low flame until somewhat thickened and the foam has mostly disappeared.

Dissolve softened gelatin in this mixture. Fold in beaten egg whites and cool, stirring occasionally until egg whites and custard no longer separates.

Pour into pudding mold rinsed with egg white or oil. Chill and unmold.

Serve topped with sweetened whipped cream, and with wafers or lady fingers.

makes 6 servings

BORSTPLAAT

(Fondants)

Borstplaat is a hard, smooth fondant, a sugar and water confection, is made in heart-shaped molds and in various colors. Chocolate initials are an eagerly awaited treats.

1 cup sugar
3 tablespoons liquid (water, milk, half and half, or light cream.
1 teaspoon butter
a few drops of flavoring or extract
a few drops of food coloring

In a small heavy saucepan, mix the sugar and liquid. Heat slowly to a boil without stirring, until the syrup registers 240 degrees on a candy thermometer.

Remove from heat immediately and add the butter, flavoring, and food coloring.

Stir vigorously until mixture thickens, ether drop from a spoon onto waxed paper or pour into greased lids, no more than 1/3 inch high. Cool to solidity.

VARIATIONS:

1. Fruit flavored borstplaat, add fruit or flavoring and appropriate coloring.

2. For coffee flavored, the 3 tblsp. of liquid should consist of 1 1/2 tblsp. strong coffee and 1 1/2 tblsp. half and half cream.

3. Chocolate flavored, add 2 tblsp. unsweetened cocoa powder to the sugar and use 3 tblsp. half and half for the liquid. Stir to dissolve any lumps before heating.

Makes 12 medium

KERSTBROOD / KERSTSTOL

Christmas Bread also known as stollen

This is a traditional recipe........ Today they add dried fruits and orange liquor for more flavor and texture. The ultimate in festive breads. The almond paste that is used in the Netherlands is called Spijs.

2 packages dry yeast	1 cup raisins, or currents
1/4 cup very warm water	or mixture of both
1/4 cup milk at room temperature,	1/2 cup diced citron
or slightly warmer	1/2 cup diced orange peel
1/2 cup sugar	or candied fruit
1/2 teaspoon salt	4 1/2 cups all-purpose flour
1/2 cup unsalted butter, softened	3/4 cup chopped blanched
3 large eggs, beat lightly,	almonds
reserving 1 egg white	2 teaspoons cinnamon

1/2 cup confectioners sugar for dusting

Mix the yeast with water and stir to dissolve. Add the milk, sugar, salt, and butter, then 2 eggs and 1 yolk from the 3rd egg. Blend well.

In a separate bowl, dust the raisins, currents, citron, and orange peel, or candied fruit with a little of flour and the cinnamon and then add the almonds.

And half the flour to the yeast mixture and stir until smooth. Cover and let rise in a warm place until doubled in bulk about one hour. The mixture is called a sponge.

Add the remaining flour and knead until smooth and elastic, about 5 minutes. knead in the fruit and nuts.

Place dough in an oiled bowl, turn the dough in the bowl, as to be sure the dough is well coated. Cover and let rise for about 30 minutes.

Divide the dough into two equal portions, and press each dough ball into a flat circle. Fold each circle over so the top half is 1-inch from the top edge of the bottom half, forming a split loaf shape.

Place on a greased baking sheet, cover with plastic wrap and let rise again, until double in size, about 30 minutes.

Bake at 375 degrees for about 40 minutes, until golden brown. Cool on wire rack and sprinkle top generously with confectioners sugar before serving.

Makes 2 loaves or 20 servings

MARZIPAN

8 ounces ground almond
8 ounces confectioners sugar
2 egg yolks - beat lightly

2 teaspoons lemon juice
3 drops almond extract
1/4 teaspoon edible rosewater

Combine almond and sugar, mix well. Add eggs, and flavoring; Mix and knead very easily.

Knead into a dough that is the consistency of play-dough.

Note: Almonds need to be blanched, the easy way is to grind them yourself.

Marzipan

2 3/4 cups almonds (soaked, peeled, dehydrated
2/3 cups raw honey
1 teaspoon almond extract
dark flax seed (optional for decoration)

Process almonds in a food processor, until flour becomes moldable. It should be right between a flour and an almond butter. Add honey and almond extract and process until it rolls into a ball. Roll into teaspoon size balls and top with flax seed stars.

MARZIPAN COOKIES

1/2 cup butter
1/4 cup sugar
food coloring

1/8 teaspoon almond flavoring
1 1/4 cups all-purpose flour

Cream butter, sugar, food coloring. Stir in flour mixing thoroughly. Shape as desired, using two level teaspoons dough to form cookies.

Place cookies on an ungreased cookie sheet. Chill 30 minutes.

Heat oven to 300 degrees. (slow bake about 30 minutes, depending on the size and thickness of the cookies), or until done, but not brown.

Makes 2 to 2 1/2 dozen

*Note: shape dough as you would using play dough, to form fruit shapes.

MUSSEL POT with TRAPPIST BEER

3 1/2 teaspoons butter
1 onion, peeled and chopped
2 carrots, peeled and sliced
2 leeks, washed and sliced
1 bunch (about 2 cups) flat leaf parsley
1 bottle (11 ounces) Trappist beer
8.8 pounds mussels
salt and pepper to taste

Rinse mussels and discard any that have broken shells. Tap the open mussel on a hard surface and if they do not close within a few minutes, throw them out also.

Chop Parsley stocks, keep the leaves apart for later. Heat the butter in the bottom of a large mussel pot and fry the onions, carrots and leeks over medium low heat, until softened, about 5 minutes.

Add the beer and bring to a boil. Add the chopped parsley stalks.

Now add the mussels and cover the pot. Allow the mussels to steam in the beer for about 5 to 10 minutes, or until the mussels are opened. DO NOT OVER COOK!

Throw out any mussels that have not opened. Season to taste. Serve the mussels with a crusty bread and salad.

Makes 4 to 6 servings

ERWTENSOEP / SNERT

(split Pea Soup)

This traditional recipe was a favorite served for New Years Day in the Netherlands.

1 1/2 cup (10.5 ounces) dried green split peas
3 1/2 ounce Dutch speklapjes (fresh slice pork belly) or thick cut bacon
1 pork chop
1 stock cube (vegetable, pork, or chicken)
2 celery stalks
2 to 3 carrots sliced
1 large potato peeled and cubed
1 small onion chopped
1 small leek sliced
1/4 celeriac cube
salt and pepper

To Serve: a handful of chopped celery leaves and rook-wurst (a Dutch smoked sausage) or smoked soft met-wurst or frankfurter / sausages.

Bring 3 3/4 pints water to a boil in a large soup pot, along with split peas, stock cube, pork chop and bacon. Put lid on the pot and leave to boil softly for 45 minutes, stirring occasionally. Skim off any froth that may form on top.

Take pork chop out of pot with tongs, debone and thinly slice the meat, set aside. Add the vegetables to the boiling broth, and leave to cook for another 30 minutes, adding a little extra water if the soup starts to catch, (stick).

Add the smoked sausage for the last 15 minutes. When the vegetables are tender,

remove the bacon and sausage with the tongs, then slice thinly and set aside.

Meanwhile if you prefer a smoother soup, puree the soup, with a stick blender.

Season to taste, add the meat back to the soup, setting some slices of rook-worst aside. Serve in bowls, or soup plates. Garnish with slices of rook-wurst and celery leaves.

* Smoked Kielbasa, smoked soft met-wurst, frankfurter or wiener sausages instead of root-wurst.

Serves 4

BITTERBALLEN

(beef balls)

Typically these are made for hors d'oeuvres, or snacks, it is a treat to have on the Christmas table, served with Jenever (a Dutch Gin)

2 pounds stew beef
1 onion
1/2 teaspoon black peppercorns
1 bay leaf
2 cloves
a few sprigs of thyme

* For Roux:
1 stick butter
1 cup flour
2 shallots chopped
1/2 quart milk
1/2 quart beef stock (made from cooking the meat)
5 sheets gelatin
salt and pepper and a little nutmeg to taste
1 bunch of flat leaf parsley, finely chopped
1 tablespoon dijon mustard

* Breading:
flour
egg
fresh breadcrumbs

Place beef in a large pan with just enough water to cover the meat. Bring to a simmer. Skim off the foam and add the onion, peppercorns, bay leaf, cloves and thyme. Allow to simmer for a few hours, until the meat is tender.

Strain the beef stock and set aside for later. Allow the meat to cool. Cut the beef into small cubes.

Make roux with butter, flour and shallots.

Use the roux to make a salpicon by adding the milk and 1/2 the beef stock, let it simmer for half an hour, stirring thoroughly.

Dissolve gelatin in cold water, and add the simmering salpicon, stirring regularly. Add the rest of the ingredients and the beef, cover with plastic wrap and let the salpicon cool in the refrigerator.

Roll heaped teaspoon of the mixture in the meat even sized balls, you should get about 60 in total. Bread them twice. Deep-fry 356 degrees.

KERSTKRANS

Christmas Fruitcake

5 ounce blanched almonds
5 ounce confectioners sugar
1 teaspoon vanilla extract
1 egg
peel of 1 lemon

1 portion puff pastry made from:
1/2 cup very cold unsalted butter
1 cup flour
1/4 cup cold sour cream
1 small (beat) egg yolk

Filling :

(can be made one month ahead)

Grind almonds with sugar in grinder or blender. Add vanilla, egg, and lemon peel. Mix well. Grind again.

Puff Pastry:

Cut butter into small pieces and add to flour. Cut butter into flour until mixture resembles small peas. Mix sour cream with egg yolk, and blend into flour mixture with a fork mixing just until it forms a ball. Wrap well and refrigerate for several hours. Allow dough to come to room temperature before working. Roll out into long strips. 1/8 inch thick, 4 inches wide.

Shape almond paste into a roll, About 1 inch thick and of nearly the same length of dough. Press 10 halved cherries at equal intervals into roll.

Reshape.

Place roll on dough, a little above center. Wet lower part of dough and wrap loosely around roll. Do not let dough overlap more than enough to seal edges with water, and brush with egg. Heat oven to 450 degrees.

Place ring in refrigerator for 15 minutes. Bake 20 minutes until golden brown.

Coat ring thinly with preserves and while still hot, with thin icing - (made with powdered sugar and a few drops of water and lemon juice). Cool on baking sheet.

When firm, carefully lift and cool on wire rack. Decorate with halved candied cherries, orange peel, lemon peel, ribbon and holly.

Makes 10 to 12 small pieces

SLEMP

2 cinnamon sticks
12 whole cloves
1 teaspoons loose black tea leaves
1/8 teaspoon ground nutmeg
1/4 teaspoon ground mace
pinch saffron
cheese cloth
cooking wine
4 cups whole milk
2 -inch strip lemon peel (bitter white pith removed)
1/4 cup sugar
1 tablespoon corn starch

Place the first six ingredients on a square of cheesecloth

and tie tightly with cooking twine.

Place milk and spice in medium saucepan. Warm over low heat

until barely simmering. Lower heat and cook for 30 minutes.

Remove spice bag.

Add sugar and stir until dissolved.

Dissolve cornstarch in 1 tablespoon cold water.

Add to milk mixture, stir until slightly thickened.

Makes 4 cups

CHAPTER

Norway / Scandinavia

The Christmas greeting is 'gul Jul', or 'Gledelig Jul', Happy/Merry Christmas.

The Tree, traditionally did not come to this area until mid 19th century.

The decorations of choice are stars, flags, Rosemailed ornaments.

Traditional Holiday festivities begin weeks before Christmas, with the brewing of the Christmas beer (Juleil). The brewing of this beer traces its roots back to the old Norse mid-winter sacrificial celebration of Joula.

Joula is a festival of lights marking the change of winter darkness to springs light. The Vikings, during this feast would toast to (SKAL) the goddess of FRYL and wish each other peace and good fortune for the coming year. In 900 A.D. King Haakon I, declared that JOULU would be held in celebration instead of FRIY.

Advent signals the beginning of the holiday season. This is a time of Religious preparation as well as holiday preparations, seasonal pork dishes, and different kinds of small cakes are prepared.

December 13th is known as LUSSINATTEN and was considered the longest night of the year, from this night (longest night) until Christmas, is the time for all manners of strange and magical happenings. Animals are given the power to talk with one another. Trolls, Gromb, Goblins, along with Lossi, a very powerful enchantress roamed these nights. The first celebration of the holiday season comes on Saint Lucia Day, which is the festival of light. A young girl dressed in a white robe with a crown of lights (candles), and a candle in her hand. She will visit schools, hospitals, and other public places to bring light into the winter darkness.

Wood is chopped to last through the first three days of Christmas. In the rule areas, the farm animals and buildings, are protected by painted crosses on the doors of the out buildings. The tradition of the Christmas Tree was introduced by Germany, the latter half of the 19th century. The tree is decorated on Christmas Eve and kept behind close doors until that evening, to be a great surprise for the children. The tradition of the Norwegian Christmas Tree decorations are small paper baskets called 'Julekurver' which is made in the shape of a heart.

Christmas wasn't actually celebrated in Norway until about 1000 or 1100 A.D. When Christianity first came to the area. Before this people celebrated Jul or Jo'l in the middle of the winter. It was a celebration of the harvest gone, and a way of looking forward to the spring. Lots of beer 'Juleol' was brewed and drank in the honor of the old pagan Scandinavian gods.

Gifts are exchanged on Christmas Eve, Santa Clause is called 'JULENISSEN', gifts are also brought by small gnomes called 'Nisse'. There are also Hobgoblins (Nisse) decorations. Children will leave a bowl of porridge for Nisse who otherwise would play tricks on the children for not doing so. Children pick up their gifts from under the Christmas Tree and read the cards from the presents out loud.

As in Finland, a sheaf of wheat is often left out for the birds to eat over Christmas, also a rice porridge is sometimes left for 'Nisse' who is believed to watch over the farm animals.

In some parts of Norway, Children like to go carol, singing. Children will often dress up like the characters from the Christmas story, such as Shepard's, wise men, and go singing from house to house in their local neighborhood. Sometimes they carry a pole with paper star hanging from the top end of the pole. Musevisa - The Mouse Song, by: Alf Proysen in 1946.

Another tradition of the Norwegian Christmas is that the families light a candle every night, from Christmas Eve to New Years Day.

Many different types of cakes, cookies and biscuits are eaten over the Christmas period in Norway. One of the most popular of the special breads is called 'Julekake', it has raisins, candies peel and cardamon in it. Rice porridge is eaten on Christmas Eve, ether as a meal at lunch time, (served with butter, sugar and cinnamon) or as a desert to the main evening meal with whipped cream through it. If you find an almond in your portion your traditionally given a pink or white marzipan pig.

Norwegians also gather for the Christmas meal of codfish, porridge, gingerbread and punch.

Ammuen Dreyer AGE 11

JULEOL

Norwegian Christmas Brew

Juleol - (English Christmas Beer) was first mentioned in Haraldskvedet from around 900 A.D. "At sea the king will drink Jol and resume Freya's game".

Today 'Jul' means Christmas in Norwegian, but the word originates from, "to drink Jol". On the occasion of the annual winter fest, people were drinking strong beer, to celebrate the sun's return and the Norse gods.

The tradition of brewing beer was introduced by 'Olaf Tryggvason', King of Norway from 995 - 1000 A.D. It is said, that Saint Martin of

Tour, came to Olaf in a dream and directed him to give the old pagan custom a Christian content.

Around the year 1000, the winter solstice, became a time when people brewed strong beer and drank to the glory of Christ and Mary. The stronger the beer the greater the honor.

He who made excellent brew was given high status. The beer should be brewed with the farms best grain, and could be seasoned with juniper berries, sweet gale, and different herbs depending on what was available. The brew was free to experiment and use new flavors to highlight personality or originality, and each regions had its own traditions.

4 to 5 gallons water
2 bottles dark beer
3 pounds (6 cups) granulated sugar
1 bottle hops extract syrup
1 tablespoon fresh yeast

Boil water and set aside until the temperature reaches 95 degrees F. Dissolve the sugar in water and add dark beer and hops extract syrup (Tomtebrygg).

Mix very well.

Remove 1 liter of liquid and stir in the yeast into it well, before pouring it back into the mixing vessel.

Fill clean beer bottles right away, and store them in a dark, and cold place for three weeks.

Skal!

KRINGLA

1 1/2 cups granulated sugar
1 egg (beat)
2 1/2 cups sour cream

4 cups all-purpose flour
2 teaspoons soda
1/4 teaspoon salt

Preheat oven to 350 degrees F.

Mix sugar, egg, and sour cream.

Measure flour by dipping method, mix flour, soda and salt.

Blend thoroughly into creamed mixture.

Divide dough in half; form each half into a long roll.

If kitchen is warm then refrigerate until ready to use.

Cut off a narrow slice of dough, roll lightly with hands on a lightly floured surface, into pencil like strips, 7 to 8 inches long.

Form by modified figure 8 by pinching ends together tightly. Bring pinched ends to center of the rings; tuck under fastening securely.

Place on lightly greased baking sheet, or parchment lined baking sheet.

Repeat with remaining dough.

Bake 12 to 15 minutes, or until lightly browned.

Makes 6 to 7 dozen cookies

BERLINERKRANZER

'Berlin Wreaths'

1 cup granulated sugar
3/4 cup softened butter
3/4 cup shortening
2 teaspoons grated orange peel
2 eggs
4 cups all-purpose flour
1 egg white
2 tablespoons granulated sugar
red candied cherries

green candied citron

Preheat oven to 400 degrees F.

Mix 1 cup sugar, butter, shortening, orange peel and whole eggs, mixing well.

Stir in flour. Mixing well til a firm dough forms.

Shape dough by rounded teaspoonfuls into ropes about 6 inches long, and 1/4 inch diameter. Form each rope into a circle. Cross ends and tucking under.

(this shape method is easier than the traditional method of tying knots).

Place on ungreased cookie sheet or parchment lined cookie sheet.

Beat egg white and 2 tablespoons sugar until foamy; brush over top of cookies.

For holly berries press red bits of cherry candies on center of knot; add little jagged leaves, cut from citron.

Bake until set, but not brown, 10 to 12 minutes.

Immediately remove from cookie sheet.

Makes about 6 dozen cookies

DANISH SUGAR COOKIES

(Like the Cookies sold in the blue tins)

1/2 cup butter
1/2 cup shortening
1 cup granulated sugar
1 egg
1/2 teaspoon vanilla
1/2 teaspoon lemon extract
2 cups all-purpose flour
1/2 teaspoon soda
1/2 teaspoon cream of tarter
1/8 teaspoon salt

Preheat oven to 350 degrees F.

Cream together butter, shortening, sugar, egg, and flavorings.

Add dry ingredients, mixing well and chill.

Shape in 1 inch balls, roll in sugar, flatten with the bottom of a glass.

May also use cookie molds.

Bake 10 minutes.

NORWEGIAN BUTTER COOKIES

1 cup butter
1/2 cup confectioners sugar
2 cups all-purpose flour
2 teaspoons vanilla

Preheat oven at 350 degrees F.

combine all ingredients, and form into balls the size of a walnut.

Press with fork, in a criss-cross design.

Bake until edges become light brown.

ROSETTES

1 egg
1 tablespoon granulated sugar
1/2 cup all-purpose flour
1/2 cup corn starch
1 cup milk
1/2 teaspoon vanilla
1/8 teaspoon salt
oil for deep frying

Beat egg, sugar, and vanilla to cream.

Mix flour, cornstarch, and salt with milk, making sure there are no lumps.

Mix milk mixture with egg mixture. Blend well.

Dip rosettes metal form into batter, then into hot oil, will release itself from form.

Brown on both sides.

Drain on paper towels then sprinkle with confectioners sugar.

NORWEGIAN SPRITZ COOKIES

(using a hand press)

3 1/2 cups all-purpose flour
1/2 teaspoon baking powder
1/2 teaspoon salt
1 1/2 cups butter, softened
1 cup plus 2 tablespoons granulated sugar
2 teaspoons vanilla
1/2 teaspoon almond extract
1 large egg lightly beat
confectioners sugar (optional)

Preheat oven at 350 degrees F.

Line cookie sheets with parchment paper.

In a medium bowl sift together flour, baking powder, and salt and set aside.

In another bowl, beat butter with sugar, vanilla and almond extract until fluffy, about 3 minutes.

Add in egg and beat until combined.

Gradually add the floured mixture to the fluffy mixture, until all is well combined well.

Spoon dough onto a hand press or cookie bag. Press dough out onto the parchment lined cookie sheet.

Making stars with a candied cherry in the center or bar types or wreaths.

Experiment with the disks, have some fun!

Bake for 8 to 10 minutes.

Makes 5 dozen cookies

GINGERBREAD

2 1/4 sticks butter, softened
3/4 cup molasses
1 1/2 cup granulated sugar
2 teaspoon cinnamon
1 teaspoon cardamon
1 teaspoon ginger
1 teaspoon cloves
3/4 cup water
5 cups plain flour
1 teaspoon baking powder

Preheat oven at 320 degrees F.

Place butter and molasses in saucepan, over low heat, and stir until the butter has melted.

Place sugar, and spices in a large mixing bowl and pour in the hot butter mixture.

Stir until sugar has dissolved.

Add water and stir well.

Stir in flour and baking powder, stir until you have a soft dough.

Wrap in plastic and let dough stand in the refrigerator at least 24 hours.

Can be stored for up to 14 days.

Take dough out and roll thin.

Cut out stars, hearts, what ever you please, have fun with it.

Bake for about 5 to 6 minutes.

Cool on a wire rack.

Store in an air tight container.

LUSSEKATTER

St. Lucia Buns

In Sweden and Norway no cinnamon or nutmeg is used in the buns, and raisins are used instead of currents.

Traditionally eaten during Advent and especially on Saint Lucia Day, December 13th. They are also prepared and eaten mostly the same as in Finland.

Traditional shapes of which the simplest is the reversed S shape.

1/2 cup unsalted butter
1 1/3 cups milk
1 teaspoon Saffron threads chopped fine and soaked in a few drops of water.
1 tablespoon active dry yeast
2/3 cups sugar
1/2 teaspoon salt
2 eggs, divided
4 cups unbleached flour and flour for kneading
raisins for garnishing

Melt butter in small saucepan set over medium heat.

Add milk and saffron, and heat, just until warm.

Pour into a bowl of an electric stand mixer.

Sprinkle yeast over the milk and let sit for 5 minutes.

Add sugar, salt, one egg, and 2 cups flour, beat with paddle attachment until smooth and well combined, about 2 minutes on medium speed.

Add final 2 cups of flour. Using dough hook, beat until mixture is smooth and begins to climb the beaters.

Transfer dough to a lightly floured surface, and knead until perfectly smooth.

This dough should have a velvety texture to it.

Place in a greased bowl and turn once to coat all surfaces, and let rise, covered in a warm place, until doubled in size, about 1 hour.

Line baking sheet with parchment paper.

Preheat oven to 400 degrees F.

Punch dough down, and roll into a cylinder 36 inches long.

Cut 18 - 2 inch pieces from cylinder. Roll each piece into a 10 inch rope.

Form each piece into an - S - spiraling the ends to form a figure - 8 -.

Transfer pieces to prepared baking sheet, let rise, covered, until doubled in size, about 45 minutes.

Brush buns with the reserved egg.

Tuck raisin into each spiral at each end of figure eight.

Bake 15 minutes or until golden brown.

Makes 18 Buns

MARZIPAN

1 cup blanched and ground almonds, (about 3 5/8 oz.) - almond flour is easiest way to get this ingredient. you can buy blanched almonds and grind them yourself.

2 cups confectioners sugar
1 tablespoon light corn syrup
1/4 teaspoon almond extract
1/2 to 1 tablespoons water

Pour almond flour and confectioners sugar into the sifter or mesh strainer over a bowl.

Sift the ground almonds and sugar together, if you prefer to hand mix them, just make sure they are completely combined.

Mix the almond extract and corn syrup, and pour them into the dry ingredients. Mix and then knead with your hands until the mixture is slightly wet, although it will not fully bind together yet.

Add 1/2 tablespoon water at first, then the rest of the tablespoon, only if necessary, working the mixture until it becomes dough-like. Shape it so that it is oblong, put dough in freezer bag and gently roll into a smooth log.

At this time you can add coloring. (pink or natural if you are making the traditional pig).

Refrigerate the log for at least one hour.

To serve, cut chilled marzipan into pieces about 1/2 inch thick.

- or -

Press marzipan into a pig mold for your holiday tradition.

RISENGRYN GROD

Norwegian Rice Pudding

1 2/3 cup water
3/4 cup long grain rice
1 quart milk
1 teaspoon salt (optional)
1 teaspoon nutmeg
1 teaspoon vanilla
1/2 cup raisins - or - 1/2 cup currents

Bring water to a boil and add rice.

Cover and lower heat to simmer for 15 minutes.

Add milk and if using them, the raisins and currents and vanilla, and then bring back to a boil.

Cover, lower heat and simmer until the rice is tender, about 20 - 30 minutes.

Optionally season with salt.

Season with butter, milk, sugar, and cinnamon.

For a sweeter rice try adding 1/4 to 1/2 cup sugar with the milk.

Robin Redmon Dreyer

KLUB

Norwegian Potato Dumplings

Potato dumplings (Klub) calls for the same ingredients as Gnocchi; potatoes, flour and eggs. The texture is similar, but taste different. It is good topped off with fresh herbs, parsley, or green onions. Serve with lots of melted butter.

5 large russet potatoes, peeled, and grated
2 large eggs
2 cups of flour
1 teaspoon salt
1 pork chop, cut into bite size pieces, or meat from a pork hock, or ham or bacon

For Serving: Butter, salt, pepper, green onion, chopped parsley.

Prepare Mixture: Place grated potatoes in a large mixing bowl. Add eggs and mix with your hands. Add one cup of flour - then gradually add the second cup of flour, keep adding flour until potato mixture sticks together. This should be about 2 cups of flour, give or take.

Form into balls: Take about 1/2 cup potato mixture, place a piece of pork chop in the middle and form into a ball, repeat until all the potato has been used.

Cook Dumplings: Bring a large pot of water to boil. Add potato dumpling one at a time. Cook for 30 minutes in simmering water. At 30 minutes, take one dumpling out and test to see if meat inside is done. If not, cook for a little longer (about 30 minutes).

For serving: Serve hot with melted butter, salt and pepper, parsley and or chopped green onion.

Makes 15 dumplings

JULEKAKE

Norwegian Punch
(Adults Only)

6 parts Wild Turkey Rye
1 part Cynar Bitter liqueurs
2 parts Bols Genever
1 part Cre'eme de-sec
2 part Triple Sec
2 parts cardamon syrup
6 parts Cold Earl Grey tea
4 parts lemon juice
cardamon pods
dried fruits

Combine all ingredients, except pods and dried fruit, in the punch bowl over one large block of ice, and serve.

Garnish with dried fruits and pods.

HOLIDAY PUNCH

Kid Safe

1 to 2 liters bottles ginger ale

1 - 32 ounce bottle cranberry juice

2 quart container raspberry sherbet

cranberries for garnishing (boil cranberries until tender, save juice for punch

1/4 cup sugar

Put cranberries in a saucepan and cover with water, and simmer until tender. While simmering berries ad the 1/4 cups sugar to sweeten berries and juice.

(if you like it a little sweeter add 1/2 cup sugar)

In a punch bowl combine ginger ale, cranberry juice, and prepared juice from cranberries and berries, add sherbet and lightly stir as you dip into glasses.

(If you like cubes also, freeze any red juice in ice cube or decorative tray, will also add flavor as it melts).

CHAPTER

Finland

In Finland, the families put up their Christmas trees on Christmas Eve, and decorate it with fruits, candy, cotton-made ornaments, paper flags, tensile, and candles to give the tree its sparkle.

Families spend hours together in the kitchen, making special dishes for this festive season. The house is also cleaned from top to bottom.

Many of the peasants will not eat their holiday meal until the birds have eaten first. For the birds, they prepare a bundle of sheaf with grain is often tied to a pole with nuts and seeds attached then tied to a pole and placed in a garden to feed the birds. The meal was begun for the family when the first star is seen in the sky.

The Christmas festivities are proceeded by a visit to the famous steam baths and then they made preparations, dressing carefully for dinner. Dinner is served between 5 to 7 in the evening.

Christmas gifts may be handed out before or after Dinner. They do not hang up stockings, but Santa Claus comes in person and is usually accompanied by a half dozen Christmas Elves to pass out the Christmas gift.

In Finland, if the children are naughty they will be punished by 'Nuuttipukki'.

Creatures from the Finnish folklore that later morphed into modern-day Santa Claus. Krampas is an other example of something that looks similar to the original Finish Father Christmas.

'Tonttu' Finland's mythical creature of Scandinavian folklore. The Tomte or Nisse was believed to take care of the farmer's home, and children and protect them from misfortune, particularly at night when the house folk are asleep.

Christmas Day Services start at 6:00 am. It is a day for family visits and reunions. In some parts of the country, the 'Star Boys' tour the countryside singing Christmas songs. As the families celebrate the season, they keep wishing each other "Merry Yule".

The main dish of the dinner meal is boiled codfish served snowy white and fluffy, with allspice and boiled potatoes with cream sauce, roast suckling pig, or a roasted fresh ham, mashed potatoes and vegetables.

After dinner the children go to bed while the adults stay up and visit with their friends and family that are visiting. They enjoy coffee until midnight.

KINKKU

Baked Ham

1 (7 to 9 pounds UNSMOKED) salt cured ham
2 large egg yolk
1 tablespoon brown sugar
6 tablespoons grainy mustard
6 tablespoon crumbled gingersnap cookies or breadcrumbs

Heat oven to 350 degrees F.

Place oven rack in the upper third of the oven.

Rinse the ham well to remove any excess salt and pat dry.

Place pork rind side up in a heavy roasting pan, and put in the oven and roast until the internal temperature on an instant read thermometer reads 160 degrees F. (about 4 1/2 hours).

Remove from oven and increase heat to 450 degrees F.

carefully slice rind off ham (in Scandinavia this crispy, delicious, heart-attack inducing crackling is often used as a side dish). Whisk together egg yolk, brown sugar, and mustard, then spread evenly over the whole ham.

Sprinkle with the crumbled gingersnaps or bread crumbs until covered.

Return ham to oven and cook for an additional 10 to 15 minutes or until golden brown.

Remove from oven and cover loosely with foil wrap and let it rest for 15 minutes.

Carve and serve warm or let it cool completely and serve cold.

LANTTULAATIKKO

Rutabaga Casserole

There are several variations of rutabaga casseroles, and if not done well, it can be very bitter. Cook for a long time, and add corn syrup and cream. The original Finnish recipe calls for molasses, but the American type, the molasses is more bitter than the Finnish molasses, so I use dark corn syrup, or even better, brown sugar and corn syrup.

2 large rutabagas
2 teaspoon salt
2/3 cup breadcrumbs
1 egg
half pint heavy whipping cream
3 tablespoons molasses or corn syrup
1/2 teaspoon ginger or cinnamon
1/4 teaspoon nutmeg
1/4 stick butter
1 small onion
1/2 teaspoon white pepper

Peel the rutabagas, chopped in fairly large cubes.

Boil water (add some salt) put in the rutabagas and boil for almost an hour or until they are super soft. Pour the water off saving 3/4 cup for later.

Smash the rutabagas.

In a separate bowl, mix egg, bread crumbs, cream, syrup and spices and let them sit for about 15-30 minutes.

Chop the onion to very small and then saute' it in plenty of butter to make it nice and golden. Then mix well with the smashed rutabagas, cream, bread crumbs and mix then add the saute'd onions.

Place in a greased casserole dish, the deeper the better.

Make spoon marks on the top of the dish to give it a decorative design; sprinkle with bread crumbs.

Bake at 400 degrees F. for less than an hour. But to get better flavor, I recommend baking at 325-350 degrees F. for about 2 to 3 hours.

RYE GINGER COOKIES

(Traditional Nordic Flowers)

1 cup butter
1/2 cup sugar
1 egg
1 cup rye flour
1 cup all purpose flour
1 teaspoon ginger
1 teaspoon cinnamon
1 teaspoon horn salt or 2 teaspoons baking powder
3 tablespoons sparkling large grained sugar

Beat together butter and sugar until creamy; mix in 1 egg.

Sift together flour and spices, the horn salt / or baking powder.

Gradually stir flour mixture into creamed mixture about 1/4 cup at a time, so as to get it thoroughly mixed. DON'T OVERWORK THE BATTER!

On a well floured surface, very gently knead cookie dough 2 to 3 times; gather into a circle, pat flat, cover with cling wrap. and refrigerate for 1 hour and up to two days.

At this stage cookie dough can also be frozen up to two months for later use.

Preheat oven to 350 degree F.

Roll out dough to 1/4 inch thickness, cut with cookie cutter and place on lightly greased cookie sheet. Sprinkle with sugar.

Bake cookies just until browned or about 10 minutes.

Remove from oven and cool on rack; store in air tight container.

JOULUTORTTU

Christmas Pastries

5 sheets frozen puff pastry
Jam of desired flavor
1 egg
Icing sugar to decorate

Take the frozen puff pastry sheets from the freezer, place them on a sheet if parchment, and let them set at room temperature for about 15 minutes (or follow package instructions).

Cut the pastry into squares about 10 x 10 inch size.

Make diagonal, about 3 cm. cuts in each corner, (like you would if making a whirly-gig or windmill), leaving the middle of the square uncut for the jam.

I don't actually cut down the corners but off the corners slightly. This way the tarts edges will be less likely to over burn.

Fold 4 of the edges toward the center of the tart and press down gently to hold them together.

Brush top of egg with slightly beat egg.

Place a teaspoon of jam in the middle of the tarts.

Bake at 400 degrees F. for about 12 to 15 minutes, until pastry has a nice color.

Let the Joulutorttu cool down then sprinkle with icing sugar,

Enjoy! Makes 10 pastries

RIISIPUURO

Rice Porridge

First of all, of course, boil rice porridge:

2 cups water
2 cups rice porridge
1 liter milk
1 tablespoon butter
1/4 teaspoon salt
1 peeled almond

Using a thick based pot, Add the rice into the boiling water, and cook for about 2 minutes or until water is absorbed.

Add milk to porridge, simmer over low heat for about 40 minutes. Stir the pudding so that it does not stick to the bottom. Reduce the heat to low, so it slowly simmers.

Finally, add salt and butter. You can add the almond to porridge.

PIPARKAKUT

Gingerbread Cookies

3/4 cup golden syrup
7 ounce Caster sugar
9 ounce butter
1 tablespoon mixed citrus peel
2 eggs
17 1/2 ounce plain flour
3 teaspoon bicarb soda
1 teaspoon salt
2 teaspoon ground ginger
2 teaspoons ground cinnamon
2 teaspoons ground cloves

Place golden syrup, sugar, butter, and citrus peel into sauce pan and bring to a boil.

Allow to cool slightly, then beat with an electric mixer, until light and slightly fluffy.

Beat in eggs one at a time.

Sift flour, soda and salt with spices together. gradually add to the fluffy mixture 1/4 cup at a time until forms a dough.

Wrap dough with cling wrap and place in refrigerator over night.

Next day:

Preheat oven to 350 degrees F.

Roll out dough as thin as possible.

Cut desired shapes using cookie cutters.

Place cookies on parchment lined cookie sheets, brush with ice-water.

Bake for 6 to 8 minutes until brown and slightly fluffy.

CHAPTER

Poland

The children of Poland receive presents twice, on "Saint Nicholas' Day", the good saint himself brings presents. On Christmas Day, it is the 'Star Man'.

The Star of Bethlehem is the most popular image in the Polish Christmas.

It is the first Star of Christmas Eve, which marks the end of the Advent fast and ushers in the time of feasting. Though Christmas in Poland is officially known as 'BOZZ NARODZENIE', it is most often referred', to as 'GWIAZDKA', which means "Little Star".

Once the star appears, a special wafer blessed by the parish Priest, called 'OPLATKI' is broken into pieces and shared by all. Finally the meal can begin.

The feast consists of 12 courses, one for each Apostle. The table is always set with one extra seat, encase a stranger, or the Holy Spirit will appear to share the meal. After the supper meal. the 'Star Man' arrives attended by the Star Boys. The Star Man examines the children in their catechism and rewards them with small presents if they do well, even if they need a bit of coaching. The Star Boys sing carols and are given a treat for their help, after the fun, all go to PASTERKA, the Midnight Mass of the Shepherds.

Christmas is one of the most festive Catholic celebrations in Poland.

It plays a major part in the Polish culture and tradition.

December 24th - Christmas Eve, the day when Christians await the birth of Jesus Christ. Even though this day is one of the most important moments in Polish tradition, Christmas

Eve is a common work day.

December 25th - Christmas Day, holiday

December 26th - Feast of Saint Stephen - the first Christian martyr, holiday

Christmas Eve, 12 fasting dishes are served, symbolizing 12 months or 12 Apostles. Historical accounts show that back in the day, particularly in the countryside, Christmas eve dinner was prepared only from the fruits of the earth: Agricultural produce and fruit of the forest, rivers, ponds, and lakes.

Meals consisted of fish, considered fasting by the church, initially eaten on Christmas Eve, with time carp was the most important meal on Christmas Eve in Poland, usually served fried, with grated horseradish or in jelly accommodated with vegetables. One of the old Polish sauces used was a grey sauce, cooked on the basis of fish blood and wine. Also BORSCHT soup made of beet root or mushrooms with dumplings filled with mushrooms, PIEROGI desserts are poppy seed rolls, honey cakes, shortcakes with almonds, nuts and raisins, as well as stewed apples, pears and compote.

CHRISTMAS TREE

The tradition of decorating the Christmas Tree came to Poland from Germany in the 18th century, before that, people would hang the top of a fur, a pine or a spruce, from the roof and place a sheaf of corn in the corner. The tree was meant to protect the house and its inhabitants from evil. Now --- the star on top of the tree symbolizes the star of Bethlehem. The decorated tree stays up until January 6th, Epiphany.

CHRISTMAS CAROLS

On Christmas Eve and during the whole Christmas Season, Poles would sing carols; traditional songs about the birth of Jesus Christ. The oldest carols date back to the 15th century. The songs have been passed down from generation to generation. The most popular songs such as 'WSRODNOCNEJ CISZY' (In the Midst of the Nights Quiet), 'LULAJZE JEZUNIU', (Sleep Baby Jesus), or 'BOG SLE RODZI', (God is Being Born) originate from the turn of the 18th century and are still sung today.

After the feast at midnight, people go to church for midnight mass, commemorating the prayers of the shepherds who waited for the birth of Jesus in Bethlehem.

PIEROGI

Polish Rice Pudding

1 quart milk
1 cup boiled rice
3 ounces seeded raisins
2 ounce currents
grated peel of lemon
1/4 teaspoon grated nutmeg
6 eggs, separated, beaten yolks
1 cup sugar
3 tablespoons of pulverized sugar
vanilla

Heat milk, add rice, raisins and currents.

Let cook 10 minutes. Add the grated peel of the lemon, and the yolks of the eggs. beat well with sugar.

Mix thoroughly, pour into a well buttered pudding - dish; let bake until done.

Beat whites to a froth with pulverized sugar, and flavor with vanilla.

Spread on pudding and let brown slightly in hot oven.

Serve with Lemon Sauce.

LEMON SAUCE

1/4 granulated sugar
2 teaspoon corn syrup
1/4 cup water
1 tablespoon butter
1 teaspoon lemon peel

4 1/2 teaspoon lemon juice
yellow food coloring if desired

In saucepan, mix granulated sugar and corn starch.

Stir in remaining ingredients.

Cook over low heat, stirring constantly, until mixture begins to thicken.

Boil and stir 1 minute, if it is too thick add just a little water to thin down.

Serve over rice.

BARSZC WIGILIJNY

Polish Christmas Eve Beet Soup

BEET SOUR (KWAS):

3 1/2 pounds beets, peeled rinsed and sliced
boiled water, cooled to luke-warm
1 slice rye bread with crust

To make beet sour:

Place beets in large crock, or ceramic bowl. Cover with the parboiled water.

Add 1 slice rye bread, pushing it under the water. Cover with cheese cloth; let stand at room temperature for 3 days. Then strain through cheese cloth, Pour into a glass jar and seal it. Store in the fridge. You may eat the strained beets or discard them.

BEET SOUP:

1 pound beets, peel, rinse, sliced
1/2 pound peeled, rinsed and sliced
vegetables,(carrots, parsnips, celery, celery root, leeks)
2 tablespoons butter

1 garlic clove mashed with a little salt
2 cups beet sour
1/4 cup strained liquid from soaking a dried mushroom
salt and pepper
sugar to taste
1 tablespoon finely chopped parsley

TO MAKE BEET SOUP:

Place beets, Wioszczna (polish vegetables), in a large stock pot.

Then add 6 cups cold water and butter. Bring to boil, reduce heat and simmer until vegetables are tender. Strain, pressing on vegetables to extract all juices.

Return the strained liquid to the pot and add 1 clove garlic mashed with

little salt, beet sour (Kwas), strained mushroom soaking liquid, salt and pepper, and sugar to taste. Bring to bail reduce heat and simmer 30 minutes.

Before serving, stir in remaining 1 tablespoon butter and 1 tablespoon chopped parsley. Labeled into hot bowls and serve with mushroom USZKA.

KOMPOT

Polish Dried Fruit Compote

Polish traditionally fix kompot for Christmas Eves 'Wigilia' dessert was made with 12 different dried fruits represents the 12 Apostle. When cooked down it becomes a type of jam that is great on any bread.

Polish dried fruit compote traditionally called stewed-fruit dessert for a traditional Christmas Eve dinner, known as wigilia.

Stewed fruit is eaten in Poland year round, But especially popular in the fall and winter. It is the summers bounty that has been dried and preserved and then constituted with sugar, water, and spices, in some cases liquor.

It is a traditional Christmas Eve dessert made with 12 different dried fruits to represent the 12 apostles. When cooked down to a thicker consistency it becomes a type of jam that is great on toast or ice cream. Also makes a wonderful gift, but must be refrigerated. This will keep for one week.

1 1/2 pounds dried fruit Plum, prune, figs, apricots, peach, apples, pears, and berries.
8 cups water
8 whole cloves
2 cinnamon sticks
lemon zest, optional
1 cup sugar, or to taste

In a large saucepan place 1 1/2 pounds various dried fruit of your choice,

8 cups water, 8 whole cloves, 2 cinnamon sticks, lemon zest if using, 1 cup of sugar, or to taste.

Bring to a boil, stirring frequently. Reduce heat, simmer, cover for 20 minutes or until fruit is tender and syrup has thickened slightly.

Add more water if you like more liquid consistency, or for a thicker compote, continue simmering to reduce the liquid further.

Cool in an ice water bath, transfer to a very clean container, you can refrigerator for up to 1 week

Serve 12

Dried fruit
1. peaches
2. Blackberries
3. Red Raspberries
4. Rhubarb
5. Cherry
6. Apple
7. Raisins
8. Prunes
9. Apricots
10. Pears
11. Figs
12. Strawberries

Robin Redmon Dreyer

KLUSKI Z KWASHA KAPUSTA

Polish Noodles and Sauerkraut

1 pound kuski type noodle, cooked and drained
1/2 pound or 2 sticks butter
1 large onion coarsely chopped
1 (32 ounce) container sauerkraut, drained
1 (14 ounce) can mushrooms, stems and pieces, undrained

Saute' onion in butter until transparent, add kraut and cook over medium-low heat for 15 minutes, stirring frequently.

Heat oven to 350 degree F.

In a large pan or bowl combine cooked noodles, kraut, and undrained mushrooms, mixing thoroughly.

Adjust seasonings if necessary.

Transfer to a large casserole dish that has been coated with vegetable spray.

Bake 45 minutes, or just until top starts to brown.

KRO'LIK DUSZONY

Polish Rabbit in Mustard with Vegetables and cranberries

3.5 ounce spicy Polish mustard
3.5 ounce boiling water
2 tablespoons apple cider vinegar
6 pressed garlic cloves
2 sprigs fresh rosemary
1 bay leaf
4 white or yellow mustard seeds
4 ounce canola oil, divided
1 rabbit dressed, rinsed, and patted dry
1 ounce butter
1.75 ounce buckwheat flour

1 large onion, chopped
6 large chopped carrots
3 medium leeks, wash well and sliced
5 ounce dry white wine
4.25 cups vegetable stocks
5 ounce sour cream
salt and pepper
5.25 ounce cranberry jam or whole cranberry sauce

MARINATE': In medium bowl mix together mustard, water, vinegar, 3 pressed garlic cloves, chopped rosemary, bay leaf, mustard seeds, and 2 tablespoons oil, then set aside.

Cut rabbit into 6 parts, rub in marinate from above, and place in a dish.

Cover with a linen cloth or plastic wrap and refrigerate overnight.

When ready to cook, remove rabbit from marinate', pat dry lightly.

In a large dutch oven or other heavy-bottomed lidded pot; heat the remaining 6 tablespoons oil and butter, dredge the rabbit in buckwheat flour and brown on both sides, cover loosely with foil and reserve.

In same pot as rabbit was browned in, add chopped onion and remaining garlic and saute' for 3 minutes, stirring frequently, add carrots and leeks and saute' 4 minutes, stirring frequently add wine, bring to a boil, reduce heat and simmer for 3 minutes, until the alcohol is evaporated.

Place the reserved rabbit pieces on top of the vegetables, add stock until rabbit is half covered.

Bring to boil, reduce heat, cover and simmer 1 1/2 hour or until rabbit is tender. Temper sour cream with a little hot pan juices, return to pot; simmer a few minutes and adjust seasoning with salt and pepper.

Serve with cranberry jam.

Robin Redmon Dreyer

ROLMOPSY

Herring for Polish Rollnops

4 whole salted herrings
2 tablespoons Polish grainy mustard or Digon
black pepper
1 large onion chopped very fine
2 medium pickles
1/2 cup white vinegar
1 cup water
1 bay leaf
3 tablespoons oil
pinch sugar

Remove the heads on the herring.

Soak in a large pan of cold water for about 24 hours. Changing water about 2 or 3 times during the 24 hours.

To clean: make sure there are no scales on the fish.

Slit the belly and remove the intestines. Remove the milt from the male herring and set aside. Remove the roe from the female and discard it.

Wash the herring cavities well.

Remove bones.

You should have 8 halves of herring fillets, spread each with some of the mustard, pepper and onion.

Place a pickle portion at the small end or large end of the fillet, as you prefer, roll up and secure with a toothpick.

Place in a clean sterilized jar. Continue the same with the remaining fillets.

In small saucepan, bring vinegar, water, and any remaining chopped onion to a full rolling boil. Let cool to luke warm. Remove milt, if using, from sack and rub it through a sieve into the vinegar mixture.

Add oil and sugar and mix well. Adjust seasonings if necessary. Pour over herring

Cover the jar and refrigerate for 3 days, at which time it will be ready to eat.

It will keep in the refrigerator for 10 days.

This can be served as an appetizer or a main course with boiled potatoes and rye bread.

MAKOWIEC

Polish Poppy Seed Roll

DOUGH:

1 package active dry yeast
2 cups warm milk
8 cups all-purpose flour
3/4 cup sugar
1 teaspoon salt
5 eggs
4 ounces (1 stick) butter, melted
2 (11 ounces) cans poppy seed filling or make your own

In a small heat proof bowl, dissolve yeast in 1/2 cup warm milk.

Combine sugar, flour, salt and eggs. Add remaining 1 1/2 cups milk, butter, and yeast mixture in a large stand mixture with paddle attachment, or by hand.

Beat until smooth.

Dough will be sticky at this point.

Scrape dough into a greased bowl.

Sprinkle top with a little flour and cover.

Let stand in a warm place, 1 hour, or til double in size.

Punch down dough and pour out onto a floured surface.

Divide dough in half, and shape each half into a rectangle.

Spread 1 can or 1/2 of filling on each rectangle and roll up like a jelly roll.

Turn ends under so filling wont pour out.

Place on parchment lined pan, let rise again, covered until doubled in size.

Heat oven to 350 degrees F.

Brush top of rolls with melted butter.

Bake for 45 to 50 minutes or until golden brown.

Remove from oven and cool.

Dust with powdered sugar

POPPY SEED FILLING:

1 pound ground poppy seed
1 cup sugar
6 ounce (1 1/2 stick) soft butter
1 cup hot milk
1 lemon rind grated

Mix all ingredients together, beat well and set aside.

BLUEBERRY PIEROGI

BLUEBERRY FILLING:

1 1/4 pound blueberries
1/2 cup sugar
1/4 teaspoon cinnamon
1 teaspoon diced lemon zest

In a large saucepan combine all ingredients over medium heat.

Allow to come to boil, reduce heat and simmer 2 minutes, remove from heat, and cool completely.

PIEROGI DOUGH:

2 large eggs
5 tablespoons sour cream
3 tablespoon vegetable oil
3/4 cup chicken broth
4 cups all-purpose flour

Combine in a large bowl, eggs, sour cream, oil, and broth, and mix well.

Add flour a little at a time, knead by hand until smooth.

Wrap with plastic. Let rest 10 minutes.

On lightly floured surface, roll out dough to 1/8 inch thickness.

using a 3 inch round cutter, cut dough. Grab scrap with plastic wrap and set aside.

Use a 1 1/2 inch cookie scoop, portion filling on all the dough circles before folding.

With clean, dry hands, fold dough over filling to create a half moon shape.

Press edges together, seal and crimping with your fingers, or use a fork as for a pie.

Bring a big pot of salted water to a boil. Reduce to simmer. Drop 12 Pierogi at a time into water. Stir once so they don't stick to the bottom of the pot.

When they rise to the surface, cook 3 minutes or until dough is done to your liking.

Remove with slotted spoon to a platter that has been spread with butter.

Serve with melted butter or confectioners sugar.

When filling pierogi use a slotted spoon to place 3 to 4 blueberries on each piece of dough. Use reserve sauce to garnish the cooked plate of crepes.

Can be frozen, freezes well.

Robin Redmon Dreyer

KOTACZ

Polish Wheal Cake

DOUGH:

7 to 8 cups unsifted, unbleached, flour
2 cups whole milk
4 ounce butter, room temperature
1 - 2 ounce cake fresh yeast
1/2 cup warm water
1/2 cup sugar
1 tablespoon salt
1 egg at room temperature

CHEESE FILLING:

1 pound large curd cottage cheese, drained well
-or- 1 pound dry curd cheese
1 large egg yolk, at room temperature
1 teaspoon sugar
1/4 teaspoon salt
additional butter

TO MAKE THE DOUGH:

Scald the milk, then put the butter into the milk to melt.

crumble the yeast into warm water, and let stand until it is bubbly, about 10 minutes.

After the scalded milk - butter mixture has cooled to no hotter than 110 degrees F.

Transfer to the bowl of a stand mixer, and add the yeast mixture, add the sugar and egg, mix well.

Add 7 to 8 cups of flour as necessary, and using the paddle attachment of your stand mixer. Knead until smooth, about 7 to 8 minutes. The dough will be soft and sticky.

Transfer to a greased bowl and let rise until doubled in size. Punch down and let rise again until doubled.

TO MAKE CHEESE FILLING:

Meanwhile, make the cheese filling by mashing the drained cottage cheese in a medium bowl to get out the lumps. Add one large egg yolk, sugar and salt then mix well.

Heat oven to 350 degree F.

Coat 3 9 x 5 inch loaf pans - or - large round pan, using coating spray.

NOW... punch down the dough, and divide among the pans. It will be a slack, almost a pourable dough, place 1/3 of cheese filling on top of each dough filled pan.

Bake for 45 minutes to 1 hour or until an instant read thermometer registers 190 degrees F.

Remove from oven, wait 10 minutes and remove from pans, rub butter over the entire crust.

Let cool completely before slicing and enjoying as is -or- with butter.

As with most breads and cakes that don't contain perspectives, this will stale quickly unless it is stored in the refrigerator and rewarmed a bit in the microwave. Can be frozen by slices in freezer bags.

PIERNIK

Polish Honey Cake

Topping:

7 tablespoon unsalted butter
1/2 cup buckwheat honey (dark honey)

1/8 teaspoon salt
1 teaspoon vanilla extract
1/2 cup almonds, slivered or sliced

CAKE:

1 3/4 cup unbleached, all-purpose flour
1 tablespoon baking powder
1/2 teaspoon salt
1/2 cup (1 stick) unsalted butter, at room temperature
5 tablespoons cane sugar
1/4 cup buckwheat honey, (dark honey)
2 large eggs, room temperature
1 teaspoon vanilla extract
1/2 cup whole milk

Place oven rack to middle of oven.

Preheat oven at 375 degrees F.

Generously butter bottom and sides of spring form pan. Line bottom with a round piece of parchment paper. Buttered parchment. Dust pan with flour, knocking out excess flour, set aside.

FOR TOPPING:

Melt 7 tablespoons butter in small saucepan. Add honey and salt, stirring until blended and bringing to a boil over medium high heat. Reduce heat to low and simmer for 2 minutes. Remove from heat, stir in the vanilla and almonds; set aside to cool.

FOR CAKE :

In medium bowl, whisk together the flour, baking powder and salt and set aside.

In a large bowl, using an electric mixer, cream together butter and sugar until fluffy. Gradually drizzle in the honey, continuing to beat until light and fluffy. Add the eggs, one at a time, beating after each addition and scraping down the sides of the bowl with spatula, as needed.

Turn the batter into the prepared pan, Distributing evenly, and smooth the top.

Pour and spread the topping evenly over the cake. Place the pan on the cookie sheet. Bake in center of preheated oven for about 35 minutes or until tested with tooth pick in center comes out clean. Cool in pan on wire rack for 10 to 15 minutes. Then turn out onto a wire rack to finish cooling completely.

Cut into wedges.

Excellent to eat as is, or dust with powdered sugar or served with sweetened whipped cream.

Makes 10 servings

CLASTO Z TRUSKAKAMI LUB JAQOWMI

Polish Berry Shortcake

1 quart berries
1/2 cup sugar

CAKE BATTER:

1 1/4 cups flour
3/4 cup sugar
1/3 cup butter
2/3 cup milk
2 eggs
2 1/2 teaspoons baking powder
1/2 teaspoon salt

---SWEETENED WHIPPING CREAM---

1 pint heavy whipping cream
1/4 cup sugar

Early in the day, prepare berries, wash, stem, place in a covered container and sprinkle with granulated sugar and place into the refrigerator. A couple times thru the day, shake the berries.

Preheat oven to 400 degrees F.

Grease and flour a 9 inch square pan or mini rounds for individual cakes.

In a small mixing bowl, with mixer, add all ingredients and beat at medium speed, scraping bowl often, until well mixed. (about 2 minutes)

Spread in prepared pan and bake for 20 to 25 minutes.

Cool completely in pan.

Just prior to serving, whip the cream and sugar.

Cut cake into 9 squares.

Then slice each square horizontally.

Place both halves on serving plate. Spoon berries on cake.

Dollop whipped cream on top of berries.

Ladle berry juice over top of cream.

Makes 9 servings

PANSKA SKORKA

The Lord's Crusts
Candy

1 cup granulated sugar
1/2 cup water
1/2 cup honey
2 large eggs at room temperature
1/4 teaspoon salt

1 tablespoon vanilla
1 tablespoon pink food coloring

In medium heavy bottomed sauce pan over medium heat, add sugar, water, and honey. Cook stirring constantly, until the sugar dissolves. Then stop stirring and use a wet pastry brush to wash down sides of saucepan to prevent crystallization of the sugar. Insert a candy thermometer, and without stirring, let the mixture come to a hard crack stage of 310 degrees F. Immediately remove from the heat to a cooler spot on the stove, let it cool 2 minutes before adding to the egg whites.

While sugar is cooking and when it reaches 252 degrees F.

Begin whipping the egg whites with a whisk attachment of your electric mixer. Whip to a soft peak stage and the change mixer paddle to a sturdier paddle attachment, because the mixture will become very stiff when the sugar mixture is added.

Once the sugar has reached 310 degrees F. and has cooled for 2 minutes, begin pouring into the beat egg whites, while mixer is running at high speed, by trickling the sugar in a thin stream into the egg whites. Beat for 10 minutes. Add salt and vanilla and beat until well incorporated.

Transport HALF of the mixture into a 9 x 9 inch pan that has been lined with parchment paper, and then coated lightly with cooking spray. Lightly coat your hands with cooking spray, and use them to press the candy into an even layer.

Add food coloring to the remaining mixture in the bowl, mix well and then spread on top of the plain white layer in the pan, again using hands that have been lightly coated with cooking spray. Refrigerate at least 6 hours or over night.

Remove candy from refrigerator, and using warm knife, loosen the candy block from the edges of the pan, and flip it out on a cutting board. Using a warm knife or one that has been sprayed with cooking spray, cut the block into 15 pieces, wrap each piece in wax paper or parchment. Panska Skorka can be stored at room temperature, in an air tight container for up to 1 week.

Makes 15 candies

GRZANIEC GALICYJSKI

Polish Hot Mulled Wine

This is popularly served outdoors when it is cold and you are enjoying the festivities of skating, sledding, sleigh rides, any outdoor winter activity.

This recipe was commonly used by the Czech, and they called it 'svarene vino', the Hungarians called it, 'forralt bor', the Serbs called it 'kuvano vino', and the Croatians say 'kuhano vino', the Bulgarians called it greyano vino, and Romanians call it vin fiert.

1 quart dry wine
1/2 cup sugar
5 partially crushed cloves
1 cinnamon stick
1 bay leaf cracked in half

In a large sauce pan combine wine, sugar, cloves, cinnamon stick, and bay leaf.

Heat to dissolve sugar, bring just to boiling point, then remove from heat.

Strain and pour into hot mugs.

CHAPTER

Asia

China, Vietnam, Philippines, Thailand, Korean, Japan

CHINA

Christmas in China celebrate by lighting their houses with beautiful paper lanterns, and decorating their Christmas trees, which they call "Trees of light" with paper chains, paper flowers and paper lanterns. Chinese children hang muslin stockings and await a visit from Santa Claus, who they call 'Dun

Che Lao Ren' which means 'Christmas old man'. Since the vast majority of china are not christian, the main winter festival in China is the Chinese New Year, which takes place at the end of January. Now officially called 'the spring festival'. It is a time when children receive new clothing, eat luxurious meals, receive new toys and enjoy a fireworks display. An important aspect of the new year celebration is the worship of ancestors. Portraits and paintings of ancestors are brought out and hung in the main room of the home.

Only about 1% of the nation is christian. The spiritual side of Christmas is naturally overlooked by many, although in recent years there has been a growth in the real reason for the holiday. Many Chinese celebrate Christmas with a lot of gift giving, It is a very materialistic holiday for those who do not have the faith. Jobs do not stop on Christmas day, and so many celebrate with a dinner, often at a restaurant on Christmas eve.

The tradition that is getting popular is the giving of apples. Many places have apples wrapped in colored paper for sale. People give apples on Christmas eve because in the language Christmas eve is called 'Pin

An Ye', which means quiet or silent night, and the word for apple in chinese is Pin Guo which sounds similar.

Some of the foods feast upon for their holiday traditions are, Chinese Duck, or duck stuffed with chunks of chicken, smoked ham, peeled shrimp, fresh chestnuts, bamboo shoots, sliced scallops, mushrooms stir-fried with slightly under-cooked rice, soy sauce, ginger, onions, whee, sugar and rice wine.

VIETNAM

Vietnam has a small population of Christians as well, due to its time under French rule. As a result, those individuals practice many of the same holiday customs as those found in Europe. Vietnamese Christian children, like their french counterparts, leave their shoes out for Santa, to deposit gifts on Christmas day.

PHILIPPINES

Having the longest Christmas in the world that starts in September. The Philippines have a multitude of traditions including the 'Misa De Gallo' (Dawn Mass), caroling, 'Monito Monita' (secret Santa) and more.

The country is also famous for its 'Parols' which are lanterns that have Christmas designs. Parols is a bamboo pole or frame with a lighted star lantern on it. It is traditionally made from bamboo strips and colored Japanese paper or cellophane paper. It represents the star that guided the wise men. It is the most popular decoration in the Philippines.

People in the Philippines are a mixture of western (USA and UK) and native Filipino traditions, so the Philippines have Santa Claus, Christmas trees, Christmas cards, and Christmas carols.

Christmas Eve is very important in the Philippines. Many people stay awake all night into Christmas Day! During Christmas Eve evening, Christians go to church to hear the last 'Simbang Gabi' or the Christmas Eve Mass. This is followed by a midnight feast called 'Nache Buena'.

The Noche Buena is a big open house, celebration with family, friends and neighbors, dropping in to wish everyone a Merry Christmas! Most households would have several dishes laid out and would normally include Lechon (roast pig), ham, fruit salad, rice cakes (bibingka), and Puto Bumbong are traditional foods and other sweets, steamed rice, and many different types of drinks.

THAILAND

Located in the South East Asia. Because of the Western and commercial influences of resent years and the Mais love for time and celebrations, many will decorate for Christmas even if they do not take an official holiday.

Children will dress up in bright colors, and schools will put on plays for the children's entertainment, complete with games, prizes, Christmas songs, and Santa Claus, who will hand out gifts to the children.

Catholics have recently try to encourage to give to those less fortunate, than themselves by organizing concerts and gift donation sites at Christmas-time. There is a great lack of teaching and understanding of the true meaningofof Christmas.

In contrast, New Years day in Thailand is a holiday. New Years is about spending time with your family and exchanging gifts. Religious Thais will go to their Buddhist temples to Tham boun (make merit) with meditation and charitable gifts. At midnight on New Years Eve. Fireworks boom, though the people will release millions of floating lanterns into the air.

KOREAN

Grandfather Santa is popular with kids in Korea (Santa Kullosu) and he wears ether red or blue Santa suit. People in Korea usually exchange presents on Christmas Eve. Only one gift is customary and sometimes it can be money. Giving actual gifts has become more popular, but giving money is still very common.

Restaurants are busy at Christmas because it is considered a romantic holiday for couples, theme parks and shows have special Christmas events. It is a popular shopping day as well.

There are more Christians in South Korea (the Republic of Korea) than in other Asian countries, such as China and Japan. So Christmas is celebrated more widely. (Christian makes up about 25 - 30 % of the population). However the other 70 % of people in South Korea are Buddhist (about 25 %) or don't have a religion at all.

Unlike Japan, Christmas is an official public holiday --- so people have the day off work and school! But they go back on the 26th which is 'Boxing Day'. There's a longer official winter break in the New Year.

Churches are decorated with lights and many have a bright red neon cross on top (all the year), so that goes very well with the Christmas lights. Most Churches will have a service on Christmas day. (Going to church has become more popular, even among non-Christians.

Some people, especially Christians, will have decorations at home, including a Christmas tree.

A popular Christmas food is Christmas Cake, but is often a sponge cake, covered in cream and bought from a local bakery, or you might even have an ice cream cake bought from 'Baskin Robbins'.

Happy/Merry Christmas in Korean is 'Meri Krismas' or 'Jeulgaeun Krismas Doeseyo'. Christians can say 'Sungtan Chukhahaeyo' to celebrate the birth of Jesus.

If you live in the 'Democratic People's Republic of Korea' Christmas will be very different. Being a Christian is 'officially' allowed, but you can go to prison, or can even be killed for being a Christian or even having a Bible.

Christians in North Korea have to meet in secret, and any celebrations of Christmas must also be held in secret.

JAPAN

Christmas was introduced to Japan by the early Christian Missionaries, and for many years, the only people who celebrated were those who turned to the Christian faith. Now the Christmas season in Japan is filled with meaning and almost universally observed. The story of the little child Jesus born in a manger is most fascinating to the girls in Japan, for they love anything to do with babies. In the scene of the Nativity, they became familiar for the first time with a cradle, for Japanese babies never sleep in cradles. Many Western customs in observing Christmas have been adopted by the Japanese. About 1 % of the people in Japan believe in the Christian faith.

Besides exchanging gifts, they also eat turkey on Christmas Day, and in some places there are even community Christmas trees. They decorate their houses with mistletoe and evergreens, and in some homes carols are sung gaily.

In Japan there is a Buddhist priest known as 'Hoteleiosho', who closely resembles our Santa Claus. He is always pictured as a kind old man carting a big pack. He is thought to have eyes in the back of his head, it is well for all children to be good while this gentleman is abroad. Santa is known as 'Santa-san'. New Years Day is the most important day on the Japanese calendar.

On New Years Eve the houses are cleaned from top to bottom, and are decorated for the morrow, when everything has been made clean and neat, the people of the house dress in their best cloths. Then the father of the house followed by the family, drives ALL the evil spirits out. He throws dried beans in every corner, bidding evil spirits leave and good luck enter.

It has been claimed that Kentucky fried chicken is now one of the most famous Christmas dinners in Japan. The demands for these celebrations are so great the people need to reserve their chicken two months in advance.

ALMOND COOKIES

1 cup all-purpose flour
1/2 cup butter, room temperature
1/2 teaspoon salt
1/4 cup plus 2 tablespoons sugar
1/2 teaspoon almond extract
1 egg yolk room temperature
1 tablespoon water
1/4 cup blanched almonds

Measure flour into a bowl. Cut in butter. work salt, sugar and flavoring in with hands. Shape in long roll 1 inch diameter; wrap in wax paper, chill about 1 hour.

Preheat oven to 400 degrees F.

Cut dough into 1/4 inch slices. Place about 1 inch apart on lightly greased baking sheet.

Brush each cookie with a mixture of egg yolk and water.

Press 1/2 blanched almond in top center of each cookie.

Bake 8 to 10 minutes, until lightly golden brown.

Allow cookies to cool slightly on the pan before removing from baking sheet, so they won't crumble.

Makes 2 dozen cookies

TERIYAKI CHICKEN WINGS

3 to 3 1/2 pounds chicken wings (about 20)

1/2 cup ketchup

1/4 cup dry white wine

1/4 cup soy sauce

2 tablespoons sugar

1 teaspoon salt

1/2 teaspoon ground ginger

1 clove garlic crushed

Cut each chicken wing at joint. (makes 3 pieces; discard tips).

Place chicken in ungreased baking dish, 9 X 13 X 2 inches.

Mix ketchup, wine, soy sauce, sugar, salt, ginger, and garlic, mix well, pour over chicken, cover and refrigerate, turning chicken occasionally, at least 1 hour.

Preheat oven to 375 degree F.

Drain chicken, reserving marinate.

Place chicken on rack in foil lined broiler pan.

Bake 30 minutes. Brush with reserve marinate.

Turn chicken; bake brushing occasionally with marinate, until tender, about 30 to 40 minutes.

Servings: 8 to 12

SWEET-SOUR PORK SAUSAGE BALLS

Meat Balls:
1 pound pork sausage
1 egg
1/3 cup fine bread crumbs
1/2 teaspoon sage

Mix sausage, egg, bread crumbs, and sage.

Shape into about 2 dozen 1 1/2 inch balls.

In an ungreased pan brown balls slowly on all sides, about 15 minutes.

Pour off grease.

Sauce:

1/2 cup ketchup
2 tablespoons brown sugar
1 tablespoon vinegar
1 tablespoon soy sauce

Combine all ingredients for sauce. Pour over meat, cover and simmer 30 minutes.

Stirring occasionally to coat meatballs. (Can be served as appetizers if meatballs are made smaller).

Serve over rice as a main dish.

Recipe:

CASHEW CHICKEN

3 whole chicken breasts
1/2 pound mushrooms

4 green onions
1 tablespoon chicken stock base
dissolved in 1 cup water
1 (4 ounce) cashew nuts
1/4 cup soy sauce
2 tablespoons corn starch
1/2 teaspoon sugar
1/2 teaspoon salt
1/4 cup salad oil

Bone chicken and remove skin. Slice horizontally into slices 1/8 inch thick.

Then cut into 1 inch squares. Arrange on a tray. Slice mushrooms.

Cut green parts of the onions into 1 inch long pieces; slice white parts 1/4 inch thick. Arrange on tray, pour chicken broth into small pitcher.

Mix soy sauce, corn starch, sugar and salt into broth in small pitcher.

Place oil and nuts into a container.

Arrange ingredients at table with an electric fry pan.

Heat 1 tablespoon oil to 350 degrees F.

Add cashews all at once. Cook 1 minute, shaking pan. Remove and set aside.

Add remaining oil and chicken, cook quickly, turning until opaque.

Add mushrooms and broth, cover and simmer 2 minutes, stir in soy sauce, and cook until thickened, stirring constantly. Simmer 1 minute uncovered.

Mix in onions, sprinkle with cashew nuts.

Serve over white rice.

CHINESE SESAME CHICKEN

2 tablespoon soy sauce
2 tablespoons toasted sesame oil
1 tablespoon sugar

1 tablespoon honey
2 tablespoons rice vinegar
1 tablespoon freshly grated ginger
2 cloves garlic minced
2 tablespoons sesame seed
1 egg beaten
3 tablespoons cornstarch
sea salt and Pepper to taste
1 pound boneless chicken thighs, trim off fat,
and cut into bite size pieces
1-2 tablespoon vegetable oil

In a bowl, combine soy sauce, sesame oil, sugar, vinegar, ginger, garlic, to make the sauce, set aside.

In a large bowl combine egg with corn starch and a generous dash of salt and pepper.

Add chicken to bowl and toss to coat, after coating let set 10 minutes.

Heat wok or heavy bottom pan, on high heat.

Add oil and coat pan.

Add the chicken and stir-fry until golden brown, about 5 minutes.

Once chicken is cooked, pour reserved sauce from bowl with soy sauce mixture into wok.

Toss to combine chicken with sauce and stir fry for a few minutes more.

As soon as sauce thickens turn off heat.

Garnish with sesame seeds, served over rice.

CHINESE STIR-FRY / CLAMS IN BLACK BEAN SAUCE

2 pounds clams
2 tablespoons Chinese fermented black beans,
rinse to remove excess salt.
1/4 teaspoon chili paste, to taste

SAUCE:

1/2 cup chicken stock broth
1 tablespoon oyster sauce
2 tablespoons light soy sauce
1 teaspoon dark soy sauce
1 teaspoon sugar
1/2 teaspoon Asian sesame seed oil

2 tablespoons peanut or vegetable oil for frying
1 1/2 tablespoons fresh minced ginger
2 teaspoons fresh minced garlic
1 Chinese leek (a large scallion),
white parts only, smash and cut into 1 inch pieces.
1 tablespoon Chinese rice wine
1 scallion cut into 1 inch pieces

Remove the clams from their packaging.

Discard all clams with broken shells, shells that are open, or who's shells do not close when tapped.

Scrub the clams well with a stiff brush.(a vegetable brush is good)

Although these are hard shell clams, you may want to soak them in salt water, to remove sand and grit, using kosher or sea salt for 2-3 hours before cooking: 1/3 cup salt to 16 cups of water is a good ratio.

Mash the fermented black beans, with the back of a cleaver or wooden spoon.

Stir in chili paste.

In a small bowl, combine the sauce ingredients. (chicken stock, oyster sauce, light and dark soy sauce, sugar and Asian sesame oil).

Heat oil in preheated wok over high heat.

When the oil is hot, add the ginger, garlic and Chinese leek.

Stir for about 10 seconds, then add black beans, and stir for about 15 seconds.

Add the clams.

Stir-fry for about 1-2 minutes, splashing with the rice wine.

You may start to hear the popping sounds of the clams opening, depending on the size and the specific kind of clams you are using.

Add the broth, and turn the heat down, cover and simmer for 5 minutes, or until all clams are opened.

Stir in green onion.

Remove the clams from the wok to the platter, discard any that did not open.

Pour the sauce over the clams.

Serve with noodles or rice.

Makes 4 servings

PHILIPPINE BUTTER COOKIES

1 cup butter softened
1 cup white sugar
3 eggs
3 2/3 cups cornstarch
1 teaspoon cream of tarter
1 teaspoon baking powder

Preheat oven to 375 degrees F.

Grease cookie sheet.

In a medium bowl, cream together, butter and sugar until smooth.

Beat eggs, one at a time, Stir in cornstarch, cream of tarter, and

baking powder until well blended.

Roll the dough into 1 inch balls and place them one inch apart on the prepared cookie sheets.

Bake 10-12 minutes in the preheated oven, or until light brown.

Remove to wire racks to cool.

THAI GINGER COOKIES

1/3 cup sesame seed
1 untreated lemon
7/8 cup butter
1 3/4 cup plus 2 tablespoon powdered sugar
1 medium egg
1 pinch salt
2 tablespoons sesame oil
2 tablespoons honey
3 1/2 cups four, and flour for rolling
2/3 - 1 cup ginger jam

Roast in a frying pan, sesame seed to golden brown, remove.

Wash lemon, dry, and finely grate peel

Sesame seed, butter, and lemon peel in small pieces.

In a large mixing bow mix, 3/4 cup powdered sugar, egg, salt, oil, honey and flour, and knead with dough hook of electric mixer until smooth.

Wrap dough in foil and refrigerate, 30 minutes.

Roll out dough on floured surface, to 1/4 inch thickness.

Cut into about 80 squares. (about 6 x 6 cm.)

With smaller cut out pieces, in shape of stars, comets, hearts, ect.

Cut out centers of 40 cookies for tops.

Line 4 cookie sheets with parchment paper, place cut out dough on cookie sheet and bake at 350 degrees F. for 6-8 minutes. Let cool on wire rack.

Cut lemon in half and squeeze out juice.

In a bowl add 2 tablespoons of lemon juice and 1 cup powdered sugar mixing well to form icing for the top of the cookies.

Put icing into a zip lock bag and cut tip out of corner.

Drizzle icing over the top part of top cookies, that have centers cut out.

Heat ginger jam enough to spread, coat bottom cookie then sandwich the top cookie onto jammed cookie. Sprinkle with powdered sugar.

Wait 1 hour before eating.

Makes 40 cookies

KOREAN BEEF BOWL

1 pound ground beef
1/2 small zucchini finely chopped or grated
12 baby carrots or 1 large carrot (can put vegetables together in food - processor)
3 whole green onions
3 large cloves garlic finely chopped
1/4 teaspoon salt
1/8 teaspoon pepper
1 tablespoon sesame oil
1/4 cup plus 2 tablespoons sweet chili sauce, or (1/3 cup brown sugar, 1 extra tablespoon soy sauce, 1/4 teaspoon red pepper flakes)
3 tablespoons soy sauce
1/2 teaspoon ground ginger

cooked white rice

Sliced green onion and cucumbers

Brown meat for 2-3 minutes and very finely chopped zucchini, carrots and garlic.

Continue to brown until veggies are tender, adding salt and pepper while cooking.

In small bowl, combine, sesame oil, sweet chili sauce, soy sauce and ginger,

Mixing well and pouring over beef and vegetable mixture.

Stir to coat and let simmer 2 minutes.

Serve hot over white rice, and top with sliced green onion.

Add cucumber on the side, also delicious.

Makes 6 Servings

JAPANESE MELON BREAD

DOUGH: KNETTEIGKUGEIN

2 1/2 cups flour
1/4 cup sugar
1 teaspoon salt
3/4 cup warm water
1 package dry yeast
1 1/3 cup room temperature butter

Mix flour, sugar, salt, and dry yeast in a bowl.

Add water, but not all at once, (otherwise the dough may be to sticky)

Knead with flour until the dough no longer sticks to surface.

Let dough rise 1 hour in a warm place, until it is doubled in size.

SECOND DOUGH: dough for outside of bread
BROTTEIGBALLCHEN

1/3 cup butter at room temperature
1/2 cup sugar
2 lightly beaten eggs
1 3/4 cup flour
1 teaspoon baking powder

Syrup, melon flavor

Cream butter and sugar together until smooth, then add eggs and melon syrup.

Stir well and add flour and baking powder. From this dough form 12 small balls.

Place in refrigerator for 30 minutes.

Knead first dough again and make 12 balls of dough with it. (KNETTEIGKUGEIN)
from the refrigerator, place between 2 pieces parchment paper, and roll out into round disks, and place on it each (BROTTEIGBALLCHEN)

Wrap each disk around ball but make sure dough is not quite wrapped up.

(otherwise the cover will tear.

Sprinkle top dough with sugar and press top of dough with a dough press or cut a shallow design into dough.

Let rise again for 40 minutes.

Bake at 350 degrees for 15 minutes.

CHAPTER

Spain

In Spain, gifts are generally opened on January 6th., on Epiphany Day (Dia de los tres reyes magos), though in some countries some receive gifts on Christmas and Epiphany, such as in Argentina and Uruguay. Christmas Eve is known as Nochebuena. A burning candle may be [laced by the door, and people may fast the entire day. In the evening when the first star is seen, they would then light bon-fires in public places. They would also attend Christmas mass or Church services, then return home to a huge Christmas feast.

The Christmas feast would most likely be made up of Christmas recipes along with traditional Spanish foods. There may be; Almond soup, roast meat, suckling pig, duck, plenty of sea food such as crab and lobster. The Christmas desserts would be Turron, and Marzipan made with honey and eggs; Provolones, which is a special shortbread cookie, and drink the Spanish equivalent of Champagne called Cava.

Christmas day is always celebrated with family and friend. visiting from house to house in one family reunion after an other. Christmas gifts are exchanged and friends and neighbors also drop by to join the celabration.

Everyone is welcome into the house, and often offered Christmas cookies.

One can always hear the traditional phrase FELIZ NAVIDAD or Merry Christmas, ringing out in greeting all day long, and often into the night.

On New Years Eve known as NOCHEVIEJA, all the main squares in Spain are lit up. The celebrations are shown. You will see people holding hands full of grapes; Legend has it, that if you eat 12 grapes at the Beginning of the New Year, you will have twelve months of good luck.

In Spain, Santa Claus is Papa Noel, and while he may be found distributing gifts, to eager children at Christmas, it is the Magi that they wait for with expectant delight.

On the 6th of January, or Three Kings Day, it is believed that the Magi, or Three Kings will bring gifts for the children, just as wise men had brought gifts to the Christ Child in Bethlehem so long ago.

The children place their shoes on the window-sill, filled with straw and carrots for the horses of the Magi, just before they go off to sleep, and parents replace the straw and carrots with gifts, for the children to find when they awake. It is also traditional on the Three Kings Day is to enjoy a desert called, 'Rosco'n de los reyes' Bread of the King), a cake which have candies, aborning it so as to give it a feel of royalty.

Adventus is Latin for Advent which means "Coming or Arrival---
This is a period of spiritual preparation for the coming of Christmas--
Christians use this time to reflect on the birth of Christ.

In western Christianity, begins on Sunday closest to November 30th thru December 24th, a period of 22 to 28 days.

Noche Buena, (Christmas Eve) for Latin american cultures, is often the biggest feast for the Christmas Season and is the Spanish Tradition annually.

In Spain / Latin America / and Philippines, the evening consists of a traditional family dinner. Roast pig, or lecho'n is often the center of Christmas Eve for feasts around the world. It is believed that this tradition dates back to the 15th century when Caribbean colonists hunted down pigs and roasted them whole, as the family gathered for Christmas Eve. In Spain the family gathers for a big meal after Christmas mass.

Spanish Hot Chocolate

6 ounces bitter-sweet chocolate chopped (at least 58 % cocoa)
1/2 cup granulated sugar
2 cups whole milk
2 cups water
1/4 cup corn starch plus 1 cup cols water
1/4 teaspoon vanilla

In a large heavy saucepan combine chocolate, sugar, milk, and 2 cups of water.

Heat chocolate over medium heat and whisk often, until chocolate is melted.

Mix corn starch into 1 cup cold water until smooth, whisk corn starch slurry into the hot chocolate. Cook over medium high heat. Mixing constantly, until chocolate mixture begins to bubble. Reduce the heat and cook for two minutes, whisking until thick. Remove chocolate from heat and stir in vanilla.

Serving in large mugs with Churros.

SPANISH CHURROS

1/2 cup butter
1 cup water
2 teaspoons coconut extract
1 cup flour
1/4 teaspoon salt
4 whole eggs
1/4 cups sugar
1/4 teaspoon ground cinnamon

Heat about two inches oil in a heavy, high side, pot over medium-high heat until the oil reaches 360 degrees F.

Mix sugar with cinnamon on a plate and set aside.

In medium sauce pot, combine 1 cup water with the butter, extract and salt, bring to a boil over high heat using a wooden spoon, stir in flour.

Reduce heat to low and stir vigorously until the mixture forms a ball. about

1 minute, remove dough from heat, and while stirring constantly.

Gradually beat eggs into dough.

Transfer churro dough into pastry bag fitted with a star tip.

Squeeze a coil of dough into hot oil. Cut the dough from the tip using a knife or kitchen shears, repeat frying 1-2 coils at a time. You can also fry them in strips and do 3-4 at a time.

Fry the churro, turning them once until golden brown, about two minutes on each side.

Transfer churro to a plate lined with paper towel to drain.

When churro is just warm enough to handle, roll them in cinnamon and sugar,

(Spain Churro are simply rolled in sugar.

SPANISH ANISE COOKIES

2 cup flour
1 teaspoon baking powder
1/4 teaspoon salt
3/4 cup sugar
1/4 cup shortening
2 eggs
2 drops anise oil

Heat oven to 375 degrees F.

Blend dry ingredients, flour baking powder, and salt.

Cut in shortening until mixture is the size of large peas.

Stir in egg and anise oil, mix thoroughly with hands.

Using half the dough at a time. roll 1/4 inch thick on a lightly floured board.

Cut into sticks 4 x 1/2 inch.

Place on an ungreased baking sheet, about 1/2 inch apart.

Brush with soft melted butter, bake 10 to 12 minutes.

Makes 3 to 4 dozen cookies

PALEO

Marzipan

Marzipan also known as Almond Paste, is an almond based confection that originated in Persia, and now is very common in European desserts. Families would make little marzipan animals, little chocolate covered marzipan sticks, and had several types of cakes and tarts that were covered with marzipan, and / or decorated with marzipan fruits.

Marzipan can be made in a loaf and served in slices, wedges, and cubes and enjoy it straight, or you can dip the slices into dark melted chocolate for a more attractive candy. The normal method of molding into shapes is to constantly dust with confectioners sugar, as you shape it like you would play-dough

Confectioners sugar makes it more pliable to hold its shape. You can also use its coloring to make its variation of fruits.

This recipe freezes well.

1 1/4 cups honey
4 cups blanched almond flour
3 egg whites

Fill sink, or saucepan, or a large bowl with cold water, throw in a handfull of ice-cubes.

Pour honey into a medium saucepan, with a candy thermometer attached to the side.

Heat honey over low heat or a medium low heat, until honey reaches 240 degrees, (this should take a long time something like 10 minutes, with no need to stir while the honey is heating).

Remove pot from heat, (but leave the stove element on, and turn to medium-low if you had it on low), and remove the thermometer from the pot. Place the bottom of the pot into the cold water. Stir the honey til it is thick and creamy, this will take 3-4 minutes, and feels like an eternity for your arm.

Stir in almond flour, and add egg whites, Place back on the heat and stir constantly 2-3 minutes, until thick.

Pour into a bowl of a standing mixer, with a paddle attachment, set mixture to low and allow to mix until cooled to room temperature (this may take about 20-30 minutes). Alternatively, you could pour out onto a clean surface (counter or baking sheet, may be lined with parchment paper since it will be very sticky), keep turning and kneading with pastry scraper until cool.

Place in a sealed container, refrigerate overnight to set.

Enjoy!

PROVOLONE

Shortbread cookies

This traditional cookie recipe is softer and more crumbly than the other Provolone versions of this cookie. This cookie is popular in Spain at Christmas time.

1 1/2 cups unbleached flour
3/4 cups raw almonds
5 ounces butter
3/4 cup granulated sugar
1/2 teaspoon cinnamon

Preheat oven to 350 degrees F.

Measure and pour flour out onto cookie sheet. Place in oven and 'toast' the flour. Occasionally stir flour around on the sheet so that it toasts evenly.

Leave in oven for about 8 minutes. Remove and set aside.

Place raw almonds on an other cookie sheet, toast the almonds until they change color just slightly.

Remove and place almonds in a food processor. Process almonds until finely ground.

Reduce oven temperature to 250 degrees F.

Cream butter, sugar and cinnamon together in a large mixing bowl, add the flour and finely ground almonds and continue mixing. The dough will be very crumbly.

Place a sheet of wax paper on a cutting board or an on an other work surface.

Press the dough together to form a round ball, then press the dough onto the waxed paper. Carefully flatten it down to 1/2 inch. use a cookie cutter to cut out the cookies.

Use a small spatula to remove the cookie from waxed paper to a cookie sheet, for baking sheet for baking. The dough is very dry and flaky.

Bake cookies on ungreased cookie sheet for 25-30 minutes at 250 degrees. remove cookie sheet from the oven and allow cookies to cool. Completely before removing from cookie sheet,

Take special care not to break them.

Makes 16 - 2 inch rounds

ROSCON DE LOS REYES

Three Kings Cake

Rosconde de reyes is a traditional dessert, served the night before or the morning of 'Reyes' or Epiphany, January 6th, Dia de Reyes or simply Reyes is the day when children in Spain receive gifts from the 'Reyes Magos' - 'Wise Men or Magi'. The three Kings who brought baby Jesus gifts. Instead of gifts from Santa Clause they receive them from the 'Reyes Magos'.

It's traditional to put several surprises inside the 'Roscon'.

A porcelain figure of a baby wrapped in foil and a dry bean is hidden in the dough. Whoever finds the baby Jesus will have good luck and will be the king of the party, but if you find the bean - pay for the cake.

4 cups unbleached flour
1/2 teaspoon salt

1 ounce yeast
2/3 cups mixed luke warm water and milk (of equal parts)
6 tablespoons butter
6 tablespoons sugar
Grate rind of 1 lemon
Grated rind of 1 orange
2 eggs
1 tablespoons brandy

Candied fruit pieces - cherries, orange, pineapple, ect....

Sift flour and salt together in a large mixing bowl. Make a well in the center of flour. set aside.

In a small mixing bowl, stir and dissolve dry yeast in luke-warm milk/water.

When dissolved pour the dissolved yeast into the center of flour.

Stir in yeast, enough flour around the bowl to form a thick batter.

With your hand grab about a teaspoon of flour from the side of the bowl and sprinkle it over the top of the batter.

Cover the top of bowl, with a kitchen towel, and keep in a warm place, away from any drafts. Allow batter to turn spongy, about 15 minutes.

In a medium size mixing bowl with a hand mixer, or whisk, to beat together the butter and sugar. The mixture should be smooth and creamy. Set aside.

Put grated orange and lemon rind, eggs, brandy and water into the bowl with flour mixture. Mix well. The dough will be sticky.

Beat flour mixture until it is sticky smooth. Beat in butter-sugar mixture and mix until dough is smooth. Dough should be formed into a ball, then covered with oiled plastic wrap. Cover bowl with kitchen towel and leave it again in a warm place and allow to rise til doubled in size. This should take about 1 1/2 hours.

** While you are waiting for dough to rise ------

Grease a large baking sheet with vegetable shortening and set aside for later.

If you use baking stone, no need to grease.

Once dough has doubled remove plastic wrap, and punch down dough. Lightly flour board of surface and place dough on it.

Knead for 2-3 minutes, then using a rolling pin, roll dough into a long rectangle about 2 feet long and, 5 to 6 inches wide.

Roll the dough on the long side into a sausage shape. Carefully place the dough into the large baking sheet or stone, and connect the edges together like a wreath or ring. If you will hide a bean or a foil wrapped figurine in the cake, now is the time to tuck it under the dough. Cover with oiled plastic wrap again, and leave in a warm place and let double in size again. This will take an hour to an hour and a half.

Heat oven to 350 degrees F. Lightly beat the egg whites in a bowl, uncover the dough and brush the egg wash over the dough; decorate the ring with the candied fruit, pushing them into the dough slightly, so they do not fall off. Place in oven and bake for about 30 minutes or until golden. Allow to cool before serving.

Makes 8 to 10 servings

CHAPTER

Mexico

People of Mexico have carried on many Christmas traditions first began in Spain.

The lights and luminaries on Christmas Eve 'La Nechebuena'.

The traditional greeting is 'Felize Navidad'.

Mexico is in central America.

They have a cultural Christmas decorated homes with red and white poinsettias and candles.

The poinsettia is native to Mexico and was incorporated into the Christmas tradition in the 17th century, when Franciscan monks used it in the connection with their Christmas celebrations, legend states that a boy named Palo was going to church in his village to visit the nativity scene; he realized he had nothing to give the Christ child. He saw some green branches that he gathered; and as he approached the manger scene, the other children laughed at him and his meager gift of weeds, but when he laid the green branches on the manger, a star shaped red flower appeared on each of the ranches. In Mexico the plant is known as "The Flower of the Blessed Night"

('La Flor De Noche Buena), because it resembles the star of Bethlehem, the red flowered plant was much admired by the 19th century. American ambassador to mexico, Joel Poinset, that he took them back to the united states, it is after him the poinsettia is named.

Children may be surprised to learn that Santa Claus plays little roll in the Mexican Christmas, giving way to the red poinsettia. The flower is a symbol of the season, as legends state a young boy, having no gift for the infant Christ, picked plain green branches to give to the newborn Messiah, which bloomed into three red poinsettias when set near his manger.

Despite the lack of a Kris Kringle in Mexico, the countries children still receive gifts.

A traditional Christmas treat is the Same as is in Spain, Rosca de Reyes, which is an oval-shaped bread covered in candied fruit. The bread contains a figurine of the baby Jesus, which is intended to symbolize the infants need to hide from King Herod.

He or she who eats the piece of bread containing the figurine, is responsible for inviting everyone to a February 2nd festival and acquiring a new dress (Ropon) for the Christ child in the families nativity scene.

The Christmas season begins on December 16th. They traditionally decorated their homes with flowers and colored paper lanterns and evergreens. A nativitie set 'Pesebre' (nativity) is also set up in the house. The nativity is the main focal point in the households Christmas. The Pesebre can be as simple as only three pieces making up the Holy family or as complex as making up the whole city of Bethlehem. Each night a procession (La Posoda) commemorates the journey of Mary and Joseph an their search for lodging for the night. In some areas, groups of villagers (Santos Peregrinos) or Holy Pilgrims, assemble each night, carrying candles, and chanting songs, they go house to house looking for lodging, at every house the pilgrims are refused; and when they have finished the procession, They return home to kneel at the nativity. After prayers are said a fiesta is held.

Children from the procession are blind folded in turn and, spun around and gets three chances to break a suspended decoration, earthenware pot, (Pinata). The pinata is filled with fruit nuts and candy, when it is broken, the children scramble to pick up the spilled goodies.

Mexicans continue to celebrate Christmas until those in the United States are relying on groundhogs to determine how long winters will last; February 2. The families will gather that day for tamales and hot chocolate.

XAVIER AGE 5

BISOCHITOS

Traditional Cookies

6 cup all-purpose family
1 tablespoon baking powder
1/4 teaspoon salt

2 cups lard
1 1/2 granulated sugar
2 teaspoon anise seed
2 eggs
1/4 cup brandy
1/4 cup granulated sugar
1 tablespoon ground cinnamon

Preheat oven to 350 degrees F.

Sift flour, baking powder and salt into a bowl and set aside.

In a large bowl, cream together lard and 1 1/2 cup sugar until smooth,

Mix in anise seed, and beat until fluffy.

Stir in eggs, one at a time,

Add the sifted flour mixture and brandy and stir until well blended.

On a floured surface, roll dough out to 1/2 to 1/4 inch thickness, and cut into desired shapes, using cookie cutters.

The traditional design is the 'Flur-de-lis'.

Place cookies on baking sheet, Mix together sugar and cinnamon; sprinkle over top of cookies.

Bake for 10 minutes in preheated oven, or until bottoms are lightly browned.

TAMALES

Christmas Chicken

A lot of Mexican families get together to do their baking and assemble mass amounts of tamales for their family feasts. This is a very popular one.

Corn husks are the most popular wrappers for tamales, which you can find in Mexican or large grocery stores.

1 - 10 ounce chicken breast
1/2 white onion, chopped
1 garlic clove, minced

2 dried chilies, stemmed and seeded
1 cup water
1 teaspoon salt
1 cup corns massa
1/2 - (10.5 ounce) can chicken broth
1/2 teaspoon baking powder
1/3 cup lard
8 corn husks, soaked in warm water, if not already packed in water.
1/2 cup sour cream

Combine chicken, onion and garlic with enough water to just cover the meat, in pot or dutch oven.

Bring mixture to a boil, then reduce heat to low, simmer til chicken is cooked through. About 1 to 1 1/2 hours.

Meanwhile, soak chilies in simmering water for 20 minutes; let cool.

Pour chilies and cooking water into a blender, and blend until smooth, season with 3/4 teaspoon salt.

Shred cooked chicken and combine 1 cup of chili mixture.

Whisk lard with 1 tablespoon broth until light.

Mix corn mesa with baking powder, and 1 teaspoon salt.

Then combine with lard mixture.

Gently mix to make a fluffy dough, add more dough if needed.

Spread dough over one side of each corn husk to about 1/4 inch thickness.

Spoon meat mixture on top of dough then fold over sides of husks to seal.

Secure with twine or string.

Place tamales in a steamer basket and steam for about 1 hour.

Remove tamale from steamer. Unwrap and top with the remaining chili sauce and a dollop of sour cream.

Makes 8

Robin Redmon Dreyer

ROSCA DE REYES

Three Kings Cake

1 - (1/4 ounce) packet active dry yeast
1/4 cup warm water
1/4 cup dried figs cut into strips, plus more for garnish
1/4 cup candied orange peel, cut into strips plus more for garnishing
1/4 cup candied lemon peel, cut into strips plus more for garnishing
1/4 cup chopped candied cherries plus more for whole for garnishing
2 tablespoons light rum
1/4 cup milk
1/4 cup sugar
1/4 cup (1/2 stick) butter, unsalted
1 teaspoon pure vanilla extract
1/4 teaspoon ground cinnamon
1 teaspoon salt
3 1/2 to 4 cups all-purpose flour
3 large eggs divided
water

In a small bowl, combine the yeast and warm water, stir to blend.

Let stand until yeast comes alive, and starts to foam, about 5 to 10 minutes.

Put all the candied fruit into a small bowl, and drizzle the rum on top.

Let stand 15 minutes to 1 hour to infuse the flavors.

In a small pot, warm the milk over medium-low heat.

Add the sugar, butter, cinnamon, salt and vanilla.

In a large bowl mix 3 1/2 cups flour, 2 eggs, yeast mixture, milk mixture and the rum soaked candied fruits.

Mix very well, until dough gathers into a ball.

If the dough is to wet, add additional flour a little at a time, if needed to form a soft dough.

Turn the dough out onto a lightly floured surface, and knead until it is smooth and elastic, about 5 minutes.

Place the dough into an oiled bowl, cover with plastic wrap or a lint free towel.

Set aside in a warm spot to rise for 1 hour.

Remove the dough from the bowl and knead on a lightly floured surface.

Using your palms, roll the dough into a long rope.

Shape the rope into a round wreath, sealing the ends together.

Insert a little doll or a coin into the bread from the bottom, if disired.

Line baking pan with foil and coat with nonstick cooking spray.

Carefully transfer the wreath to the prepared baking sheet.

Preheat oven to 350 degrees F.

Beat the remaining egg in a small bowl with 1 tablespoon water, to make an egg wash, and brush the top of the bread, and decoratively garnish the top of the wreath with more candied fruit, and bake for 35 to 40 minutes, until the cake is golden.

Cool on a wire rack before slicing

Makes 8 Servings

RUM RAISIN RICE PUDDING

1 cup short grain white rice
4 cups non fat milk
4 sticks cinnamon
1 can sweetened condensed milk
1 vanilla bean, split and scraped
3/4 cup dark rum
1 cup golden raisins

Wash rice under cold running water, until water runs clear and drain well.

Bring milk to a boil with the cinnamon stick, add rice, return to boil and reduce to simmer. Cook 12 to 15 minutes, or until just barely soft throughout.

Stirring occasionally. Add sweetened condensed milk and vanilla bean and continue to simmer very slowly, covered, for about 15 additional minutes or until rice is plump and tender and sauce is the consistency of heavy cream.

Chill is a bowl over ice water to stop cooking.

Place rum and raisins in a heavy bottomed pot, and simmer over low heat until raisins have plumped and rum is almost gone. Set aside to cool and fold into chilled rice pudding.

Serve with a sprinkle of cinnamon.

MEXICAN HOT CHOCOLATE

1 1/2 ounce unsweetened chocolate
1/4 cup sugar
1 tablespoon plus 2 teaspoon instant coffee
1/2 teaspoon ground cinnamon
1/4 teaspoon ground nutmeg
dash salt
3/4 cup water
2 cup milk whipped cream

Heat chocolate, sugar, coffee, cinnamon, nutmeg, salt and water in a 1 1/2 quart, saucepan over low heat, stirring constantly, until chocolate is melted and mixture is smooth.

Heat to boiling, reduce heat. Simmer uncovered, stirring constantly, 4 minutes,

Stir in milk, heat through, just before serving, beat with hand beater until foamy. Top each serving with whipped cream.

CHAPTER

England

Families in England share many customs wit the United States throughout the Christmas season. Christmas trees are decorated, carols are sung, and many dine on traditional meals and all the trimmings. Father Christmas bears many similarities to Santa Claus and leaves gifts in stockings, (and sometimes pillowcases) laid out by children on Christmas Eve.

The traditional greeting is "MERRY CHRISTMAS"

The traditional tree did not come to England until 1841, when Prince Albert had one brought into the palace and decorated for his wife Victoria and his children. The tradition quickly caught.

Throughout the United Kingdom, December 26th starts the 12 days of Christmas. The 26th of December is known as Boxing Day, where the alms or the poor boxes were traditionally opened, and the funds were given out to the poor.

This was also when the servants were given the day off from work, so they were able to celebrate Christmas with their families. For the next 12 days, there are parties, pantomime shows, children's plays, musicals about well known fairy-tales, audience participation is greatly encouraged, and other types of entertainment, which ends on January 6th.

England is the home of Charles Dickens, author of the story, "The Christmas Carol".

England had the first known Christmas card personally made and sent in 1840.

Father Christmas is England's' Santa, derived from the pagan spirit (HERN) who appeared in the 'Murmmer's' plays. He has a long white hair and beard, and dresses in a long red and green robe, that is decorated with holly, mistletoe and ivy. On his head he wears a wreath made of the same plants.

Legend says that Father Christmas originally dropped coins down the chimney, and that the coins would be lost if there were no stockings hanging on the mantels of the fireplaces. Some even hang their socks at the foot of their bed.

Children sent letters to Father Christmas by writing them and then burning them in the fireplace. It was thought, that the wishes were sent in the smoke.

On Christmas Eve the children would leave out carrots for Father Christmas's reindeer, and minced pies and brandy or hot drink for Father Christmas.

On Christmas morning the children would open the gifts in their stockings, then later they would open the gifts under the tree.

For Christmas dinner - At each place setting there were noise makers called 'crackers'. Tom Smith invented this tradition in 1850, as a way of selling more of his confections. Crackers are wrapped in fancy paper, and at each end there are pull-taks, when pulled, there will be a loud crack, and inside the cracker may be a paper hat, a toy and some candy. In most English homes, before the meal is served they pop their crackers and must put on their hats and enjoy their candy before eating their meal.

England gave us such foods as, fruitcake, trifle (sponge cake), Christmas puddings, minced pies, roast potatoes, and mince meats.

OLD-FASHIONED PLUM PUDDING

During the first week in Advent, the housewives in some parts of England prepare the fruits and other ingredients for the plum puddings they will serve on Christmas day, because it means good luck, each family member takes a turn stirring the yuletide pudding.

1/2 pound currents (1 cup)
1/2 pound brown sugar (1 cup)
3 cups course bread crumbs
6 eggs beaten until very light
1 1/2 teaspoons nutmeg
1/2 teaspoon cloves

1/2 cup brandy
1/2 pound raisins (1 cup)
1/2 pound suit chopped (1 cup)
1 1/2 teaspoon cinnamon
3/4 teaspoon allspice
1/2 cup white wine
1/4 pound (1/2 cup) finely cut citron
1/4 pound (1/2 cup) candied orange peel

Place all ingredients in a large bowl, mix well, using both hands.

Pack into one large melon mold, cover tightly.

Place on a trivet in a deep-well cooker or a kettle filled with enough water to come to 2/3 way up the sides of the mold.

boil 4-8 hours, the longer the better.

Remove pudding from mold, allow to cool a while.

Clean mold thoroughly and place slightly cooled pudding back in the mold.

Prick pudding with a knife o knitting needle.

Sprinkle with 3 tablespoon brandy, repeat this again at the end of one week.

Keep pudding covered so it will not dry out.

When ready to eat, reheat in the water bath as before, boil for 2 hours.

Remove from mold, pour 2 tablespoon brandy over the pudding, light with match, and carry flaming to your awaiting guests.

CHRISTMAS STEAMED PUDDING

1 cup boiling water
1 cup chopped cranberries, or cut-up raisin
2 tablespoons butter
1 1/2 cup flour
1/2 cup sugar
1 teaspoon baking soda

1 teaspoon salt
1/2 cup molasses
1 egg

cream sauce or hard sauce

Pour boiling water on cranberries, stir in butter.

In a large bowl mix flour, sugar, baking soda and salt.

Add to flour mixture water cranberries, molasses, and egg.

Mixing all ingredients well.

Pour into a well greased 6 cup mold, cover tightly with aluminum foil.

Place mold on rack in a dutch oven, half-way up mold with water, cover with dutch oven. Keep water boiling over low heat until wooden pick inserted in center comes out clean, about 2 hours.

Remove from dutch oven, let set in mold for 5 minutes, unmold.

For a dramatic finale, flame the steamed pudding.

Heat 1/4 cup brandy in a small long handled pan, ignite with long match.

Pour over warm unmolded pudding

The alcohol in the brandy burns off and the flavor remains.

YORKSHIRE PUDDING

1/4 cup drippings from beef roast
1 cup all-purpose flour
1 cup milk
2 eggs
1/2 teaspoon salt

Mix flour, milk, eggs, and salt until smooth.

Heat oven to 425 degrees F.

In the oven, heat baking pan, 9x9x2 inches.

Measure drippings from roast, place hot drippings into pan;

pour in pudding batter.

Bake until puffed and golden brown, about 25 minutes.

Cut into squares and serve with roast beef.

Makes 9 servings

BRITISH RASPBERRY TRIFLE

Of the many sweet puddings from the British Isles, the elaborate concoctions - oddly enough called "Trifle"! - is a very popular holiday dessert.

1/2 cup sugar
3 tablespoons cornstarch
1/4 teaspoon salt
3 cups milk
1/2 cup dry white wine
3 egg yolks, beaten
3 tablespoon butter
1 tablespoons vanilla
2 packages (3 ounce each) Lady Fingers
1/2 cup raspberry preserves
1 package (12 ounces) frozen raspberries, thawed
1 cup whipped cream
2 tablespoons sugar
2 tablespoons toasted slivered almonds

Mix 1/2 cup sugar, cornstarch, and salt in a 3-quart saucepan; gradually stir in milk and wine.

Heat to boiling, over medium heat, stirring constantly.

Boil and stir 1 minute.

Stir at least half of the hot mixture into the egg yolks.

Blend into hot mixture in saucepan.

Boil and stir 1 minute.

Remove from heat; stir in butter and vanilla.

Cover and refrigerate at least 3 hours.

Split ladyfingers lengthwise into halves; spread each half with raspberry preserves.

Layer 1/4 of the ladyfingers cut side up, half of the raspberries and half of the pudding in 2 quart serving bowl; repeat.

Arrange remaining ladyfingers around the bowl in an upright position, with cut sides toward center.

Cover and refrigerate.

Beat whipped cream and 2 tablespoons of sugar, in a chilled bowl until stiff, spread over desert.

Sprinkle with almonds.

GINGERBREAD

1/2 cup butter
1 cup brown sugar
2 eggs
2 cups sifted flour
1 teaspoon cinnamon
1 tablespoon baking soda
1/2 teaspoon salt
1/2 cup boiling water
1/2 cup dark molasses

Cream the butter til fluffy, add sugar and cream again.

Beat in eggs, one at a time.

Sift flour, cinnamon, soda, salt and ginger; sift again.

Stir together boiling water and molasses.

Add to the butter - egg mixture alternately with the dry ingredients, Mix well.

Pour into buttered 8x10 inch pan.

Bake at 350 degrees F.

About 40 minutes, or until tests done.

ENGLAND'S SNOWMAN BUNS
OR
A NEW YEARS BREAD

1 package active dry yeast
3/4 cup warm water (105-115 degrees F.)
1/3 cup sugar
1/4 cup shortening
2 eggs
2 teaspoons ground nutmeg\
1 teaspoon salt
3 - 1/2 cups all-purpose flour
24 currents
1 egg slightly beaten

Dissolve yeast in warm water in large mixing bowl.

Add sugar, shortening, 2 eggs, nutmeg, salt, and 2 cups flour.

Beat on low speed, scraping bowl constantly, about 30 seconds.

Beat on medium speed, scraping bowl occasionally, about 2 minutes.

Stir in remaining flour, until smooth.

Cover; let rise in a warm place until doubled in size, about 45 minutes.

Stir down dough by beating 25 strokes.

Turn out onto a well floured surface; cut into 12 equal parts.

(each part will make one snowman)

Shape 1/4 of each part into a 4 inch oval, for the body.

Shape 1/2 of the remaining dough into a ball for the head.

Pinch a tiny piece for the nose.

Shape remaining dough into 4 inch roll, and cut into halves for the arms.

Arrange 3-inches apart on a parchment lined cookie sheet.

Let rise until double in size, about 45 minutes.

Press in two currents for the eyes, and three for the buttons.

Brush with beaten egg, and bake at 350 degrees F.

Bake about 15 minutes

Makes 12 Snowmen

CHRISTMAS BRUNCH TEA SCONES

2 cups all-purpose flour
2 tablespoon sugar
1 tablespoon baking powder
1/2 teaspoon salt
1/3 cup dried currents
6 tablespoons butter
1 egg beaten
1/2 cup milk
1 slightly beaten egg

In a bowl, thoroughly stir together the flour, sugar, baking powder and salt.

Stir in the currents.

Cut in the butter until the mixture resembles course crumbs.

Add 1 beaten egg and milk, stir just until dough clings together.

Knead dough gently on lightly floured surface. (12 to 15 strokes)

Cut the dough in half, Shape each half in a ball and or roll to 6 inch circle about 1/2 inch thick.

With a sharp knife cut each circle, into 6 to 8 wedges.

Place wedges on a parchment lined baking-sheet.

(do not have sides of wedges touching)

Brush scones with slightly beaten egg.

Bake at 425 degrees F.

Bake for about 12 to 15 minutes or until deeply golden brown.

Makes 12 to 16 Scones

EUROPEAN SHORTBREAD BISCUITS

1/4 cup firmly packed brown sugar
2 tablespoon sugar
1/2 cup butter
1 cup all-purpose flour
1/2 teaspoon salt

Heat oven to 300 degrees F.

In a large bowl, beat brown sugar, sugar, and a half cup butter until light and fluffy.

Stir in flour and salt and mix well.

On a floured surface roll out dough 1/4 inch thick.

Cut with 1 to 1-1/2 inch cookie cutter.

Place on ungreased baking sheet.

Bake for 10 to 20 minutes, or until very light golden brown and set.

Remove from cookie sheet and cool completely.

SUGARPLUM COOKIES

3/4 cup sugar
1/2 cup butter softened
1/2 cup shortening
1 egg
2 1/2 cups flour
1 1/2 teaspoon vanilla
1/2 teaspoon baking powder
1/8 teaspoon salt
3/4 cup cut up candied or dried fruit

Creamy Icing

Mix sugar, butter, shortening, and eggs.

Stir in flour, vanilla, baking powder, and salt.

Heat in oven 375 degrees F.

Shape dough by teaspoon fulls around fruit to form balls.

Place about 1 inch apart in parchment lined cookie sheet.

Bake until delicately browned, about 12 to 15 minutes; cool.

Spread tops of cookies with creamy icing.

Decorate with colored sugars, non pareils, or chopped nuts

Creamy Frosting:

1!/2 cups confectioners sugar
1/2 teaspoon vanilla
2 to 3 tablespoons water as needed for desired thickness

Mix together sugar, vanilla, and 2 tablespoons water creaming well, adding more water if needed for desired consistency.

Makes about 7 dozen cookies

ROAST GOOSE WITH BROWN POTATOES

1 goose 9 to 11 pounds
4 to 6 large potatoes, prepared and cut into halves
Salt and pepper
Paprika

Wash and from fat off goose.

Rub cavity of goose lightly with salt.

Fasten neck skin of goose to back with skewer.

Fold wings across back with tips touching.

Tie drumsticks to tail.

Prick skin all over with fork.

Place goose breast side up, on roasting rack in a shallow pan.

Roast uncovered at 350 degrees F.

Roast until done, 3 to 3 1/2 hours. Remove excess fat from pan occasionally.

One hour and fifteen minutes before goose is done, place potatoes into roasting pan around goose, brush potatoes with goose fat, sprinkle with salt, pepper and paprika.

Place a tent of foil over goose to prevent excessive browning.

Goose is done when drumsticks are tender.

ROAST LEG OF LAMB

5 to 7 pound leg of lamb
Garlic sliced into slivers
Salt and pepper

Do not remove fell (paper-like covering)

Make 4-5 slits in lamb with a knife,

Insert slivers of garlic into slits.

Sprinkle on salt and pepper.

Place lamb fat side up, on rack, in shallow roasting pan.

Insert meat thermometer so tip is in center of thickest part of lamb, and does not touch bone, or rest in fat.

Do not add water.

Roast uncovered in a 325 degree F. oven. until thermometer reaches

170 degrees F. about 2 1/2 hours for about a 5 pound leg.

About 3 1/2 hours for 7 pound roast.

Lamb can be roasted to 140 degrees F. for rare -or- 160 degree F. for medium.

Allow to set for 15 to 20 minutes before carving.

YORKSHIRE BEEF

1 pound ground beef
1 can (15 ounce) tomato sauce
1/4 cup chopped green pepper
2 tablespoons flour
1 teaspoon dried parsley flakes
1/2 teaspoon salt
1/4 teaspoon pepper
1 cup shredded cheddar cheese (about 4 ounces)
2 eggs
1 cup milk
1 tablespoons oil
1 cup flour
1/2 teaspoon salt
2 tablespoons chopped green onion

Heat oven to 425 degrees F.

Cook and stir ground beef in a 10 inch skillet until brown.

Stir in tomato sauce, green pepper, 2 tablespoons flour, parsley flakes,

1/2 teaspoon salt, and pepper.

Heat to boiling stirring constantly.

Boil and stir 1 minute.

Pour into ungreased baking pan, 9x13x2 inches.

Sprinkle cheese on top.

Beat eggs, milk, and oil, 1 cup flour, and 1/2 teaspoon salt with hand beater, until smooth; pour over cheese.

Sprinkle with green onions.

Bake until golden brown, 25 to 30 minutes.

Serve immediately.

ENGLAND'S OLD-FASHIONED MINCEMEAT PIE

4 pound lean Beef
1 pound beef suet
4 cup seedless raisins
2 cups currents
1 cup diced citron
1 cup diced orange peel
1/2 cup diced lemon peel
1 cup chopped figs
2 1/2 cup sugar
2 teaspoons salt
2 teaspoon nutmeg
2 teaspoon cinnamon
2 teaspoon allspice
1 teaspoon cloves
5 cups brandy
4 cups sherry

Cut the meat into chunks and simmer for about an hour and a half, or until tender, in just enough water to cover.

Cool and grind through a coarse blade of a meat grinder.

Grind the suet. Mix well with the remaining ingredients except for brandy and sherry.

After mixing well, add enough brandy to make a thick soupy mixture.

Place in an earth-ware container / crock, cover and let stand for at least one month. (check in a week to see if the mixture seems dry, if it has absorbed most of the liquid, moisten it with sherry.) check every two weeks, adding alternately, brandy or sherry.

As mincemeat absorbed the moisture. It will keep indefinitely without refrigeration, but after six weeks or so you may seal it in a glass jar.

Makes about 9 quarts

RAISIN SAUCE

1/2 cup packed brown sugar

2 tablespoons cornstarch
1 teaspoon dry mustard
1 1/4 cups water
2 tablespoons lemon juice
1 cup raisins

Mix brown sugar, cornstarch, and mustard in 1 quart saucepan.

Gradually stir in water and lemon juice; add raisins.

Cook over medium heat, stirring constantly, until mixture boils.

Cool and stir 1 minute.

Makes about 1 1/2 cups

HOT CHOCOLATE

4 heaping tablespoons unsweetened cocoa
4 heaping tablespoon sugar
1 cup hot water
7 cups milk

In saucepan combine cocoa and sugar, stir in the hot water and

place the pan over moderate heat, stirring continuously, until mixture begins to boil.

Immediately stir in milk and continue stirring until the milk is hot but not yet boiling.

Remove the pan from heat and with a wire whisk beat the cocoa for 15 seconds, until it is smooth and frothy, pour into mugs immediately.

CUSTARD EGGNOG

SOFT CUSTARD:

3 eggs slightly beaten
1/3 cup sugar
dash salt

2 1/2 cups milk
1 teaspoon vanilla

1 cup chilled whipping cream
2 tablespoons confectioners sugar
1/2 teaspoon vanilla
1/2 cup rum
1-2 drops yellow food coloring
ground nutmeg

Mix eggs, sugar, and salt in a heavy saucepan.

Stir in milk gradually.

Cook over low heat, stirring constantly, until mixture just coats metal spoon, 15 to 20 minutes.

Remove custard from heat;Stir in vanilla.

Place saucepan in cold water until custard is cool.

(If custard curdles beat vigorously with hand beater until smooth)

Cover and refrigerate at least 2 hours, but no more that 24 hours.

Just before serving, beat whipping cream, confectioners sugar, and vanilla in a chilled small mixer bowl until stiff.

Stir rum, 1 cup whipping cream into chilled custard.

Pour eggnog into small punch bowl.

Drop remaining whipped cream on mounds on top of eggnog.

Sprinkle nutmeg on top of mounds of cream.

Serve immediately.

WASSAIL

1 gallon apple cider
1 teaspoon whole allspice
1 teaspoon whole cloves
2 - three inch cinnamon sticks

2/3 cups sugar
orange slices studded with cloves

Heat cider, allspice, cloves, cinnamon sticks and sugar to boiling.

Reduce heat, cover, simmer 20 minutes.

Strain punch and pour into a heat proof punch bowl.

Float oranges in bowl.

Makes: 32, 1/2 cup servings

CHAPTER

Christmas In America

U.S.A.

Contemporary 'Santa Claus' was born in America, thanks to artists, poets, writers, legends and the changes through the sands of time.

Santa Clause is said to be the Dutch word for Saint Nicholas, Sinterklas, although the Dutch brought him to the United States in the 17ᵗʰ century, but he did not become an important person until the Novelist, Washington Irving, put him in a novel in 1809. This first Santa was known as Saint Nicholas - he did smoke a pipe, but he flew around in a wagon, with no reindeer. He did not have a red suit or live in the North Pole, but he did bring presents to the children each year.

In 1863, he was given the name Santa Claus and wore the red suit, smoked a pipe, and had reindeer and sleigh.

Today Christmas Celebrations still vary greatly between regions of the United States. This is because of the variety of the nationalities that have settled here.

In Pennsylvania, the Mavarian's build a landscape, called Putz - under the Christmas Tree, While in the same State, the Germans are given gifts by 'Belsnickle', who taps them with his switch misbehaved.

Early European settlers who brought many traditions to the United States, many settled in the early days in the south, these settlers would send distant greetings to their neighbors by shooting firearms and setting off fireworks. In Hawaii this practice is still used, Santa arrives by boat and Christmas dinner is eaten out doors.

In Alaska, boys and girls with lanterns and poles, carry a large form of a star, from door to door; followed by Herod's men who try to capture the star.

They sing carols and are invited in for supper. Colonial doorways are decorated with pineapple which is a symbol of hospitality.

Polish Americans, on Christmas Eve, spread hay on their kitchen floor, and under the table to remind them of the stable and the manger. When they make up the table for dinner, two extra places are set up for Mary and the Christ Child in case they should knock at the door and ask for shelter.

American homes are decorated with holly and evergreens and mistletoe, most have a tree set up with tensile, ornaments and electric lights, some string popcorn and candy canes.

In America the traditional Christmas dinner is generally roast turkey, with vegetables and sauces. For desserts, it is rich fruity Christmas puddings, with brandy sauces, minced pies, pastries, cases filled with a mixture of chopped dried fruit.

The majority of Americans celebrate Christmas with the exchanging of gifts, and greetings with visits from friends and family. For many Christmas starts on Christmas Eve.

Before 1850 many US citizens did not dream of Christmas at all.

The Christmas that Americans celebrate today, seems like a timeless weaving of custom and feeling, beyond the reach of history. But yet the familiar mix of carols, cards, presents, treats, trees and the many Santa's and holiday traditions that have come to define December 25th in the United States is a little more that one hundred years old.

America did not even conceive of Christmas as a National holiday until the middle of the last century. The creation of the American Christmas was a response to social and personal needs, that arose at a particular time in history, in this case, a time of sectional conflict and civil war, as well as the unsettling process of urbanization and the beginning of industry. The holidays new customs and meanings helped the nations to make sense of the conflict and confusion of the era, and to secure, if only for a short while each year, a soothing feeling of unity.

In colonial times, Americans of different sects, and different national origins kept the holiday (or did not) in ways that carry over from the old world, Puritans for instance, attempted to ignore Christmas because nothing was said in the Bible about the topic. Virginia planters, took the occasion to feast, dance, gamble, hunt, and visit, acting on what they believe to be the old Christmas Customs in English manors. Even as late as the early nineteenth century, many Americans, Churched or unchurched, northerners or southerners, hardly took notice of the holiday at all.

By mid-century, however, new conditions had begun to undercut most local customs and create needs for common and visible celebrations, communication, and transportation revolutions made once isolated part of the country, actually aware of each other. Immigration played an important part in the ethnic and religious settlements that had been a part of America from its beginning. Moral, Political, and economic tension mounted among east, west and south, raising new question s about the nature of the union itself. Science challenged religion, new wealth and larger markets superseded old. Population increased, the pace of life accelerated.

The swirl of change caused many to long for earlier times, the times when they imagined the old and good values when people upheld peaceful communities.

It also made them reconsider the notion of 'community' in larger terms, on the national scale, but modeled on the ideals of a family gathered at the hearth, it is at this cross-roads of progress and nostalgia, Americans found in Christmas, a holiday that ministered to their needs. The many Christmas's celebrated across the land began to resolve into a more singular, and widely celebrated home holiday.

This new revised Christmas of our time, afforded a retreat, from the realities, of contemporary life, but cast in contemporary terms. Americans varied old themes and wove new symbols into the received fabric, thus created something of their own. The American holiday often embraced the often contradictory strains of commercialism and artisanship, as well as nostalgia and faith in progress, defined the late nineteenth century culture. It's relative lack of theological or Biblical authority - what had made it an anathema to the puritans - ironically allowed Christmas to emerge as a highly ecumenical event in a land of pluralism, it became a moment of idealized national self definition.

Not surprisingly, the strongest, impetus for such a holiday came from those areas most profoundly affected by the various social, economic and technological revolutions of the antebellum era. Especially in northern cities, where the intimacies of village and town cultures, had been most forcefully challenged by city and factory, the felt need for more explicit symbols of common purpose, and these ends, and even to forge a national culture. New Years Eve, the Fourth of July and especially

Thanksgiving had their merits, and partisan, but Christmas emerged as the most logical and effective choice. By the 1850's it had captured the Northern imagination and was making inroads in the south.

The Civil war intensified Christmas appeal. It's sensational celebration of family matched the yearnings of soldiers and those they left behind. Its message of peace and good will spoke to the most immediate prayers of all Americans, yet Northern Victory in 1865 as much as the war situation itself determined the popularity and shape of the America's Christmas, Now unchanged in the sphere of national myth-making and in control of the publishing trade, customs and symbols of Yankee origin and preference came to stand for the American Christmas.

Each custom had its own history, and and only over time merged with others to create a full create a full blown national holiday.

As early as 1832, 'Harrist Martineau', (from New England) had identified what would become, what was the most familiar symbols of the American Christmas. It was the Christmas tree. By the 1850's many Americans, not just New Englander's, had fallen in love with the custom. The media introduced the custom, even more widely, inspiring Americans throughout the nation to adopt the tradition as their own.

As the tree grew in popularity in front parlors, it also assumed a place in the market. By the 1950's, town squares began to fill with trees, cut for seasonal profit; even in homes of the 'Hebrew Brethren'. "Christmas trees bloomed", noted a Philadelphia News paper in 1877. By 1900, one American in five was estimated to have a Christmas tree.

At first the decoration of these fragrant evergreens reflected folk tradition. People added nuts, strings of popcorn, or beads, oranges, lemons, candies and home made trinkets. However Newspapers, and magazines, raised the standards for ornaments.(on suggestion:cotton batting dipped in thin gum arabic then diamond dust made a beautiful frosting for the new tree branches.) Home- made ornaments gave way to more uniform and sophisticated ones, the old style was overtaken by the urge to make the tree a show piece for the artistic arrangement of the glittering baubles, the stars, the angels, ect...

Free decorating soon became big business. As early as 1870, American business men began to impart large quantities of German made ornaments to be sold on street corners and then in toy shops and variety stores, vendors hawked glass ornaments and balls in bright colors, tin, cut in many shapes, and wax angels with spun glass wings. So many charming little ornaments can now be bought ready to decorate Christmas trees, "that it seems almost a waist of time to make them at home," one advertisement declared.

The rise of Christmas cards revealed other aspects of the new holiday's profile. P.H. Pease, a printer and variety store owner who lived in Albany, New York, distributed the first American made Christmas cards in the early 1850's.

A family scene dominated the small card center but unlike the English fore-winner (itself only a decade older), the images on each of the four corners made no allusion to poverty, cold or hungry. Instead pictures of Santa, Reindeer, dancers, Christmas presents of all kinds, and Christmas banquets of food, all expressing a season of joy.

'Louis Prang' a German immigrant to America in 1850, and owned thirds of the steam presses for printing in America. In 1873, at an international expo-sition, the wife of the London agent suggested he add Christmas greetings to his trade cards, when Prang introduced these new cards into the United States in 1875, proved so successful that they could not meat demand. In 1880 Prang sponsored annual competitions for Christmas card designs to promote and educate public on decorative art. By 1890 cheep imitations from his native Germany drove Prang from the Christmas card market entirely.

More and more Americans resorted to sending Christmas cards, instead of the older custom of writing letters, or making personal visits. Cards became a staple in the December mail. In 1882 post officials thought Christmas greeting cards were only a fad that would pass, and to their surprise, it never faltered but grew and grew. Christmas cards made modest, yet suitable presents.

Decorated trees and cards were the only window dressing to the custom of gift-giving that blossomed in 1870's thru 1880's. Gifts had played a pig part in Christmas's of the past.

The getting and giving of gifts provided a means of social change, gift giving has been very important to the consumer economy. In the 1920's, 30's and 40's, merchants had noticed the grow role of gifts in the celebration of Christmas, by late 1850's imaginative importers, craftsmen and storekeepers, reshaped the holidays to meet their own ends, even as shoppers elevated gift giving in their holiday at home. The magazine 'Harper's' gave early voice to link between gifts and givers in

1856: 'Love is the moral of Christmas..... what are gifts but the proof and signs of love'!

Saint Nick / Santa Claus was the symbol of gift giving in 1820's in 'Clement Moore's' poem, "A Visit From St. Nicholas". By the 1850's and 60's artiest and writers have given a wide circulation of the American Saint that Moore had introduced. 'Thomas Hast's' drawings widened the popularity of Santa in the late 19th century. Moore had already supplied the eight reindeer to pull the sleigh. Nast gave him a workshop and ledgers to record children's conduct. He made Santa taller and dresses him in red. To this, Nast and others added a home at the north pole, elves, a wife and even by some accounts, children.

XAvier   Age 5

These amplifications imported to Santa a more human and credible and idealized troublesome aspect of the nations material and spiritual life. For example the charming notion of Santa and his helpers supplied all the Christmas toys encoded a highly romantic vision of American capitalism. This Santa reigned without opposition over a vast empire. The world of practicality he prospered as a highly successful manufactures and distributor of toys. From his fir coat to his full girth, he resembled the notions gelded age presents and its well-fed captains of industry.

Labor conditions were idealized as well. A work force of skilled and reliable elf-laborers helped secure Santa's place in the of American business, These North Pole Elves were not unlike immigrants working in the Nations sweatshops. The best of them worked hard and unselfishly.

Their existence made a maxim in that hard work and a cheerful attitude benefited all.

Santa was a Robber Baron in reverse. Other than acquire wealth, he shed it yearly. He never purchased gifts, but (with Elves help) made his own to give away without regard for financial profit. Rewarding the most innocent and naive of all the children. Santa Clause exemplified the realm of dreams, hopes, wishes and belief, not from realities and compromises necessary to negotiate contemporary life.

So powerful was the symbol of Santa Clause that a number of writers and preachers worried that he had become a substitute and rival to Jesus.

Centuries earlier, Puritans had expressed the same fear about Saints in general. Although the faith not only of Puritan Calvinist but of all Christians had modified over the intervening years, America's protestant culture still looked upon an iconography human-like embodiment of Christmas with great suspicion.

The fear that children might equate Santa with Jesus or God, however, missed an important part, In an age of science, Santa, while not a religious figure, per se', represented a palpable medium for which children and adults in the late nineteenth century America could experience and act upon spiritual impulses. Santa allowed one to give and get and also believe.

In 1897, 'Virginia O'Hanlon', asked a plain question from the 'New York Sun' reporter a simple question, "Is there a Santa Clause?" "Yes Virginia there is a Santa Clause." Came the reply. The answer, though was not a lie designed to satisfy a youngster's curiosity, but an example of faith itself. "Virginia your friends are wrong," the editor wrote, "They have been affected by the skepticism of a skeptical age. They do not believe except they see." Without Santa, he argued.

"There would be no childlike faith then, no poetry, no romance to make tolerable this existence.... nobody see's Santa Clause, but that is no sign there is no Santa Clause. Nobody can conceive or imagine the wonders there are unseen and unseeable in the world".

It is in the brief December season that Americans using the language and the objects of their culture, recapture ideals and act according to their better selves. In this sense the nations Christmas truly brings together the cultures two most disparate yet similarly unbound projects - to seek wealth and secure salutation.

ROAST TURKEY

8 to 12 pound turkey
salt
butter

Remove neck and giblets from cavity of thawed or fresh turkey.

Rinse turkey well and pat dry with a paper towel.

Rub cavity of turkey lightly with salt. (do not salt if turkey is to be stuffed)

Stuff turkey just before roasting, not ahead of time.

Fill the wishbone area with stuffing first.

Fasten neck skin to back with skewer.

Fold wings across back with tips touching.

Fill body cavity lightly. (Do not pack)

Stuffing will expand while cooking.

Tuck drumsticks under band of skin at tail or tie together with heavy string, then tie to tail.

Place turkey breast side up, on rack, in shallow roasting pan.

Brush with butter.

Insert meat thermometer into thickest part of breast meat and does not touch bone. (Do not add water)

Roast uncovered at 325 degrees F. oven for 3-1/2 to 4-1/2 hours.

Make sure the meat thermometer reached 185 degrees F.

When the turkey begins to turn brown, place a tent of foil over turkey to finish cooking.

GIBLET GRAVY

neck, gizzard, heart, liver of turkey
1/2 teaspoon salt
1/4 teaspoon pepper
water
1/2 cup drippings from turkey
1/2 cup all-purpose flour

Cover turkey gizzard, heart and neck with water.

Sprinkle with salt and pepper.

Heat to boiling, reduce heat to simmer.

Simmer uncovered until gizzard is fork-tender, 1 to 1-1/2 hours.

Add the liver the last 5 to 10 minutes of cooking; drain.

Reserve broth for gravy.

Cut-up giblets.

Refrigerate broth and giblets until ready to use.

Pour drippings from roasting pan into a bowl.

Return 1/2 cup drippings to pan.

Stir in 1/2 cup flour, cook over low heat, stirring constantly until mixture is smooth and bubbly; remove from heat, add enough water to reserved broth to make 4 cups.

Stir in flour mixture.

Heat to boiling, stirring constantly. Boil and stir 1 minute.

Stir in giblets; sprinkle with salt and pepper.

Beat until giblets are hot.

Makes 4 cups

OLD FASHIONED BREAD STUFFING

1-1/2 cups chopped celery with leaves
3/4 cup finely chopped onion
1 cup butter
9 cups soft bread cubes
1-1/2 teaspoons salt
1-1/2 teaspoon dried sage leaves
1 teaspoon dried thyme
1/2 teaspoon pepper

Caramelize celery and onion in a 10 inch skillet until onion is tender.

Stir in about 1/3 bread cubes. Pour into deep bowl. Add remaining ingredients; toss, stuff turkey just before roasting.

Mill stuff a 12 pound turkey.

Makes 9 pounds stuffing

WHITE AND WILD RICE MEDLEY

1/2 cup slivered almonds
1/4 cup uncooked wild rice
1 jar (2-1/2 ounce) sliced mushrooms drained
2 tablespoons chopped green onions
1/4 cup butter
1 tablespoon instant bouillon
2-1/2 cup boiling water
3/4 cup uncooked regular white rice

Cook and stir almonds, wild rice, mushrooms, and green onions in butter until almonds are a golden brown. (10 to 15 minutes)

Pour wild rice mixture into ungreased 1-1/2 quart casserole.

Stir in instant bouillon and water.

Cover and bake at 350 degrees F. for 30 minutes.

Stir in regular rice, cover and cook until liquid is absorbed, about 30 minutes longer.

GLAZED BAKED HAM

5 to 8 pound ham (fully cooked smoked picnic)

whole cloves
1/4 cup honey
1/2 teaspoon dry mustard
1/4 teaspoon ground cloves

Orange slices and maraschino cherries for garnish (if desired)

Place fully cooked smoked shoulder fat side up, on rack, in shallow roasting pan.

Insert meat thermometer so tip is in thickest part of meat, and does not touch bone, or the rest of fat.

Bake uncovered in 350 degree F. oven until done, 25 to 30 minutes per pound, until thermometer registers 140 degrees F.

About 30 minutes before ham is done, remove from oven; drain.

(saving drippings)

Cut uniform diamond shapes on the fat surface of ham.

Insert whole clove into each diamond.

Mix honey, mustard, and ground cloves; spread on ham and bake 30 minutes.

Decorate ham with orange slices and maraschino cherries if desired.

GLAZED CARROTS

1-1/4 pound fresh carrots (about 8)
1/3 cup packed brown sugar
1/4 cup butter
1/2 cup honey
1/2 teaspoon grated orange peel

Cut carrots crosswise into 2-1/2 inch peaces, then into 3/8 inch strips.

Heat 1 inch salted water (1 cup water to 1/2 teaspoon salt) to boil.

Add carrots, cover, heat to boiling.

Reduce heat and heat to boiling, 18 to 20 minutes and then drain.

Cook and stir brown sugar, butter, honey and orange peel in 10 inch skillet till bubbly.

Add carrots and cook over low heat, stirring occasionally, until carrots are glazed and heated through about 5 minutes.

GREEN BEANS WITH ALMONDS

3 packages (9 ounce each) frozen cut green beans
3/4 cup water
2 tablespoon butter
8 ounce slice almonds
1/2 teaspoon salt
1/8 teaspoon pepper

Heat beans and water in a 3-quart saucepan; reduce heat.

Cover and simmer, stirring occasionally, until tender, about 10 minutes, drain.

Toss beans with butter, almonds, salt and pepper

SCALLOPED CORN

2 tablespoons melted butter
2 tablespoons sugar
salt and pepper
2 eggs beaten
1-1/2 cups evaporated milk
3/4 cup crushed crackers
1 can cream corn
1/4 cup Finley chopped onion

Mix all well, together and Bake at 350 degrees F.

Cook for 1 hour.

HOLIDAY BAKED YAMS

1 (40 ounce) canned yams
1 (8-1/2 ounce) can crushed pineapple juice
2 tablespoons light brown sugar
2 tablespoons butter melted
3 tablespoons chopped pecans
3/4 cup mini marshmallows

Drain yams, mash well.

Drain pineapple; reserve juice. add juice to yams.

Add sugar and butter; beat well.

Stir in pineapple and pecans.

Coat inside of 1-1/2 quart casserole with 'Pam' spray.

Spoon in mixture.

Bake for 20 minutes at 350 degrees F.

Sprinkle with marshmallows.

Bake 10 minutes longer.

Serves 8

APPLE SALAD

This is a traditional recipe used from my family for 5 generations of Christmases. When we had any family gathering this was a dish you could always depend upon being placed upon the table. I don't know who taught my mother but I remember this being at reunions, but anyway, My mother taught us to make this and we taught our girls and the next generation has started to leave home and this is one of the recipes taken with them. I hope this will have a traditional place at your table.

3 cups diced apples with peel (Fuji or gala work best)
2 cups sliced, seedless grapes
1 cup thinly sliced celery
1/2 cup chopped walnuts or pecans
1 tablespoons granulated sugar
Miracle whip salad dressing
Marshmallows if desired (miniature marshmallows)

Combine the apples, grapes, celery and pecans together.

Sprinkle the sugar over the fruit and shake the bowl to collect on the fruit to draw juices.

Start with 2 tablespoons salad dressing, mixing into the fruit, (the amount will depend on how juicy the fruit is) when you have the desired consistency of salad, throw in a hand full marshmallows. (the amount to your liking)

Toss and chill.

Makes 6 to 8 servings

CHRISTMAS EVE FRUIT SALAD

1 can (11 ounces) mandarin orange segments, drained
1 can (8-1/4 ounce) sliced beets, drained
1 can (8-1/4 ounce) pineapple chunks
2 tart red apples cut up
1 banana sliced

1 tablespoon lemon juice
Shredded lettuce
1 tablespoon sugar
1/4 cup chopped peanuts
1/4 cup salad dressing
2 tablespoon milk

Place orange segments, beets, pineapple, (with syrup) apples and bananas in a bowl.

Add lemon juice; toss gently, let stand 10 minutes;

Drain.

Arrange mixture on a platter of shredded lettuce.

Sprinkle with sugar and peanuts.

Mix salad dressing and milk.

Drizzle over fruit.

BREAD PUDDING FROM "1685"

2 cups bread cubed (4 or 5 slices)
1/2 cup raisins
2 cups milk
3 tablespoons butter
1/3 cup sugar
dash salt
1 teaspoon vanilla
2 egg
1/2 teaspoon nutmeg

MERINGUE:

2 egg whites
dash salt
4 tablespoon sugar

Current Jelly

Cut bread into 1/2 inch cubes, crust and all, and placed in a well-buttered 1 quart baking casserole.

Sprinkle with the raisins and mix lightly.

Scald the milk and stir into it, while heating, the butter and sugar.

Beat eggs slightly with a fork, add the salt, nutmeg, and vanilla and stir into the milk mixture.

Pour over the bread cubes.

Set casserole in a pan of warm water.

Bake for 1 hour in a 350 degree F. oven, or until knife inserted in center comes out clean.

Dot surface with jelly.

Beat egg whites until stiff, then add salt and sugar, a little at a time, beating until smooth and glossy.

Spread over pudding and bake in a 325 degree oven until lightly browned.

Serve warm or cold.

The jelly and meringue may be omitted, and the pudding served with cream, or chocolate or lemon sauce.

HARD SAUCE

1/2 cup butter softened
1 cup confectioners sugar
2 teaspoons vanilla
1 teaspoon rum

Beat butter in a small mixing bowl, on high speed until smooth, about 5 minutes.

Gradually beat in confectioners sugar, and vanilla or rum.

Refrigerator 1 hour.

SWEET POTATO CRESCENT ROLLS

My sister would always make these for our Christmas Holidays, our brother would always try to bargain away a few to take home for later. These melt in you mouth. Before Jena made them, I do believe mom made them, just not very often.

1 package active dry yeast
1 cup warm water (105 to 115 degrees F.)
1 cup luke warm mashed sweet potatoes
1/2 cup shortening
1/3 cup sugar
1 egg
1-1/2 teaspoons salt
5 to 6 cup flour
Soft butter

Dissolve yeast in warm water in a large bowl.

Stir in sweet potatoes, shortening, sugar, eggs, salt and 3 cups flour.

Beat until smooth.

Stir in enough remaining flour to make dough easy to handle.

Turn dough onto a lightly floured surface, knead until smooth and elastic.

This takes about 5 minutes.

Place in a greased bowl; turning dough once, with greased side up.

Cover and let rise in a warm place, until doubled in size, about 1 hour. (dough is ready if indention remains when touched)

Punch dough down; divide into 3 equal parts.

Roll each part into a 12 inch circle on a floured surface.

spread surface with butter, cut into 12 wedges then roll up tightly,

Beginning at rounded edges, place rolls with points underneath on greased cookie sheet; and curve slightly. Let rise until double 30 to 45 minutes.

Heat oven to 400 degrees F.

Bake until golden brown.

BUTTERMILK BISCUITS

1 cup all-purpose flour
1 teaspoon baking powder
1/8 teaspoon baking soda
1/8 teaspoon salt
1/3 cup buttermilk or sour milk
2 tablespoon cooking oil

Stir together flour, baking powder, soda, and salt in a medium bowl.

Stir together buttermilk and oil, then pour over flour mixture and

mix well.

Knead dough gently, on a lightly floured board 10 to 12 times.

Roll or pat dough to 1/2 inch thickness.

Cut with a 2 inch biscuit cutter, dipping cutter in flour before each

cutting and place dough on ungreased baking sheet.

Bake at 450 degrees F. for 10 to 12 minutes, until golden,

Serve warm.

Makes 8 biscuits

HOLIDAY BREAKFAST BREAD

2 cups flour
2 cups sugar
1 teaspoon soda
1 teaspoon salt
1 teaspoon cinnamon

3 eggs, slightly beaten
1 1/2 cup oil
1 cup chopped pecans
1 cup coconut
2 cups dried bananas
1 large can crushed pineapple, drained
1 1/2 teaspoon vanilla

Mix flour, sugar, soda, salt, and cinnamon in a large bowl.

Add beaten eggs and oil.

Then add pecans, coconut, bananas, drained pineapple and vanilla,

Mixing well. Prepare 2 loaf pans.

Bake at 350 degrees F.

Bake for 1 hour to 1 hour 20 minutes.

PUMPKIN BREAD

3 cup sugar
1 cup oil
3 eggs
2/3 cup water
3 cup flour
1 teaspoon cinnamon
1 1/2 teaspoon salt
1 teaspoon nutmeg
2 teaspoons baking soda
1 tablespoon baking powder
2 cups pumpkin
1 cup chopped nuts

Beat together sugar, oil, and eggs in a large bowl.

Sift together flour, cinnamon, salt, nutmeg, baking soda, and baking powder.

Add sifted dry ingredients, alternately with water beating after each addition, add pumpkin and nuts, stirring well.

Pour into greased loaf pans.

Bake at 350 degrees F.

Bake for 90 minutes or until knife inserted in center comes out clean.

THUMBPRINT COOKIES

1/2 cup butter
1/4 cup brown sugar (packed)
1 egg separated
1/2 teaspoon vanilla.
1 cup floured
1/4 teaspoon salt
3/4 cup finely chopped nuts

Jelly or tint confectioners icing

Heat oven to 350 degrees F.

Mix butter, sugar, egg yolk, and vanilla thoroughly.

Measure flour and salt; stir in.

Roll dough into a ball, (1 teaspoon per ball).

Beat egg white slightly with fork.

Dip balls in egg white.

Roll in nut.

Place about 1 inch apart on ungreased baking sheet.

Press thumb gently down in center of each.

Bake 10 to 12 minutes, or until set, cool, fill thumb

print with jelly or tint icing.

Makes 3 dozen cookies

CHRISTMAS COOKIES

1 pound butter
1 1/2 cup sugar
2 eggs
1/2 teaspoon vanilla
5 cups flour
Course red or green sugar for garnish

Preheat oven to 375 degrees F.

Cream butter. Add sugar a little at a time, beat till fluffy.

Add vanilla, mix well.

Add eggs, one at a time, beating well after each addition.

Mix in flour, and blend well.

Force mixture through a pastry bag, fixed with medium or large star tube,

onto a buttered cookie sheet. (it may be necessary to chill the dough before

forming the cookies).

Sprinkle with colored sugar.

Bake for 8 to 10 minutes or until delicately brown.

CANDY WINDOW SUGAR COOKIE CUTOUTS

I would like to share with you that my daughter, Katie is big on making Gingerbread houses each year. This is one of the methods she used to practice on her windows before she tackled the real thing. play with this method, be creative, and have fun.

1/3 cup butter
1/3 cup shortening

2 cups flour
3/4 cup sugar
1 egg
1 tablespoon milk
1 teaspoon baking powder
1 teaspoon vanilla
dash salt
3 ounce hard candy, finely crushed

Powder sugar icing

Preheat oven to 350 degrees F.

Cream together, butter, sugar, shortening, until soft, adding egg and milk blending well.

Gradually add salt, baking powder, vanilla, stirring again, adding last the flour gradually, making sure to blend well between each addition.

Divide dough in half- cover and chill 3 hours.

On lightly floured surface, roll each half of the dough to 1/8 inch thickness, using 2 to 3 inch cookie cutter.

Cut dough into desired shapes.

Place on foil lined cookie sheet.

Cut out a small shape in the center of cookie.

Spoon some candy in the center of each cookie.

Bake for 8 to 10 minutes.

Cool cookies on foil, then peel off foil.

Makes 36 to 48 cookies

HOLIDAY WHITE FRUIT BARS

2/3 cup shortening
1/2 cup sugar
2 eggs, separated

1 tablespoon sherry flavoring
1/4 teaspoon almond flavoring
1 3/4 cups flour
2 teaspoon baking powder
1 teaspoon salt
1 cup cream (20% butter fat)
1/2 cup flaked coconut
1/4 cup chopped citron
1/2 cup chopped blanched almonds
1/4 cup cut pecans

Icing

Preheat oven to 350 degrees F.

Mix together shortening, sugar and egg yolks, add flavorings and blend til fluffy.

Blend together dry ingredients and gradually add to the creamed mixture.

Gradually add in the coconut, citron and nuts.

Beat egg whites until stiff peaks form; fold into dough

Spread into greased oblong 9x13x2 inch pan, bake about 30 minutes.

Spread with icing while still warm.

When cool cut into squares, or bars.

Cookies improve with mellowing, so bake at least 24 hours before serving.

Makes 2 1/2 to 3 dozen bars

CANDY CANE COOKIES

1 cup shortening
1 cup sifted confectioners sugar
1 egg
1 1/2 teaspoons almond extract
1 teaspoon vanilla
2 1/2 cups all-purpose flour

1 teaspoon salt
1/2 teaspoon red food coloring

1/2 cup peppermint candy crushed
1/2 cup granulated sugar

Preheat oven to 350 degree F

In a bowl mix 1/2 cup crushed peppermint candy and

1/2 cup granulated sugar, and set aside.

Mix shortening, sugar, egg and flavorings thoroughly.

Mix flour, and salt; stir into shortening mixture.

Divide dough in half.

Blend food coloring in half of the dough.

Roll into 4 inch strips (using 1 teaspoon dough) from each color.

For smooth even strips, roll them back and forth on a lightly floured surface.

Place strips side by side, press lightly together and twist like a rope, for best results, complete cookies one at a time.

If all dough of one color is shaped first, strips become to dry to twist.

Place on ungreased baking sheet, curve top around to form top of the cane.

Bake 9 minutes until golden browned.

While still warm remove from baking sheet with spatula.

Sprinkle with candied sugar mixture.

Makes 4 dozen cookies

CHOCOLATE NO BAKE COOKIES

This is a cookie I grew-up with, It seemed that every time mom made them it was like eating candy. Mom would make these at Christmas-time and my brother Gregg would go wild for them and at the age of 60, he will ask for these over any gift. This will make wonderful Christmas gifts and package well.

2 cups sugar
1/2 cup cocoa
1/2 cup milk
1/2 cup butter
1 teaspoon vanilla
3 cups quick oats

Mix sugar, cocoa, and butter in a saucepan, bring to a full-boil; boil for just one minute, stirring often.

Remove from heat.

Immediately, stir in oats and then add vanilla; quickly drop by spoonfulls onto wax paper, and let cool until harden.

EARLY AMERICAN SEED CAKES

1 cup butter
1/3 cup sesame seed
1/2 cup butter
1 cup sugar
1 egg
2 tablespoons water
2 cups flour
1 tablespoon baking powder
1/4 teaspoon salt

Brown Butter Sesame Seed Icing

Preheat oven to 375 degrees F.

Brown 1/2 cup butter and 1/3 cup sesame seeds in a medium saucepan over low heat until golden brown, remove from heat.

Mix 1/2 cup butter, sugar, and egg thoroughly.

Add 2 tablespoons sesame seed from browned butter to sugar mixture.

Blend in water.

Sift flour, baking powder, and salt together.

Gradually add flour to sugar mixture. Mixing well.

Drop by teaspoonfuls dough onto ungreased cookie sheet.

Flatten with the bottom of a greased glass, dipped in sugar.

Bake about 10 minutes or until lightly browned around the edges

Cool completely and Ice.

SESAME SEED ICING:

3 cups confectioners sugar, sifted
3 tablespoons milk
1 teaspoon vanilla
remainder browned sesame seeds

Blend confectioners sugar, milk, vanilla, into sesame seed, mixing well.

Stirring til smooth.

OLD-FASHIONED FRUIT CAKE

3 cups all-purpose flour
1 1/3 cups sugar
2 teaspoons salt
2 teaspoons ground cinnamon
1 teaspoons baking powder
1 teaspoon ground nutmeg
1 cup orange juice
1 cup vegetable oil
4 eggs
1/4 cup dark molasses, or dark corn syrup, or dark honey
3 cups golden raisins
8 ounce pitted dates, cut into halves (1 1/2 cups)
5 ounce whole red and green candied cherries (3/4 cup)

5 ounce red and green candied pineapple, cut up (1 cup)
8 ounce whole Brazil nuts or pecan halves (1 2/3 cup)
Sweet glaze, optional

Preheat oven to 275 degrees F.

Line 2 loaf pans, 9x5x3 or 8 1/2 x 4 1/2 x 2 1/2 inch with greased aluminum foil.

Beat together in large mixing bowl, oil, eggs, molasses, sugar and salt.

In a separate bowl blend flour, cinnamon, baking powder, and nutmeg.

Gradually blend flour mixture into liquid mixture.

Scraping bowl occasionally, beating on medium speed for 3 minutes.

By hand mix in raisins, dates, cherries, pineapple and nuts.

Incorporating

Spread into prepared pans.

Incorporate through batter well.

Bake until wood pick inserted in center, comes out clean, 2 1/2 to 3 hours.

If necessary cover with aluminum foil, during last hour of baking, to prevent excessive browning.

Remove from pans; cool.

Wrap in plastic wrap, or foil, then refrigerate 3 to 4 weeks or freeze.

Before serving, drizzle with sweet glaze.

SWEET GLAZE:

2 tablespoon light corn syrup,
1 tablespoon water

In a sauce pan heat syrup and water just to a boiling, cool to warm.

MARY BALL WASHINGTON'S GINGERBREAD

(1784)
This recipe was found in a worn-out cookbook of George Washington's
Mother.

1/2 cup water
1/2 cup dark brown sugar, firmly packed
1/2 cup light molasses
1/2 cup honey
1/4 cup sherry
1/2 cup warm milk
3 cup sifted flour
2 tablespoons ground ginger
1 1/2 teaspoon ground cinnamon
1 1/2 teaspoons ground mace
1 1/2 teaspoon ground nutmeg
1 teaspoon cream of tarter
3 eggs, beaten well
2 tablespoons grated orange peel
1/4 cup orange juice
1 cup raisins
1 teaspoon baking soda
2 tablespoons warm water

Preheat oven to 350 degrees F.

Cream butter until light.

Add brown sugar and cream again.

Add molasses, sherry, honey, and milk and beat very well.

Sift flour, cinnamon, ginger, mace, nutmeg and cream of tarter together.

Add alternately with beaten eggs to the butter mixture.

Add juice, orange rind, raisins and baking soda dissolved in warm water.

Pour into a buttered 13 x 9 inch pan, lined with buttered wax paper.

Bake 45 to 50 minutes, until cake is firm in center.

Cut into squares.

Makes 12 servings

CHOCOLATE MIRACLE WHIP CAKE

My Mother always made this on our birthdays and on holidays. I believe it was the best part of the Holiday. Mom lives in Idaho now and the rest of the family is in Indiana, but when she comes home she always makes a miracle whip cake. My Grandchildren loves the icing on this cake more than the cake.

2 cups all-purpose flour
1 1/2 teaspoon soda
1 1/2 teaspoons baking powder
4 tablespoons cocoa
1 cup sugar
1 cup miracle whip
1 teaspoons vanilla
1 cup water

Preheat oven to 350 degrees F.

In a separate bowl, sift together flour, soda, baking powder, set aside.

In a large mixing bowl, mix together cocoa and sugar to incorporate easily.

Mix together flour mixture and cocoa mixture.

With a mixer, mix in miracle whip, vanilla and water, mixing well.

Pour into a prepared pan, and bake for about 25 minutes or until pick inserted in center comes out clean.

Ice with Mom's White Butter Icing.

WHITE BUTTER CREAM ICING

This is the icing Mom always makes, and as I grew up it was such a treat for mom to make us the graham cracker sandwiches with this icing. and since I have left home she has made some changes in this recipe by adding peanut butter.

1 cup sifted confectioners sugar
1/4 cup salted butter
1 tablespoon milk
1 teaspoon vanilla

In a small mixing bowl with hand mixer, whip butter and add confectioners sugar milk and vanilla. Beat until nice and smooth. If it is to stiff, add a teaspoon milk. If icing is too thin add just enough sugar to make the desired consistency.

Makes about 1/2 cup icing

CHRISTMAS COCONUT CAKE

2 cups all-purpose flour
1 1/2 cups granulated sugar
3 1/2 teaspoons baking powder
1 teaspoon salt
1/2 cup shortening
1 cup milk
1 teaspoon vanilla
4 egg whites
2/3 cups flaked coconut

fruit filling, (can be a favorite jam)

1 cup whipping cream
1/4 cup confectioners sugar
3/4 teaspoon almond extract

Preheat oven to 350 degrees F.

Grease and flour 2 - round 9 inch layer pans.

Beat flour, confectioners sugar, baking powder, salt, shortening, milk and vanilla in a large mixing bowl on low speed.

Scraping bowl constantly, 30 seconds.

Beat on high speed, scraping bowl occasionally, 2 minutes.

Add egg whites, beat on high speed, about 2 minutes, scraping bowl occasionally.

Stir in coconut, pour into pans, bake until wooden pick inserted in center comes out clean, 30 to 35 minutes; cool.

Fill layers and frost top of cake with in 1-inch of edge with filling or jam.

Beat whipping cream, powdered sugar and almond extract in a chilled bowl until stiff.

Spread tops and sides with whipped cream.

Refrigerate.

MERRY'N BRIGHT LEMON CAKE

1 1/2 cup granulated sugar
2 cups cake flour
2 teaspoon baking powder
1 package (3 ounce) lemon gelatin
3/4 cup milk
2/3 cup light cooking oil
2 tablespoons lemon extract
4 large eggs separated

Preheat oven to 350 degrees F.

In one mixing bowl, sift 1 1/4 cups sugar, flour, baking powder, and gelatin together.

In an other bowl, combine milk, oil, and lemon extract.

Beat liquids into dry ingredients, until batter is smooth.

Beat egg yolks into the batter, one at a time.

Whip egg whites until stiff (not dry) with 1/4 of granulated sugar.

Fold the egg whites lightly but thoroughly into the batter.

Grease ring pan and dust with flour.

Spoon batter into pan and bake for 40 to 50 minutes, until cake springs back lightly to the touch.

Turn out immediately onto a wire rack.

glaze top with a drizzle icing after cool.

FRESH PUMPKIN PIE

1 pastry lined 9 inch pie tin
3/4 cup brown sugar
1/2 teaspoon salt
3/4 teaspoon cinnamon
1/4 teaspoon ginger
1/4 teaspoon cloves
1/4 teaspoon nutmeg
1 1/2 cup prepared fresh pumpkin
1 1/2 cup rich milk
2 beaten eggs

Chill pie shell.

Preheat oven to 450 degrees F.

Combine brown sugar, salt, and spices, mixing well.

Mix the remaining ingredients and with a whisk, mix well.

Pour into chilled pie shell.

Bake for 15 minutes, then lower heat to 325 degrees F. for an additional 30 minutes or until knife inserted in

center comes our clean.

Serve with whipped cream or ice cream.

PECAN PIE

9 inch unbaked pie crust
3 eggs
2/3 cup granulated sugar
1/2 teaspoon salt
1/3 cup butter melted
1 cup light corn syrup
1 cup pecans

Preheat oven to 375 degrees F.

Beat together eggs, sugar, salt, melted butter and light corn syrup.

Now mix in pecans.

Pour into pastry lined pan.

Bake until set and pastry is browned for about 40 to 50 minutes.

HOT CINNAMON CIDER

My daughter Katie has started a tradition of making this recipe each year on Christmas day, we truly enjoy it and the whole family looks forward to her making it each year.

half gallon fresh apple cider
2 cinnamon sticks

You want to bring this to a boil in a dutch oven on the stove, boil about 10 minutes then take out cinnamon sticks and keep warm in a crock pot.

If you use cider in the store you will want to add some flavor, you may want to try this.

3 quart
1/3 cup red cinnamon candies
1 tablespoon whole allspice

heat all in a dutch oven bring to a boil, reduce heat to simmer 5 minutes, remove allspice and serve.

Makes 24 - 1/2 cup servings

MAMIE EISENHOWER'S FUDGE

4 1/2 cups granulated sugar
2 tablespoons butter
pinch salt
1 tall can evaporated milk

Bring all the above to a boil for 6 minutes, stirring constantly.

Put into a large bowl:

12 ounce semi-sweet chocolate chips
1 pint marshmallow cream
2 cups nut meats

Pour boiling syrup over chocolate, marshmallow cream, and nuts.

Beat until chocolate is melted, and pour into pan.

Let set about 2 hours before cutting.

Store in a tin box.

CANDIED GRAPEFRUIT PEEL

Grapefruit peel with the membrane pealed out,

and cut into 1/4 inch strips.

(2 cups)

Boil 20 minutes and drain.

Boil 20 more minutes in fresh water, drain again.

Cook 20 minutes in a light syrup, bubble along.

Drain: roll in sugar, lay on wire rack to dry.

BUTTERMILK CANDY

This recipe was retrieved from my Great Grandmother, Ethel Flora Thackery Swango's recipe box; was dated September 23, 1923

2 cup sugar
1/2 cup buttermilk
1 tablespoon butter
1/2 cup nut meats

Cook sugar, buttermilk, and butter to a soft stage on a candy thermometer.

Add nuts then beat until thick.

Pour into a greased pan and mark. I believe this is an 8 or 9 inch square pan.

When cool cut into squares.

CHAPTER

Pagan Beliefs

YULE WINTER SOLSTICE / PAGAN CHRISTMAS on December 25th Long ago, under the light of a star, a savior was born unto mankind, of a gentle virgin Mother. Shepherds from nearby fields attended the miracle. As an adult he acquired 12 disciples, and people called him 'The Good Shepherd'.

His name was 'Mithra of Persla' and he lived 100's of years before Jesus, but easily could have next 'Osiris - or - Krishna - or - Zoroster.

HAPPY SATURNALIA EVERYBODY

Christmas is the Pagan holiday yule. Christians may think Christmas has to do with the birth of Jesus, but he was not born on December 25th, and has also been a religious holiday for pagans of ancient and modern times, as Yule or Winter Solstice.

'YULE' was the traditional name for the celebrations around the 25th, the festivals lasted for 12 days, which are now considered the 'Twelve Days of Christmas'. The origins of the word Yule seemed to originate from the Anglo Saxon word for sun and light. Most likely regarding the birth of the sun, from the shortest day. In many places fire or candles were kindled to burn through the twelve days that marked the festivity.

Many of the symbols of Christmas echo its aspect of rebirth and hope in darkness. Holly was thought to be important because it retains its greenery rough the winter months, and as such is a symbol of summer life in the winters darkness. Holly was the male symbol of this greenery, and Ivy was the female, the two, often placed together as a 'Fecundity' at the dark end of the year.

There was also a belief that evergreen plants and trees were refuges for the woodland spirits through the winter months. Evergreen trees were a symbol of life.

Yule (Pronounced EWE-elle) is when the dark half of the year, relinquishes the light half. Starting the next morning at sunrise, the sun climbs just a little higher and stays just a little longer in the sky each day;

Known as the 'Solstice Night', or the longest night of the year, much celebration was to be had as the ancestors awaited rebirth of the oak king, the sun king, the giver of life that warmed the frozen earth and made her to bear forth from seeds protected through the fall and winter in her womb.

Bonfires are lit in the fields, and crops and trees were "Wassailed" with toasts of spiced cider.

Children were escorted from house to house with gifts of clove spiked apples and oranges which were laid in baskets of evergreen boughs and wheat stalks dusted with flour. The apples and oranges represented the sun. The boughs were symbolic of immortality, the wheat stalks portrayed the harvest, and the flour was the accomplishment of triumph, light and life. Holly, mistletoe and ivy not only decorated the outside, but also the inside of the homes. It was to extend invitation to natures spirits, to come join the celebration. A sprig of holly was kept near the door all year long, as a constant invitation for good fortune to pay a visit it the residents.

The ceremonial yule log was the highlight the festival. In accordance to tradition, the log must ether have been harvested from the householder's land, or given as a gift... it must never have been bought. Once dragged into the house and placed in the fireplace, it was decorated in seasonal greenery, doused with cider and ale, and dusted with flour, before set ablaze they must put a piece of chard log from last year with the new log (kept just for this purpose). The log would burn throughout the night, then smolder for 12 days.

As the 12 days come to an end, the yule log will then ceremoniously be put out, and then a piece of chard wood is saved for the next year. ASH is the traditional wood of the yule log, it is the sacred world tree of the Teutons, known as YGGDRASIL, an herb of the sun, ash brings light into the hearth at the Solstice.

The Pagan Santa, his name was Odin and was considered to be the god of yule, (a pagan midwinter festival) by many of the German people. The legend of Odin spoke of a great long bearded man who flew through the sky with the aid of an eight-legged horse. The horse was not only rumored to fly, but also could leap long distances as well. Children in these ancient days would leave carrots, sugar and straw in their shoes for Odin's flying horse. Their shoes were carefully placed near the chimney. Odin was said to reward children for their kindness with food, sweets or presents.

The evergreen tree is the symbol of the green to come at the rebirth of mother earth. In ancient Egypt, they laid gifts under palm trees during the winter celebration. In ancient Rome they used the Fir tree, (called the Baal Berlth) as a testimony to the pagan messiah, Baal Tamar.

The Pagan messiah Baal Tamar, in classic literature, Nimrod is sometimes called Ninus, but Ninus was probably, in fact Nimrods's son, the builder of the city of Nineveh. Nimrod's wife was Semiramis, the queen of heaven, and sometimes her husband is called Ninus, while other times, Ninus is said to be her sun. The confusion is related to the story of Nimrods deification. The legend said, Nimrod was killed, and resurrected as his wife's son, a feat which could be orchestrated only by a god, thus began the mother / son cult religions. Semiramis sometimes called Rhea, came to be known as the 'Great Mother of the Gods', while her son Ninus or Bacchus or Tammuz (Ezekiel 8:14) was known as the 'Lamented One'. Tammuz is sometimes called 'Adonis' or 'Dronysus, other variations of the Babylonian gods of Rhea and Tammuz included Ceres (or Irene) and Plutus in Greece; Isis and Osiris in Egypt; Fortuna and Jupiter in pagan Rome; Isi and Iswara in India; Cybele and Deoius in Asia; Shing Moo in China; Goddess Mother and Son in Tibet. ALL derived from Rhea and Tammuz. In some literature, it is believed that Tammuz was known as Hercules the Lamenter, and he was sometimes confused with the Shem in the bible or at least with being his descendant. Some believe that Crishna if the Hindus, and the Buddha in Japan are also deviations of these same Babylonian gods.

Baal-Bereth is the father of the yule season and the yule (xmas) tree.

The Christmas tree now so common among us, was equally common in pagan Rome and pagan Egypt, that tree was the palm tree, in Rome it was the fir, the palm tree denoting the Messiah as Baal-Tamar, the fir referring him as Baal-Berith.

The Christmas tree as has been stated was generally at Rome a different tree, even the fir, but the very same idea was implied in the palm tree, was implied in the Christmas fir, for that covertly symbolized the new born god as Baal-Berith, "lord of the covenant" and thus shadowed forth perpetuity and ever lasting nature of his power, not that after having fallen before his enemies, he had risen triumphant over them all.

All world religions origins is in Babylon at the tower of babel, Which means, "Gate of God." In the book of Genesis 10:8-12. Nimrod means "He Rebelled."

His own mother Semiramis bore him a son Tammuz. His mother/wife known as Queen of heaven, the mother of deity. After Nimrod's execution by shem, he reincarnated to his son Tammuz and worshiped as "Sun God", this is how the origins of trinity began. Ancient pagans choose evergreen tree (x-mas) for it never died, green forever, and Egyptians build their pyramids in the shape of the Christmas tree.

In Egypt they worshiped Nimrod as a palm tree, referring to him as the Messiah "Baal-Tamar." Among the most ancient of Baal-Bereth, "Lord of the Fir tree." He evolved into Baah-Berith, "Lord of the Covenant." In ancient Rome, where they also worshiped the fir tree, they called him "Baal-Berith"

Origins of the Candy Cane

The Candy Cane origins date back to Egyptian and Babylonian times as part of Ancient rituals. The Egyptians loved sugary treats, "Hard Candies" made from lemon, cinnamon, or peppermint flavors were popular in Egyptian and Babylonian times in the shape of the Pharaoh's crook, was to honor their pharaoh.

Herbs Played a major part in the Egyptian Medication

The Egyptians were the firs to recognize the health benefits of honey, cinnamon, and mint, not only a food source but as medicine.

The plant medicines mentioned in the Ebus papyrus for instance include opium, cannabis, myrrh, frankincense, fennel, cassia, senna, thyme, henna, juniper, aloe, linseed, and castor oil--through some of the translations are less than certain. Cloves of garlic have been found in Egyptian burial sights including the tomb of Tutankhamen and in the sacred underground 'Temples of the Bulls' at Saqqara. Many herbs were steeped in wine, which was then drunk as an oral medicine.

The 25th of December was observed in Rome as the day when the victorious god reappeared on earth and was healed at the 'Hatalis invicti solis,' "The Birth-day of the Unconquered sun," Now the yule log represents the dead stock of Nemrod, known as the sun god, but cut down by his enemies; the Christmas tree represents 'Nimrod-the slain', god reborn, the ancient practice of kissing under the mistletoe bough, most common to the Druids was derived from Babylon, and was a representation of the Messiah, "The Man The Branch." The mistletoe was regarded as a divine branch - a branch that came from heaven, that grew upon a tree that sprung out of the earth. Nimrod, the god of nature, was symbolized by a great tree, but having been cut down and killed in his prime, he was now symbolized as a branches tree stump; called a yule log, then the great serpent came and wrapped itself around Nimrod (the stump). Miraculously, a new tree appeared at the side of the stump, which symbolized Nimrod's Resurrection and victory over death.

Pagans in German countries used the reindeer as a symbol of the horned god that they worshiped.

Baal-Berith was known also as "Lord of the Covenant" and as "The God Berith", he was a popular god and was worshiped in Canaan, Philistia, and Shechem. He was the protector of the covenant between Shechem and some neighboring canaanish towns, which were originally independent, but were at length brought under subjugation by the Hebrews - any Israelite who might be dwelling in Shechem would be simply or protected strangers, and not contribute to Abimelech. It was there that 'Gaal' first came forward as a leader of a rebellion, and within it precinct the inhabitants of the tour of Shechem (the acropolis) found a temperary refuge from Abimelech at the the close of the revolt. Baal-Berith was also known as "God of the Community".

The "Entire" Earth is lying in the power of ancient Babylon and the Spell cast by Nimrod and his mother.

The Babylonians centered the birth of god 'Tammuz' on the winter solstice and god Nimrod would visit the evergreen trees of the people and leave gifts upon them. The early Christian Church founded upon the exchange of gifts because of its Pagan origins. People refuse to give up their old pagan religions though. Ultimately around 700 years ago the Christian Church decided to attribute the gift exchange to symbolize the gifts given to Jesus by the three wise men. It took the Church 1300 years to finally "borrow" the pagan ritual of gift exchanging and called it their aeon.

Baby Jesus? Notice the pagan symbol for the sun is the (Halo, Nimbus) and the suns rays -- notice the "T" for Tammuz who was born in Babylon on December 25th.

Notice holly for the 'Holly god Saturn' who's birthday is also December 25th, the first sun god of Babylon.

The Romans and Saturnalia celebrations are even credited with the tradition of kissing under the mistletoe was used as a means to get a pretty girl to kiss you during the celebration and alternately instigate an orgy.

The Druids in Scotland and Ireland also believed mistletoe was a symbol of flirtation, a husband and wife desiring a child would hang the mistletoe around their bead during intercourse.

The yule day have Babylonian origins, yule is the chaldee name for an infant of little child, December 25th was called 'Yule Day' by pagan Angelo-Saxon ancestors. The night preceding yule day was known as 'Mothers Night'.

The Mesopotamian were polytheistic, their chief god was Marduk. Each year, as winter arrived, it was believed that Marduk would do the battle with the monsters of chaos.

"Christmas" was invented to compete with the pagan celebrations in December. The 25th was a sacred day for both Romans and the Persians, whose religion was Mithraism, one of Christianity's main rivals. The Church adopted many of the pagan rituals in their attempt to make the religion more attractive to converts.

It wasn't until 350 AD that the Bishop of Rome, Julius, chose December 25th as the observance of Christmas. This was obviously influenced by the ancient Romans year end festivities to honor Saturn (their harvest god) and Mithras (the god of light). The Roman feast of Saturnalia was a seven day festival in honor of the deity Saturn.

As Christianity spread, the Church became alarmed by the continuing practice among it's flock of indulging in customs such as this Saturnalians feast, "if you can't beat 'em join 'em" mentality began and slowly but surely the pagan ritual of using greenery to decorate homes moved from being prohibited as idolatry to becoming an accepted custom of the festivity.

Another tradition at the saturnalian, involved exchanging candles, clay dolls, and other small gifts.

PAGAN SYMBOLISM

YULE:

Rebirth of the sun, The longest night of the year, the winter solstice, planning for the future.

SYMBOLS OF YULE:

yule log, or small yule log with 3 candles, evergreen boughs or wreaths, holly, mistletoe hung in the doorways, gold pillar candles, baskets of clove studded fruit, a simmering pot of wassel, poinsettias, Christmas cactus.

HERB OF YULE:

Bayberry, Blessed thistle, evergreen, frankincense, holly, laurel, mistletoe, oak, pine, sage and yellow ceder.

FOOD OF YULE:

cookies, caraway cakes soaked in cider, fruit nuts, pork dishes, egg nog, ginger tea, spiced cider, wassel, or lambs wool ale, sugar, nutmeg, roasted apples.

INCENSE OF YULE:

Pine, ceder, bayberry, cinnamon.

COLORS OF YULE:

Red, green, gold, white, silver, yellow, green, orange.

STONES OF YULE:

Rubies, bloodstone, garnet, emeralds, diamond.

ACTIVITIES OF YULE:

Caroling, wasseling the trees, yule log, decorating the yule tree, exchanging of presents, kissing under the mistletoe, honor kris kringle - the Germatic pagan god of yule.

SPELL WORKING OF YULE:

Peace, harmony, love and increased happiness.

December 25th - is the birthday of several pagan gods.

HORUS (Egypt 3000 BC)

ATTIS (Greece 1200 BC)

MITHRA (Persia 1200 BC)

KRISHNA (India 900 BC)

DIANYSUS (Greece 500 BC)

TAMMUZ (Babylonian)

SATURN/CRONOS (Roman / Greek)

DEITIES OF YULE:

Goddesses- Brighid, Isis, Demeter, Gaea, Diana the great mother

GODS- Apollo, Ra, Odin, Lugh, The oak king, The horned one, The green man,

The divine child, Mabon

CHAPTER

Religions

CHRIST IN CHRISTMAS

As Christians, we celebrate Christmas, because of the birth of Jesus.

We know that all praise and glory belong to Jesus. The world around us wants to diminish the true meaning of the Christmas season, with the focus placed on spending money and make-believe stories. With all the flashy stuff this world has to offer, it may seem, that focusing on the true meaning of Christmas will leave us and our children underwhelmed. While we know the true JOY comes from knowing Jesus, there are so many wonderful ways to keep Christ in Christmas; thus making the celebration memorable!

THE CHRISTMAS STORY

LUKE 2:6-20

And so it was, that, while they were there, the days were accomplished that she should be delivered. And she brought fourth her first born son, and wrapped him in swaddling cloths, and laid him in a manger; because there was no room for them in the inn.

And there were in the same country shepherds abiding in the field, keeping watch over their flock by night. And, lo, the angel of the Lord came upon them, and the glory of the Lord shone round about them: and they were sore afraid.

And the Angel said which unto them, Fear not: for, behold, I bring you good tidings of great joy, which shall be to all people. For unto you is born this day in the city of David a Savior, which is Christ the Lord. And this shall be a sign unto you: Ye shall find the babe wrapped in swaddling cloths, lying in a manger.

And suddenly there was with the angel a multitude of the heavenly host praising God, and saying, Glory to God in the highest, and on earth peace, good will toward men.

And it came to pass, as the angels were gone away from them into heaven, the shepherds said one to another, Let us now go even unto Bethlehem, and see this thing that has come to pass, which the lord has made unto us. And they came with haste, and found Mary, and Joseph, and the babe lying in a manger.

And when they had seen it, they made known abroad the saying which was told them concerning this child. And all they that heard it wondered at those things which were told them by the shepherds.

But Mary kept all these things, and pondered them in her heart. And the shepherds returned, glorifying and praising God for all the things that they have heard and seen, as it was told unto them.

Cheyanne Dreyer

KEEPING CHRIST IN CHRISTMAS

Dear Billy Graham,

Christmas, is still weeks away, but already I'm dreading it.

It's such a busy time for our family, and we always end up spending more than we should. I know we ought to keep Christ in Christmas but how can we?

---Mrs. C.F.

"Dear Reader: Yes, now is a good time to remind ourselves to keep Christ in Christmas--- and not only keep him there but make him its center.

After all, Christmas celebrate the most important event in human history: the moment when God stepped out of eternity into time.

Think of it! At Christmas, the God who created the whole universe came down from heaven and became a baby -- Jesus Christ.

How can you make Christ the center of your Christmas? First take time each day to pause as a family and thank God for sending his son into the world. Also take advantage of other opportunities to focus on him (for example, through special programs in your church or community).

Take time to plan now for the coming weeks. Make a Christmas budget -- and stick to it. Plan your time also. Don't let the holiday season overwhelm you, but instead let your life be overwhelmed by the wonder of what Christ has done for us.

Billy Graham
November 17, 2004
Tribune Media Service

CHRISTIAN

DEPICTION OF THE NATIVITY OF JESUS

also called: Noel, Nativity, X-mas, yule

OBSERVED BY:

Christian, Many non-Christians

TYPE:

Christian cultural

SIGNIFICANCE:

Traditional remembrance of the birth of Christ Jesus

OBSERVANCES:

Church services, Gift Giving, Family and other Gatherings, Symbolic Decorating

DATE: December 25th

Western Christianity and some Eastern Churches, Secular World
January 7th

Some Eastern Churches

January 6th

American Apostolic and Armenian

Evangelistic Churches

January 19th

Armenian Patriarchate of Jerusalem

FREQUENCY:

Annual

RELATED TO:

Christmas Tide, Christmas Eve, Advent, Annunciation, Epiphany,

Baptism of the Lord, Nativity Fast, Nativity of Christ, Yule,

Saint Stephens Day

ADVENT - THE TIME BEFORE CHRISTMAS

Before Christmas, many Christians use the time of Advent to prepare themselves to get ready to celebrate the joy of Christmas, when Christians celebrate the birth of Jesus, who they believe is the Son of God.

-------Advent is normally a period of four Sundays and weeks before Christmas.

-------In many Orthodox Catholic Churches Advent lasts for forty days starting on November 15th.

-------In orthodox churches which celebrate Christmas on January 7th, Advent starts on the 28th of November.

-------During Advent many people fast (don't eat certain foods). The types of food that people give up depends upon their church traditions and where in the world they may live.

AFTER CHRISTMAS -- THE 12 DAYS OF CHRISTMAS AND EPIPHANY

-------After Advent, traditionally, Christmas celebrations (and often a feast) Started on Christmas Day and lasted for 12 days - so they were known as "The 12 Days Of Christmas". The celebrations finished on the evening of January 5th, which is better known as 'The 12th Night'.

-------Throughout history, the 12 days of Christmas were a time of feasting and fun.

-------Following the 12th Night on the 6th of January is Epiphany, when people remember the Wise men (also called the three kings) who visited Jesus and / or baptism of Jesus.

-------Epiphany / Twelfth Night is also the time when it was traditional to take down the Christmas decorations, although some would leave them up until Candlemas.

CANDLEMAS - THE END OF CHRISTMAS

After both Christmas and the Season of Epiphany, the end of the Christmas celebration comes on February 2nd, forty days after Christmas, with Candlemas.

Candlemas also known as the presentation of Jesus at the Temple or the feast of the purification of the virgin (or Mary) is when some Christians remember the time Mary and Joseph too baby Jesus to the Jewish Temple in Jerusalem to give thanks to God for giving them a Son.

-------The name Candlemas comes from "Candle mass" because in many Candlemas Services the candles are 'blessed', and used in the churches in the coming year or are given out to people to use in their homes for their private prayers.

-------In many Catholic Churches, It's the time for people to remember and renew promises they've made to the Church and celebrate some of the prophesies which were given about Jesus.

-------In many Eastern Orthodox Churches, an all night vigil is held the night before the candle blessing ceremony. In the morning the candles are blessed and given to people.

THE MEANING OF CHRISTMAS

Wise men came from the East, perhaps Persia. They saw the Babe-a Babe whose tiny hands were not quit long enough to touch the long heads of the cattle, and yet hands that were steering the reins that keep the sun, moon, and stars in their orbits. Shepherds came, and they saw the baby's lips that did not speak, and yet lips that might have articulated the secret of every living man, that hour. They saw the Baby's brow under which was a mind and intelligence compared with which the combined intelligence's of Europe and America amount to naught.

One silent night, out over the white-chalked hills of Bethlehem, came a gentle cry. The great ones of the earth did not hear it, for they could not understand how an infant could be greater than man. At the Christ Child's birth, only two groups of people heard that cry; the shepherds, who knew they did not know anything and the wise men who knew the did not know everything.

Let us reach out at this Holy Christmas season to except Christ with humility and love.

Author Unknown

25 ADVENT PROMISES FROM GOD

1. HOPE - Romans 15:13
2. HIS WORD IS FLAWLESS - Psalm 18:30
3. CREATED IN GODS IMAGE - Genesis 1:27
4. KNOW ME - Psalm 139:1
5. REDEMPTION - GALATIANS 3:13
6. MERCY - Psalms 145:9
7. HEARS PRAYER - Jeremiah 33:3
8. LOVE - John 3:16
9. SALVATION - Romans 10:9
10. WISDOM - James 1:5
11. STRENGTH - Isaiah 41:10
12. FORGIVENESS - I John 1:9
13. SUPPLY OUR NEEDS - Philippians 4:19
14. GRACE - Ephesians 2:5
15. JOY - John 15:11
16. OMNIPRESENT - Deuteronomy 31:6
17. GOD WORKS FOR GOOD - Romans 8:28
18. PROTECTION - Psalm 32:7
19. VICTORY - James 4:7
20. PLANS OF HOPE - Jeremiah 29:11
21. REST - Mathew 28:11
22. PEACE - John 14:27
23. GUIDANCE - Psalm 32:8
24. JESUS IS LORD - Isaiah 9:6
25. NOTHING IS IMPOSSIBLE - Luke 1:37

CHAPTER

Legends and Myths

LEGENDS OF CHRISTMAS

From Advent to Christmas to Epiphany, the holiday herald's time-honored traditions and customs the bring the sight and sounds of the season to life throughout Europe and the world. TRULY, it is, the most wonderful time of the year. As we gather with friends and family this holiday season to recount the stories of Christmas, let us not forget from whence we came. Lets take a journey through the past and present of Christmas Legends and Traditions.

Countless legends cluster about Christmas. The Yuletide season is glorified in song and stories that stir the mind and touch the heart.

SAINT NICHOLAS

Saint Nicholas was the original name for Santa Claus, he was the patron saint of many people and places. He was a real person, the Bishop of Myra, an ancient city of Asia Minor, in the fourth century. He is especially loved by the Russian peasants, because he protected the week and the poor against the strong and rich. According to a legend the people in the seaport village of Venice adopted him as their patron after he had stopped a terrible storm at sea while on a voyage to the Holy Land.

Boys depend on him because Nicholas once brought back to life young boys who had been cut up by a wicked innkeeper and salted in a cast of brine. Young girls have a special place in their hearts for him. Once on one occasion he tossed 3 bags of gold into a window of a home where three sisters lived. They had no dowry, (which is a gift the wife brings to the husband when they are wed.) Therefor could not find husbands without a dowry (money). Some say, the pawn shop's three gold balls stand for these three bags of gold, so pawn brokers claim him as their saint.

THE LEGEND OF LA BEFANA

The legend of La Befana explains how this elderly woman came to be the one to bring gifts to the children of Italy on Epiphany Eve. The old woman, a very particular housekeeper, was visited one day by the Wise men, who sought directions to Bethlehem. They offered to take the woman with them to pay homage to the Baby Jesus, but she declined, to busy cleaning her house to be bothered.

In time the woman came to regret her decision and set out after the wise men, only to get lost herself. Though she never found the wise men or the Baby Jesus, she still wanders the world searching, leaving gifts with the children of each house she passes by in honor of the one child she missed.

There is a similar legend in Russia about a woman called Babushka; both women bring coal to bad children.

THE LEGEND / TRADITION OF THE YULE LOG

The tradition of the yule log has very deep pagan roots. Celts, Teutons, and Druids burned the massive logs in winter ceremonies in celebration of the sun. The selection of each season's yule log was of the highest importance and surrounded by ceremony, as the log was to start the celebration fires and lasts for the duration of the winter festival.

In the Christian era, the log was often cut on February 2 (Candlemas Day), then set outside to dry during the late spring and summer; sometimes it was soaked in spices and decorated in greenery. Often a piece of the previous year's log was used was used to light the new log. In Scandinavia this saved piece had the additional significance of representing good will from Thor's lightning bolt would not strike burned wood, and that their houses were safe from lightning as long as they had this yule brand.

When Christianity emerged in Europe, the yule log remained popular in England and Scandinavia. In order to justify this pagan ritual, church officials gave it a new significance, that on the light that came from heaven when Christ was born. The log was lit on Christmas Eve and left burning throughout twelve days of Christmas.

In some parts of France the yule log was presented as the source of children's gifts. The log was covered with cloth and brought into the house, where the children whacked it with sticks, beseeching it to bring fourth present. When no presents came, the children were sent outside where they were to confess their sins that they committed that year; when they returned, the log was uncovered, surrounded by gifts.

Changes brought by the Industrial Revolution finally made the yule log impractical. Few had the time or space for the preparation it required, and the small fireplaces of the city could not accommodate such a massive thing. Like the boar's head, the huge yule log became, for most people, an emblem of the past.

LEGEND OF THE ANIMALS

It was told, at the night of Jesus' birth was the darkest ever known, but when the child was born a great light spread across the skies. At that moment the cattle keeled down in the stalls of the little manger. They spoke to each other. A cock crowed, "Christ is born!" and the animals whispered, "Let us all worship together."

Every year at midnight on December 25th, cattle all over the world kneel in adoration.

It was also said that when the infant Jesus cried, his mother could not sooth him. A small brown bird fluttered through the door and sitting on Mary's shoulder, piped a few notes. The child Jesus was so surprised that he stopped crying. The bird continued to sing and the notes became sweeter, while the infant smiled and slept.

From that time on, the birds have the been gifted with most trilling of bird songs. Blessed with the glory of that night, he became the Nightingale.

LEGENDS OF THE HOLLY

Everything associated with Christmas is legendary. There is the Holly which, as its name suggests, was holy. Wherever holly was hung it drove away evil spirits, and brought beauty into the house. Because its leaves remain green, in twas considered a symbol of everlasting life.

Holly was also sacred for another reason. The sharp pointed leaves were used for Christs crown of thorns, and the berries were white until they were stained with his blood.

An other legend is told of how the Holy family was fleeing from the soldiers at night. The family hid behind a leafless holly bush for protection.

That night the holly bush grew leaves and sharp thorns to hide the family. Ever since the holly bush has leaves all year round.

Once again legend also has it that holly sprang from the footsteps of Christ as he walked the earth. The pointed leaves were said to represent the crown of thorns Christ wore while on the cross and the red berries symbolized the blood he shed.

LEGEND OF THE MISTLETOE

The mistletoe, too has spiritual significance; while other plants are rooted in earth, the mistletoe grows in air. When it is brought indoors it bestows blessings and radiates love. People who kiss beneath it are assured of happiness throughout the coming year.

Mistletoe was used by Druid Priests 200 years before the birth of Christ in their winter celebrations. They revered the plant since it had no roots yet remained green during the cold months of winter.

The ancient Celtics believe mistletoe to have magical healing powers and used it as an antidote for poison, infertility, and to ward off evil spirits.

The plant was also seen as a symbol of peace, and it is said that among Romans, enemies who met under mistletoe would lay down their weapons and embrace.

Scandinavians associated the plant with 'Frigga', their goddess of love, and it may be from this that we derive the custom of kissing under the mistletoe. Those who kissed under the mistletoe had the promise of happiness and good luck in the following year.

THE LEGEND OF THE CHRISTMAS ROSE

One of the most charming legends concerns the origin of the Christmas Rose. The story is told of a little peasant girl who tended sheep near Bethlehem. When the three kings came by, she sent along and watched as the monarchs laid their gifts at the foot of the manger. She, too, would, have liked to have added something for the new born babe. But she was poor and had nothing to give. She wept and, when the kings departed, she started to follow them, still weeping. Before she had gone a step an angel appeared and touched the earth with his forefinger. Immediately the ground was covered with Christmas Roses, pure white, perfect in form and fragrance. The girl picked an armful and turned back to the manger. She was about to lay them before the crib when the holy child opened his eyes. Ignoring the royal offerings left by the kings, little Jesus smiled at the girl and reached for the flowers.

THE LEGEND OF THE CHRISTMAS TREE

The tradition of the Christmas tree came to Germany. There it was a fir-tree celebrated in that favorite song 'O Tannenbaum'. The idea of lighting the tree has said to have come from Martin Luther, who placed candles on the candles on the branches, suggesting that the Christ child had brought the light of love to mankind. Trimming the tree became a happy as well as a hollowed custom.

It would seem that immediate ancestor to our Christmas tree of today would be the paradise tree. In the Medieval Church calendar, December 24th was 'Adam and Eve Day'. On this day many plays would act out the fall of the first two humans to make clear the meaning of Christ's birth the next day, the coming of the "Second Adam" to redeem the failure of the original. A main set piece of this play was the paradise, the tree from which Adam and Eve ate against God's command. It being winter, the tree consisted of the fir tree, hung with apples. The custom became popular in households throughout Germany.

The custom of the Christmas tree became more widely accepted in 1844 when Prince Albert, Queen Victoria's consort, sat up a tree and started the fad that has since became a tradition.

The first tree in America were probably introduced by Germans. During the revolutionary war, Hessian who were German mercenaries, fought on the British side. These less-than-welcome visitors probably set up the first American Christmas tree.

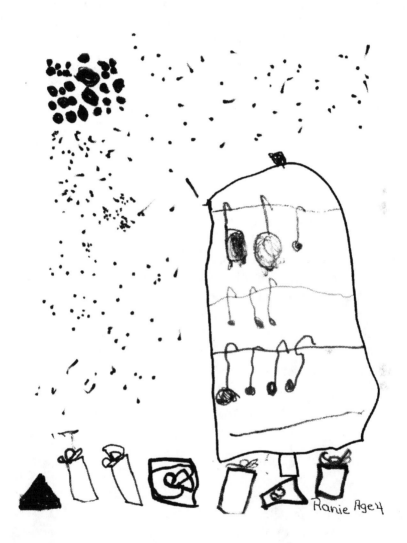

THE LEGEND OF THE CANDY CANE

A candy maker in Indiana wanted to make a candy to help us remember what Christmas is all about, He made Christmas Candy Canes.

He started with a stick of pure white hard candy. White for the purity and sinless nature of Jesus, the hard candy is to symbolize the solid rock foundation of the Church and strength of the promise of God.

He made it in the form of a "J" for Jesus, and to represent the staff of the good shepherd. He included red stripes to represent the suffering he endured at the end of his life, or the blood he shed for us.

THE LEGEND OF THE KINDRED BLACK

In parts of Spain and Italy, the Nativity scene includes the usual suspects-Mary, Joseph, the Shepherd and sheep of course, the baby Jesus, but there is often another figure included, the CAGANER, A traditional figure from the 18th century, EL CAGANER, literally means "the crapper" or "the shitter". He is a small porcelain figure of a peasant wearing the traditional catalen red cap, the Barratina and he is squatting with his pants around his ankles, and defecating onto the ground. The Caganer is seen as good luck because he fertilizes the earth, insuring a good harvest in the upcoming year.

The legend was that if a country family did not put a caganer in their nativity scene, they would have a very poor year harvest. This figure is never in front of the nativity as that would show a lack of respect. He is huddled in a corner, under a bridge, behind a tree, and each morning of the holiday season some families have the children hunt for him as part of a game.

THE LEGEND OF THE SAND DOLLAR

There's a pretty little legend
That I would like to tell,
Of the birth and death of Jesus
Found in the lowly shell.

If you examine closely,
You'll see that you'll find here
Four nail, holes and a fifth
Made by a Roman spear,

On one side the Easter lily,
Its center is a star
That appeared unto the shepherds
And lead them from afar.

The Christmas Poinsettia
Etched on the other side
Reminds of his birthday
Our happy Christmas tide

Now break the center open
And here you will release
The five white doves awaiting
To spread good will and peace.

This simple little symbol,
Christ left for you and me
To help us spread the gospel
Through all eternity.

THE LEGEND OF THE SPIDER

The Ukrainian's, spiders and webs represent good luck and their Christmas trees are decorated with artificial webs to usher in luck and good fortune for the new year.

The legend goes, that the children of a widow living in a cramped and cold hut, tended a pine cone seedling until it grew into a tree so they could have a Christmas tree that year. When the time came to decorate it however, the widow, destitute, had to disappoint her children by telling them that decorations would not be possible again that year. The children expected their fate but cried as they went to sleep that cold Christmas Eve. The household spiders, hearing the children's sobs, spun intricate and beautiful webs all over the tree, throughout the night. In the morning, the children awoke to the sunlight glistening off the webs and the children cried out to their mother to come and see their decorated tree. As the rays of sun continued to climb the tree, the webs turned to silver and gold, and the family never wanted for anything again.

THE LEGEND OF THE CHRISTMAS STOCKING

The most popular legend about why stockings are hung at Christmas, goes something like this:

A recently widowed man and father of three girls was having a tough time making ends meet, even though his daughters were beautiful he worried that their impoverished state would make it impossible for them to marry. St. Nicholas was wondering through the town, where the man and his daughters lived, and heard villagers discussing that families plight. He wanted to help but knew the man would refuse any kind of charity directly. Instead, one night, he slid down the chimney of that man's house, and filled the girls recently laundered stockings, which happened to be drying by the fire, with gold coins, and then he disappeared.

The girls awoke in the morning and were overjoyed upon discovering the bounty. Because of St. Nick's generosity, the daughters were able to wed, and their father could rest easy that they would not fall into lonely disrepair.

Although the date of the story is unknown, the origin and date is most widely referenced when it comes to the history of the Christmas stocking.

CHRISTMAS STOCKING LEGEND # 2

Some say it was from a time when fresh fruit was difficult to come by and finding an orange in your stocking was a huge treat. But a different version of the beautiful-daughters-distraught-father legend swaps the gold coins left by Saint Nicholas with three gold balls left in each stocking. Understandably, the solid gold balls tradition isn't so easy to replicate; that's why their citrus look-a-like have found their way into stockings along side, chocolates and trinkets, but hopefully not coal or switches!

LEGEND OF THE SILVER PINE CONE

There was once a very poor family with very little food or wood to keep them warm...... The mother decided to go into the woods and gather pine cones to sell for food and use some to keep them warm.... She picked up the first cone and heard a voice say, "Why are you taking my pine cones?" It was an elf, the woman then explained the whole story...... With a smile, the elf told her to go to the next forest, there she would find a better bunch of pine cones.... Off she went, and when she reached the forest, she was very tired.... She set her basket on the ground and pine cones began falling into it.... She gathered them up and returned home, and when she sat them down, every pine cone turned into silver coins. So to this day always keep a silver pine cone on your hearth for legend has it, a silver pine cone will bring good fortune your way.

LEGEND OF THE ACORN

Legend of the acorn have thought to bring good luck in Germany, Acorns are also believed by the Germans, to represent the rebirth of life as witnessed through the coming of Jesus Christ. Early German Christmas trees were covered in acorns to commemorate this gift of life and luck.

LEGEND OF THE CHRISTMAS OWL

I'm a little Christmas owl
Please hang me on your tree,
I wont say much while I'm here
But my eyes have much to see.

When Santa starts to check his list
You know he checks it twice,
He sends this owl to be his eyes
And see WHooooooo's naughty or nice!

So every time you see an owl
With his eyes so wide and bright,
Be on your best behavior for
That owl is Santa's sight.

Robin Redmon Dreyer

LEGEND OF THE BIRDS NEST

An old Christmas legend long ago,
great happiness and good fortune
came to those who chose a Christmas tree
with a birds nest in its branches.

LEGEND OF THE CHRISTMAS WREATH

Long ago an orphan boy
Sought comfort from the cold
In a Church where all bore gifts....
Riches of silver and gold,

Though the boy had no gift,
He would not despair,
For his life had been filled
In blessed grace and prayer.

He took a holly branch and tied
A circle in a crown,
Then brought it to the church
And at the alter laid it down.

The wreath began to sparkle
As brilliant berries glowed above,
A testament to the strength of prayer
And Gods encircling love.

THE LEGEND OF THE ROBIN'S RED BREAST

A little brown bird shared Bethlehem's stable with the holy family.
One night as the family slept, the little brown bird noticed their fire
was going out, and she flew from the rafters and fanned the fire with
its wings throughout the night in order to keep the baby Jesus warm...
In the morning she was rewarded with a bright red breast as a symbol
of love for the New Born King.

THE LEGEND OF THE CHRISTMAS BLANKET

May the warmth of the Christmas blanket
keep you safe and well.
May the spirit of the season
In your heart begin to swell.
You are friends we love and cherish
And we hope this year you'll find
The special peace that Christmas brings.
It is truly one of a kind.
We hope you like this blanket
It's our Christmas gift to you!
May it warm your heart and home,
Now - and all year through.
We thank-you for your kindness
We have one thing that's left to say
Happy Christmas friends and neighbors.
Have a happy Holiday!

THE LEGEND OF THE CHRISTMAS CAT

There was no snow in Bethlehem _ _ Instead the small cat watched a star -spangled sky from her perch in the window of a stable _ _ _ _ She liked the stable, for it was a warm, safe place to raise her furry babies, and the innkeeper sometimes left scraps for her to nibble. Tabby wasn't particularly distinctive, and most humans didn't look at her twice, after all, her short, grey-black fur was quite common. But Tabby's striped coat hid a heart bigger than cats twice her size.

This night though, Tabby was out of sorts, for she has not been able to hunt and "catch" dinner. Travelers had poured into town for days so noisy they disturbed decent cat folks rest. Why, they invaded Tabby's quiet stable, a place she had share before with with only other furry creatures. Tabby hadn't minded the human couple, they were more calm than most.

She left that morning for her rounds, but when she returned to her stable was packed with people. From her perch on the window, Tabby watched the last of the strangers leave. She slipped from the window and padded inside and froze. Meewwww, meewwww cried a tiny voice....

A kitten Tabby's ears turned this, way and that, to find the sound of the kitten's voice. It came from the manger, intent or mewling that rose from within. Tabby was drawn by the kitteny sound... though she knew her own babies were grown to cat-hood. She tip-toed slowly and passed by woolly burro, a warm cow and other animals......

The woman looked up and saw the striped cat. "Oh little cat," she murmured.... "My baby cannot sleep, and nothing calms him this night," she sighed and turned back to the manger. "How grateful I would be if you could bring him sweet dreams," As Tabby watched, each stable animal stepped forward and tried to sooth the woman's baby, but the kittenish sounds continued, and finally Tabby could contain herself no longer, first she washed herself, paws, face, behind the ears to the very tip of her tale {so not to offend the child's mother} and then she shyly stepped forward_ _ _ _ she leaped gracefully into the manger and stared at the face of the most beautiful baby {human or kitten} she had ever seen.

He cooed and smiled, waving his tiny hands at the Tabby and she very ts carefully drew her claws and settled down beside him. Forgotten was the empty tummy, she could only hear her heart calling out to this sweet human kitten...... Then Tabby began to purr.

This wondrous cat-song filled the stable with over-whelming emotion. The animals listened in awe, and the mother smiled as her baby quieted and went to sleep.... The mother placed her hand on the tabby's head_ _ _ "Blessings upon yo, tabby cat, for this sweet gift given my child," she said, and where she touched Tabby' brow, there appeared an 'm' the sign of Madonna's benediction.

From that day forward all proper tabby cats are honored with an 'm' on their brow for the great service preformed that first Christmas night, and Christmas nights often find Tabby cats staring into the nights, purring as they recall a very special ancestor once sang to sleep the Christ child.

Unknown Author

Legend of the Christmas pickle

The legend of the Christmas pickle was supposedly attributed to the Germans, though few Germans ever heard of it and its real origins remain a mystery.

In 1880, F.W. Woolworth in the United States began importing glass ornaments for Christmas trees, often in the shapes of fruits and vegetables, it's theorized that some may have been pickle shaped. At some point after that, families in the U.S. began a tradition where the pickle ornament was the last to be hung on the tree On Christmas Eve, after the children went to bed. The first child to find it Christmas morning got to open the first gift, got an extra gift in some iteration of the tradition is simply blessed with good luck in the coming year.

2. PICKLE LEGEND

A decedent of a soldier who fought in the American Civil War (John Lower) a (Hans Lauer perhaps?) Born on Bavaria in 1842 wrote to tell about a family story that had to do with a Christmas pickle, according to family lore, 'John Lower was captured and sent to prison in Andersonville, Georgia... In poor health and starving, He begged a guard for just one pickle before he died; the guard took pity on him and found and found a pickle for John Lower,

According to family legend --- John said that the pickle --- by the grace of God --- gave him the mental and physical strength to live on. Once he was reunited with his family, He began a tradition to hide a pickle on or in the depth of the Christmas tree. The first person to find the pickle on Christmas Christmas morning would receive a year of good fortune.

Found By: Rita Mace Walston

The Legend of the Names of the Christmas Elves

In the Pegen times of Scandinavian, people believed that house gnomes guarded their homes against evil, although these gnomes were almost benevolent, they quickly could turn nasty when not properly treated, so it was told. Throughout the centuries they were ether loved or loathed. Some people even believed they were trolls and cannibals. The perception of gnomes largely depended upon whether a person was naughty or nice.

When Christmas became popular again as a festival season in the middle - 1800's Scandinavian writers such as Thile, Toplius, Rydberg, sketched gnomes' true role in modern life: fairies that are somewhat mischievous, but the true friends and helpers of Father Christmas (Santa Claus), they are Christmas Elves.

Living in Lapland

At one stage it was thought the elves lived in 'Father Christmas' (Santa's) village in North Pole. However in 1925 It was discovered that there are no reindeer in the North Pole, but there are lots in Lapland, Finland. Nobody has actually seen their village because the passage to it is a secret that it is known only to Father Christmas and the elves, we know that it is somewhere on the KORVATUNTURI mountain in SAYUKOSKI county of Lapland, Finland which is on the Finish - Russian boarder.

On January 6th the elves light up their torches and come down from their secret village in the mountain to play in a secret field to celebrate the last day of Christmas.

The Names of the Elves

The elves are the Children of GRYLA and LEPPALUDI, their father and mother. Some people say there are 13 elves, some say 9 some say 6. They are very clever and help Father Christmas to design the toys that children an grown-ups order by post, e-mail, or texting. We know at least 6 of the duties they have, including looking after the reindeer. Here it is with their westernized names:

BUSHY EVERGREEN - is the inventor of the magic toy-making machine.

SHIMMY UPATREE - is Father Christmas's (Santa) older friend and co-founder of the secret village in Lapland.

WUNORSE OPENSLAE - designed Father Christmas's sleigh and maintains it for top performance. (It is believed that the reindeer reach speeds faster than Christmas tree lights.) He also cares for the reindeer.

PEPPER MINSTIX - is the guardian of the secret of the location of 5 other Christmas villages.

SUGARPLUM MARY - is head of the sweet treats and assistant to Father Christmas's wife, Mrs. Clause, also known as Mary Christmas.

ALABASTER SNOWBALL - is very important. He is the administrator of the naughty and nice list.

THE LEGEND OF THE CHRISTMAS STAR

A diamond shines no brighter
Than that lovely Christmas Star,
It shines it all its brilliance;
Its seen from near and far,

A symbol of the Christ Child
As he lay upon the hay,
It tells to all the waiting world,
A King was born that day.

A Bethlehem star keeps shining
Give us faith and hope and love,
Keep our thoughts forever turning
To the savior up above.

Give us strength, hope and courage,
To do our best by far,
And never falter in our faith.
As we watch that Christmas Star.

The Star of Bethlehem, often found at the top of a Christmas tree or on a plate of Christmas cookies, is strictly Christian origin.

The nature of the star mentioned in the Bible remains a mystery. For an account of the ongoing debate regarding its mythical of factual status.

LEGEND OF THE ICICLE

One beautiful night very long ago,
The Savior was born in a winter snow.
The angels in heaven look down on his birth,
As their tears of happiness fell on the earth.
God wanted a reminder of the love he brings,
And the joyful tears at the birth of our King
So he caught their tear In his powerful hands,
And spread them as crystals across the land.

Author Unknown

THE 12 DAYS OF CHRISTMAS

The popular song, "The Twelve Days Of Christmas" (originated between the years of 1558-1829) is often thought of as a delightful - thought - nonsensical part of the Christmas Season. However, according to legend, it is actually a song used by Christian parents during the religious wars of the 16th century in England to teach their children the catechism clandestinely. Each symbol has a specific meaning to teach one part of the Christian faith. And whether or not this is historically accurate. The song can certainly be used in this fashion.

One commentator ((Dennis Bratcher)), said it best: "While some have tried to debunk this as an 'urban myth' out of personal agendas, others have tried to deal with this account of the songs origin in the name of historical accuracy. There is little solid evidence ether way." Some church historians affirm this account as basically accurate, while others point out apparent historical and logical discrepancies....

Perhaps when all is said and done, historical accuracy is not really the point. Perhaps the more important is that Christians can celebrate their rich heritage, and Gods grace, through one more avenue this Christmas. Now, when they hear what they once thought was a secular nonsense song, they will be reminded in one more way of the grace of God working in transforming ways in their lives and in our world. After All, is that not the meaning of Christmas anyway?

Also, it's a popular misconception that the twelve days of Christmas land before Christmas day, rather they are the twelve days between

Christmas and Epiphany celebrated on January 6th, the day we celebrate the arrival of the wise men to worship and bring gifts to the baby Jesus. It's a fantastic season!

MY TRUE LOVE

"My true love" refers to God himself, the giver of all good gifts. The "Me" who receives the presents symbolizes every baptized person.

THE FIRST DAY OF CHRISTMAS - A PARTRIDGE IN A PEAR TREE

Partridge in a pear tree is Jesus Christ
This refers to Jesus. Another partridge, when in the presence of a predator, is willing to risk injury and death to save her chick. This image points to Christ's death on the cross to save his people and echoes Jesus' lament over Jerusalem; "Jerusalem, Jerusalem, you who kill the Prophets and stone those sent to you, how often I have longed to gather your children together, as a hen gathers her chicks under her wings.... (Luke 13:34)

THE SECOND DAY OF CHRISTMAS - TWO TURTLE DOVES

The two turtle doves represent, Old and New Testament, which together give full story of God's creation, his love for his people, how his people broke their relationship with God, his plan to redeem them, and what is to come as they are reunited with God and how they will worship him forever.

THE THIRD DAY OF CHRISTMAS - THREE FRENCH HENS

There are two versions of what the three french hens stand for. Some say they are three biblical virtues the author Paul espoused in 1 Corinthians 13:13...

Faith, Hope, Joy

Others claim the three french hens represent the three precious gifts the wise men brought: Gold, Frankincense, and Myrrh, and inspire us to bring our best to Christ.

THE FOURTH DAY OF CHRISTMAS - FOUR CALLING BIRDS

The four calling birds stands for gospels that call all peoples to Christ.
Mathew, Marl, Luke, John

THE FIFTH DAY OF CHRISTMAS - FIVE GOLDEN RINGS

Five Golden rings represent the Torah, which call the Pentateuch, the five books of the Bible. These books give a rich history of God's people and point to God's grace in spirit of their unfaithfulness.

THE SIXTH DAY OF CHRISTMAS - SIX GEESE A LAYING

The six geese represent the six days of creation.

THE SEVENTH DAY OF CHRISTMAS - SEVEN SWANS A SWIMMING

The seven swans tell of the seven gifts of the Holy Spirit gives, described in {Romans 12:6-8} Prophecy, Service, Teaching, Exhortation, giving, Leading and Compassion.

THE EIGHTH DAY OF CHRISTMAS - EIGHT MAIDS A MILKING

The eight maids are the eight Beatitudes, Jesus preached in {Mathew 5:3-10}.

1. Blessed are the poor in spirit, for theirs is the kingdom of heaven.

2. Blessed are those who mourn, for they will be comforted.
3. Blessed are the meek, for they shall inherit the earth.
4. Blessed are those who hunger and thirst for righteousness, for they will be filled.
5. Blessed are the merciful, for they will be shown mercy.
6. Blessed are the pure at heart, for they will see God.
7. Blessed are the peacemakers, for they will be called the children of God.
8. Blessed are those who are persecuted because of righteousness for theirs is the kingdom of God.

THE NINTH DAY OF CHRISTMAS - NINE LADIES DANCING

The nine ladies are the nine fruits of the spirit that distinguishes the character of a follower of Christ; Love, Joy, Peace, Patience, Kindness, Generosity, faithfulness, Gentleness and Self Control. {Galatians 5:22}

THE TENTH DAY OF CHRISTMAS - TEN LORDS A LEAPING

The ten lords are the ten commandments God gives his people to show them how to live.

THE ELEVENTH DAY OF CHRISTMAS - ELEVEN PIPERS PIPING

The eleven pipers are the eleven Apostles who remained faithful to Jesus: Simon Peter, Andrew, John, Philip, Bartholomew, Mathew, Thomas, James son of Alphaeus, Simon the Zealot, Judas the son of James, the number of Apostles are eleven, NOT, twelve because the twelfth, Judas Iscariot who betrayed Jesus.

THE TWELFTH DAY OF CHRISTMAS - TWELVE DRUMMERS DRUMMING

The twelfth drummers are the Apostles creed, one of the most widely accepted creeds across Christendom, includes twelve points of doctrine that outlines what Christians believe:

1. Believe in God the Father almighty, creator of heaven and earth.
2. I believe in Jesus Christ, His only son, our lord.
3. He was conceived by the power of the Holy Spirit, and born of the virgin Mary.
4. He suffered under Pontius Pilot, was crucified, died and was burred.
5. He descended to the dead, On the third day he rose again.
6. He ascended into heaven, and is seated on the right hand of the Father.
7. He will come again to judge the living and dead.
8. I believe in the Holy Spirit.
9. The Holy Catholic Church, the communication of the Saints.
10. The forgiveness of sins
11. The resurrection of the body
12. And life everlasting

Amen

RINGING OF THE BELLS

Christmas bells ring out the happy news of the Savior's birth from the belfries of the grandest Cathedrals, from the tiny steeples of humble country Churches, and from the hands of carolers making their joyous rounds. Bells have been a big part of the Christian churches since the fifth century, when church bells began to be used in Italy to call worshipers to service. The were first heard in the churches of France in the middle of the sixth century; and in 680,

The first church bell was rung in England by Benedict, Abbot of Weymouth. Soon missionaries carried bells to other parts of Britain; and a Saxon king, Egbert, is reported to have decreed that all church services be announced by ringing bells.

Because of their original association with the churches, bells acquired a sacred character, and passages from the Bible were often engraved on them. One tenor bell, dedicated to St. Nicholas at a church in England, had an inscription: "Pray For Our Children, Pray For Our Sailors. Pray For Our Town. I to the church the living call and to the grave do summon all." The bells were treated with special respect and care by the church members; and in some churches, the bells were actually given names, anointed and baptized. In 1878, the chimes of London's St. Paul's Cathedral were blessed.

Bells were a familiar part of everyday life even in the days before the birth of Christ. Their ringing announced events of importance and enhanced special celebrations. And as Christianity spread, the ringing of church bells became a familiar sound to Christians the world over. Church bells still chime on many occasions throughout the year, but at no time is their sound so clear or their ring so joyous as when they sound out in celebration of the Christmas miracle.

BELLS AND MORE JOYOUS NOISEMAKERS

This is also a holdover from pagan times, bells and other noisemakers were believed to frighten away evil spirits. As part of the midwinter solstice festivals, bell-ringing activities were very rowdy, mixing some fun in with serious intent. As late as the 1890's in the U.S., children thought of Christmas and noisemakers as nearly synonymous. The demise of the tiny, wildly popular Christmas firecracker may have as much to do with the parent's eardrums as it may have been with safety concerns.

Bells however_____particularly church bells_____ remained a staple of the holiday. Today their peals serve as unmistakable heralds of the arrival of the Christmas season.

RUDOLPH THE RED_NOSE REINDEER

The Chicago-based Montgomery Ward Company, department store operators, had been purchasing and distributing children s coloring books as Christmas gifts for their customers for several years.

In 1939, Montgomery Ward tapped one of their own employee's to create a book for them, thus saving money. 34 year old copy-writer Robert L. May, wrote the story of Rudolph the Red-nose Reindeer in

1939 and 2.4 million copies were handed out that year. Dispite the wartime paper shortage, over 6 million copies had been distributed by 1946, Then in 1948 a short nine minute cartoon was shone in the theaters.

A VIKING STORY

This story tells us when Christianity first came to Northern Europe, three personages representing virtues were sent from heaven to place lights on the original Christmas tree. They were Faith, Hope, and Charity. There search was long for they were required to find a tree that was as high as hope; as great as love; as sweet as charity; and one that had the sign of the cross on every bough. Their search ended in the forest of the North for they found the fir. They lighted it from the radiance of the stars and it became the first Christmas tree.

When the Holy family was pursued by Herod's soldiers, many plants offered them shelter. One such plant was the pine tree. When Mary was too weary to travel longer and the family stopped at the edge of the forest to rest. A gnarled old pine which had grown hollow with it's years invited there to rest within its trunk--then it closed its branches down and kept them safe until the soldiers had passed. Upon leaving, the Christ Child blessed the pine and the imprint of his little hand was left forever in the tree's fruit--the pine cone.

If the cone is cut lengthwise the hand may still be seen.

THE LEGEND OF ROSEMARY

Rosemary is a revered ceremonial herb symbolizing remembrance, friendship and fidelity. It was thrown into, or placed on graves and presented to those that grieved (as a sign that the deceased will always be remembered). It was also woven into a brides wreath, used to decorate church and was presented, tied with ribbons, to the bridesmaids and guests. Anne of Cleves wore a rosemary wreath when she embarked on her ill fated marriage to Henry VIII.

The floor of the church was strewn with it at Christmas and, as a poor man's incense, was burnt in place of the real thing. Housewives spread it on the floor at Christmas!

There are many legends surrounding rosemary but perhaps the best known is that it will never grow higher than Christ and if it outlives the 33 years of our Lords life, will grow outwards rather than upward.

Another legend claims the flowers originally white, only changing to blue when Mary, on the flight from Egypt, through her blue cloak over a bush, changing its color at the same time as giving it its distinctive fragrance. A variation of this legend says when the Holy Family fled to Egypt, they stopped to rest on a hillside, by a little stream where Mary washed the Baby's cloths.

She spread his tiny garments on a fragrant bush to dry in the sun. For its humble service, the plant was named rosemary, and God rewarded it with delicate blossoms of the same heavenly blue as Mary's robe.

For St. Thomas Moore, whose garden was lavishly planted with rosemary, and Shakespeare Ophelia, the herb symbolized remembrance. During exams, Greek students wore rosemary in their hair to aid their memories. It was cultivated in monastery gardens for food and medicines. According to medieval legends, Rosemary decorating the altar at Christmas time brings special blessings to the recipients, and protection against evil spirits. It was used to garnish the boar's head at the Christmas feast.

CHAPTER

Saint Nicholas

WHO IS SANTA CLAUS?

Jolly Old Saint Nicholas, Father Christmas, Kris Kringle, Santa,
Where did he come from? It turns out our beloved icon originates
from a Bishop in the Church in the 300's. Legend says that Saint
Nicholas (Bishop) gave money to the poor and later the Church declared
December 6th to be Saint Nicholas Day. In the early 1800's St. Nicholas,
now known as Santa Claus, from the Dutch 'Sinter Klaas' became
popular in the United States. Many of our modern traditions around
Santa comes from an anonymous poem published in 1823 called "A
Night Before Christmas".

(In Present Day Turkey) Asia Minor a man named Nicholas led
a church, as the Bishop of Myra in the 300's. Beyond this, little has
been found about this particular Saint. However, many legends have
developed over the centuries, Facts probably stand behind a few of these
legends, but regardless of their history, the legends have shaped the way
people view St. Nicholas today.

Legends say that Nicholas was born on Patara to wealthy parents.
After multiple miracles as a young child, the people of Myra made
him the Bishop. He was imprisoned during the Diocletian persecution,
then released after Constantine came to the throne.

After his release, Nicholas found the Arian heresy defending the
doctrine of the deity of Christ. One document written over 500 years
A.D., claims

'Thanks to the teaching of Saint Nicholas' the metropolis of Myrna
alone was touched by the filth of the Arian heresy, which it firmly
rejected as a death - dealing poison, one intriguing, but almost surely
fictitious, account says he traveled to the 'Council of Nicaea' and

confronted Arius personally by slapping him in the face. Other stories tell of a pilgrimage to Egypt and Palestine during which he walked on water to save a sailor, raised a dead man to life, and miraculously escaped the plot of a treacherous sea captain.

Due to many of these legends, Nicholas quickly became one of the most popular Saints in the Church. He is the patron Saint of the Mariners, merchants, bakers, travelers children, all of whom looked to him for protection. Churches were named after him (400 in England alone during the late middle ages). Miracles were attributed to him, and in 1087 a group of men took his bones from a sepulcher in Myra to Bari, Italy which quickly became the popular place of pilgrimage for Christians in the west.

The best known St. Nicholas story involves a poor widower with three daughters. Lacking dowries for his girls, the widower feared that they would wind up in slavery or prostitution. Nicholas had compassion on the family and secretly used his wealth to help them. He dropped bags of gold through their window in the middle of the night to provide the needed dowries. Some versions of the story say he dropped them through a chimney and another has one of the bags end up in a stocking that one of the girls had hung on the fireplace to dry.

December 6th was the traditional day of the death of St. Nicholas. The Church proclaimed the day as St. Nicholas Day. Over time people began to give gifts in his name on December 6th or the Eve of his feast day. Other customs developed, such as visits to children, when Nicholas brought token presents and inquired to see if children had been naughty or nice, 'his riding over houses at night on a white horse, and children leaving shoes out to collect gifts..

After the reformation, Protestants largely abandoned St. Nicholas. They taught that each believer can go directly to God through Jesus Christ and needed no help from the saints. As part of this belief, the reformers rejected Catholic feasts, like St. Nicholas Day. In Germany, Martin Luther substituted Christ Kindl (the Christ Child) for St. Nicholas as the bringer of night-time gifts, his visit was moved from December 6th to Christmas Eve on December 24th.

Christ kindl eventually became re-pronounced as Kriss Kringle, ironically is now considered another name for Santa Claus.

When many Protestants rejected Saint Nicholas as a gift giver, other adult figures arose to replace him, including 'Old Man Winter in Finland', 'Father Christmas in England'. During the 14th century when America's ideals of Santa Claus morphed from a more disciplinary Churchman into a grand fatherly gift giver, these other Christmas figures were transformed as well, becoming, kindly, elderly, conveyors of presents for children.

Santa Clause as the Americans know him, is about 200 years old. Most Americans in the Colonial period. However the Dutch in the Colonial period, however, the Dutch reform had continued to observe Christmas, and brought many of their traditions including St. Nicholas, to New Amsterdam, (now New York).

During the early 1800's, a group of New York businessmen began to introduce Saint Nicholas into American Culture. In 1809 Washington Irving (1783 to 1859) Author of 'Rip Van Winkle' and 'The Legend of Sleepy Hollow', wrote another influential work, a history of New York, under the Pseudonym, Diedrick Knickerbocker. In hiss of New York, which was prominently a Dutch City, and Irving mentioned Saint Nicholas 15 times throughout the book, Irving was also drawing upon the Dutch folklore to renew a tradition. Irving's Saint Nicholas flew over trees in a horse drawn wagon, and slid down chimneys to deliver gifts. He even gave a 'wink' before disappearing.

Then in 1823, an influential poem was published anonymously in a Troy, New York newspaper. It was originally titled, "A Visit From Saint Nicholas," "The Night Before Christmas" became one of the most famous poems. Often they were attributed to Clement Clarke Moore, a New Yorker and friend of Washington

Irving. The poem reshape Saint Nicholas and the American Christmas. Many ideas common to the contemporary Santa mythology were first introduced in this poem.

For example the poem created, the idea of Santa riding the sleigh, rather than a horse or a wagon. Reindeer appeared for the first time, there are eight of them, and they are named. Saint Nick visits with gifts on Christmas Eve, other than the eve of Saint Nicholas Day, as has been the custom in Europe for centuries. This slight change, helped move gift giving to the center of Christmas tradition. Rather than drawing the appearance of wearing the traditional Bishops attire, the poem St Nick, was a lovely jolly, plump, magical old man, with twinkling eyes, rosy cheeks, and a round belly, that shook when he laughed like a bowl full of jelly.

About the same time St. Nicholas was taking on a new form. In New York City, the Dutch phrase Sinter Klaas (Dutch for St. Nicholas) was taking its English form, Santa Claus. Santa Clause began to be used in advertising after 1820, but a number of images of Santa Clause appeared, each wildly different than from the others. During and after the civil war, Thomas Nast's famous picture of Santa Claus in 'Harpers Weekly', presented him with a "jolly face", full beard, wide belt around his rotund waist. Nast introduced more traditions common today. For example, he became a North Pole toy maker, with Elves for assistance, who received letters from children, and ate delicious treats that children left in their homes for him to gobble up on Christmas Eve.

"By the early 1900's Santa Clause was an omni-present part of the North America Christmas Scene." His image has become more fixed, however he was still wearing red, blue and various other colors until Coca-Cola commissioned commercial artist, Haddon Sundblom to paint multiple images of Santa Claus for their marketing between 1931 to 1964.

These images fixed Santa's image as a red and white Santa, perfect for marketing, with the red and white Coca-Cola. Contrary to some claims, Coka-Cola DID NOT invent Santa! Their nearly universal advertising merely "helped put the finishing touches on Santa Claus who already had become mostly standardized."

By the twentieth century, Saint Nicholas had morphed into Santa Claus in the United States, he had been detached from his Churchly roll, became mainly a secular symbol of giving (or consumption) and was more popular than ever.

AMERICAN SANTA - Red velvet hat, jacket and pants with white fur trim around brim of hat, cuffs of sleeves and pants cuff, as well as the trim of coat with white gloves, black patented leather boots and belt with gold buckle. Carries a red bag full of toys.

SWEDEN SANTA --- Olive wool cap with wreath of holly around its brim, olive TOMTE green mid. length coat, with green pants, brown boots. carries a bag of toys.

IRELAND SANTA - Green hat, red/green plaid band around the hat with a red - plume feather - red waist coat, green vest, red/green plaid - knelt and cape - green stockings, black shoes.

FINLAND SANTA - Red long floor length coat with white embroidery, red gloves, JOULUPUKKI pointed red hat with a red pom pom on the end lays to the side over his shoulder, red boots.

GERMAN SANTA White floor length robe, trimmed in gold, gold crown shaped CHRISTKIND - like the popes hat, brown boots, gold belt.

WEIHNACHTSMANN - Red floor length robe, trimmed with white fur at hood and wrists, brown boots, belt and carries switches in his belt carrying gifts.

RUSSIA - Dressed in red robes (like a wizards robe) trimmed in white D'YED MOREZ fur, his beard is snow white, bushy and long. Delivers toys FATHER FROST door to door.

ITALY - Dressed in a red floor length robe, red hat that comes to a BOBBO-NATALE point with fur trimming the sleeves and edges around coat and around ears of hat. Black boots and sash tied his robe. leaves gifts under the tree.

HOLLAND - He wears the traditional Bishops robes. Red cape with red SINTERKLAAS Bishops hat all trimmed in gold. with a white gown trimmed AND in gold, black boots, and sash. Rides a white horse.

BLACK PETE - dressed in Spanish attire. Santa's helper.

NORWAY - Wears a red knit cap and a red knit pull-over sweater with NISSE white blousy shirt under sweater, olive green pants, black boots. Considers to be a 'brownie' or 'hobgoblin or 'gnome.

SANTA'S SLEIGH AND REINDEER

The popularity of Santa and his reindeer is largely due to Clement C.
Moore, who put the two together in his successful poem "A Visit from St. Nicholas." But Moore was not the first to pair Santa with hoofed friends.

Before Moore published his poem, there had been a number of less successful books that portrayed Santa flying around in a sleigh pulled around by one reindeer. This concept had long been popular in Russia, where Father Frost arrived in the villages in a reindeer-drawn sleigh. The Norse god Wodin was said to ride his horse was said to ride his horse Sleipner through the air to make sure people were behaving; in Holland St. Nicholas rides Sleipner to this day.

Today, Rudolph, "the red-nosed reindeer" is by far the most popular of Santa's nine; he is also the youngest (or at any rate the most recent arrival).

The first eight reindeer were introduced by Moore in 1823; Rudolph did not come along until 1939, in a story by Robert L. May. Rudolph's notoriety owes much to the popularity of the Gene Autry song "Rudolph the Red-nose Reindeer," released in 1949 and a holiday classic to this day.

Cheyanne ♡

CHAPTER

Making Christmas Traditions

Anything you do over and over becomes a tradition

****

Traditions are an important part of leaving a heritage past down from generation to generation.

My son and his wife started a Christmas Eve thyme night with his wife and their children, and when his wife had died, that tradition continued and was the memories the four children grasped, to continue the memories. The traditions you make with your families are the memories you build.

There are many ways of making traditions that will create lasting memories for your family. I this chapter I would like to share some with you.

Christmas traditions build unity and love, acts of service and thoughts of Christ.

We all think of traditions at Christmas time. It is also a time to share with our friends and neighbors. How about taking a plate of homemade cookies to a shut-in or offer to help them with their shopping.

It is a good time for the family to do fun things together. Just to get in the car and see all the Christmas lights in the neighborhood or visit one of the live nativity scenes in the area.

One of the traditions in Europe was the Yule Log which warmed the house during the cold Christmas night. It was ceremoniously brought into the house and to the fireplace and lit with the remnants from the log of the previous year. This was to erase trouble from the past and bring good fortune. Today the yule log takes the form of a traditional French cake shaped like a log, a perfect finish to a Christmas feast.

STOCKING TRADITIONS

In 1913 the 'Dennison Manufacturing Company' started selling stockings and crepe paper to decorate their homes.

When you celebrate Christmas what is your stocking of choice?

I have my Grandmothers and Great-Grandmothers, It is so nice to see them hanging next to mine, and then my children's, and now my grandchildren's, the change is awesome!

As far back as 1823, when Clement Clarke Moore (or possibly Henry Livingston Jr.) wrote "A Visit From Saint Nicholas," stockings were hung by the fireplace awaiting a visit from Santa Claus. At the end of the Poem, St. Nick, filled all the stockings and then turned with a jerk / and laying his finger aside of his nose / and giving a nod, up the chimney he rose."

Stocking have been an essential part of the Christmas tradition for centuries except briefly in the mid- 1800's, when the 'New York Times' wrote that Christmas Trees almost completely supplant them as a tradition of choice.

In 1918, catalogs were selling pre-made decorated stockings for people to purchase specifically for the Christmas Holiday.

A STOCKING FOR JESUS

On Christmas Eve each year, every member of the family takes a paper and writes down one thing they want to give Jesus the following year. For example:

I am going to try to 'never miss a day of scripture reading', or 'I am going to have a better attitude and believe in myself', or I'm going to 'work on forgiving_____ and repenting for my anger'. ECT............

The following year, on Christmas Eve, the family gathers to pull out their gifts to Christ from the previous year, read them and see how well they did. Then, everyone does it again!

THE WHITE STOCKING

'Twas the night before Christmas as I walked through the house,

Not a creature was stirring, not even a mouse.

The presents were wrapped and placed under the tree.

I paused, tired, excited, and then giggled with glee.

The stockings were hung and were beautifully filled.

No one had been forgotten, though the credit card was billed.

As I looked at the scene, with the stockings on the ledge

I noticed one was empty, the one on the edge.

Where's the spirit of - what have I done?

The children's stockings are all full, except for this one,

It was the stocking intended for the child of Bethlehem.

The stocking for Jesus that was hung up with them,

Of all the people at Christmas, that night be forgotten,

How could I not remember the "Father's Only Begotten"?

Only He had been left out of the festivities.

As we planned and prepared all, for our families.

As I pondered, I realized this just was not right!

It was His birth that was being celebrated, after this night.

I resolved then and there to remember to remember the lord

And quickly made changes that were easy to afford.

I hung the white stocking in a special place in our home,

And corrected the atmosphere to provide a more spiritual tone

On Christmas morning I gathered the family together

And each of us wrote on a special piece of paper,

We gave Jesus a gift which we placed in the stocking,

A sincere change of heart, not there for the mocking.

The white stocking hung in our home as a symbol for us.

Of the true meaning of Christmas - the savior, the Lord Jesus,

So take your white stocking and hang it with pride

Remember the savior, put his gift inside.

STOCKINGS FROM DAD'S DRAWER

For some people pulling stockings out of dad's drawer - the bigger the better to have Saint Nicholas fill, to others who have personalized decorated maybe even hand-made, foot shaped bag to have year after year. It has even been a tradition the Military took with them into the field of battle in 1944, it was noted that they hung them from their rifles.

CHRISTMAS JAM

Don't boil yourself
in the Christmas jam
of unwise spending
and special cram....
Preserve your fruit
with the spiritual
things and the lasting
joy of the holiday
season-----

Author Unknown

CHRIST IN CHRISTMAS

Teach your children about the birth of Christ-- Participate as a family and keep these values, not only at Christmas but all year through.

One way, we kept Advent very near our hearts, you can participate in your church or you can have the (4) candles at your home and participate as a family at YOUR chosen time, and each week when lighting a candle, reading a portion of scripture that goes along with that week.

MAKE A TRADITIONAL TREASURE HUNT

Treasure hunt is a fun way to spend time as a family, and children love treasure hunts. There is nothing quite as exciting as searching the house, knowing that a gift is waiting somewhere. To celebrate Advent each year, wrap little trinkets, chocolates and books, hide each morning. Then write a simple rhymes for each day, then offer clues for the search.

BAVARIAN TRADITION "BRIDES TREE"

This is a Tradition I want to do as my Grandchildren start getting married. I found you can get the 12 piece ornament set on Amazon. This is a beautiful wedding or shower gift and comes in a white satin box.

"Old" Bavarian tradition is a so called 'Brides Tree' upon which a dozen special ornaments are hung to ensure a better life for the married couple.

The 12 ornaments and their symbolic significance are:

Angel (Gods Guidance)
Bird (Joy)
Fish (Christ's Blessings)
Flower Basket (Good Wishes)
Fruit Basket (Generosity)
Heart (True Love)
House (Protection)
Pine Cone Faithfulness)
Rabbit (Hope)
Rose Affection)
Santa (Good Will)
Tea Pot (Hospitality)

Hand blown glass ornaments in these forms are still produced in Bavaria.

Robin Redmon Dreyer

PEPPERMINT PIG TRADITION

In Germany A marzipan pig traditionally given as a gift or as a stocking stuffier between Christmas and the New Years Day to bestow good fortune on friends and loved ones in the coming year. You can make the pig or purchase them at a confectioners shops. They can be dipped in chocolate or flavored with peppermint. Pigs were good luck, this was started during the Victorian ere.

You smash the peppermint pig with a mini hammer after Christmas Eve dinner and share the pieces around the table, to receive good luck for the rest of the year.

ACTIVITIES YOU CAN USE TO BUILD YOUR CHRISTMAS TRADITION

Are you celebrating Advent? What is Advent?

10 ways to celebrate Advent that you may consider having a fun and Christ centered Christmas.

Celebrate Advent, because, Christ has come, and He is coming again!

1.) Make up an Advent calendar,{with 24 slots for 24 days} Be creative, you see many on 'Pinterest' and in stores, but you can be creative, by working together you are forming or strengthening your bonds together with Christ Jesus.

2.) You could have an scripture Advent calendar, by using your refrigerator or a large chalkboard you will put up one scripture each day up on the fridge, as we count down to Christmas. You will also put one question ether pertaining to your lives, relating to the scripture - or - to scripture itself. If your children have looked up the scriptures and give you the answer to the question, you may then treat them to a piece of candy.

** You don't have to spend a lot of time in these activities, because our lives are so busy or you don't want the activity to become work, but like fun..

3.) You can also buy the cardboard Advent calendar with the little chocolates in them, the are inexpensive and convenient, sold most anywhere during the holiday.

4.) You can pick up an Advent devotional for busy families, at any book store and they are short and have a discussion question with each short story.

5.)You can find yourself a nativity sticker book for your child and use it each night with discussion. If you buy it enough ahead you can plan out your 24 days - be sure you have 24 stickers.

ADVENT #2

The Advent calendar is very important in your Christian growth, as well as adding a traditional aspect to your holiday. It builds anticipation and plants memories that grow each year.

An Advent calendar can simply be a small banner, made with (for example) a felt Christmas tree and 24 pockets just big enough for a piece of candy and a scripture, or a tiny ornament that you would place on the felt tree until by the 24th the tree will be filled. It's fun to watch each day as the tree fills with the ornaments knowing Christmas Day grows closer - (the ornaments may or may not be a Christmas symbol)

A FAMILY WHO BAKES TOGETHER STAYS TOGETHER

My children are grown now, but I know that my two sons and my daughter has carried the tradition of holiday baking on with their own children, and I love to sit back now and admire their handy work in the kitchen. Even though I would make loads of candies, cookies and decorated cakes, there were so many other things in the kitchen that could be done.

My daughter has a beautiful little girl, our Ranie June. They make a Gingerbread house each year as part of their holiday tradition; my daughter Katie always makes the gifts for the family's on both her side and her husbands side. I love seeing the expressions on the faces of those receiving the baked goods. So the big thing is, my mother did holiday baking with me, me with my children, my children with their children and so the tradition has gone for three generations extending to the fourth; from here it becomes a legacy.

It is fun after a season preparing cookies, candies and breads; you begin to sort, box and prepare for the gifting, it is so fun to make it a family thing and helps the children to feel they are a part of the giving.

CAROLING

If you belong to a church, they may go caroling, if you don't, you can gather family members and friends together, and go caroling as a group, but making this a tradition is doing this joyful experience year after year. everyone enjoys hearing others sing these traditional carols and there are so many places that would gladly have you come and sing for them (such as hospitals, nursing homes, elderly living, malls, clubs and lodges, door to door where you live) there are so many options and you may also be able to set up dates and times a year in advance depending on where you live. Before you decide to go to a public place to sing, be sure to call ahead, make sure there is an opening for your group.

THYME NIGHT

Choose a night with family or family and friends and each year choose a thyme, have everyone dress to the thyme, research the foods and fix what would go with the thyme, games can be arranged to the thyme and entertainment.

My oldest son and his family has done this for about ten years or more, they have always had their parties on Christmas Eve, but when His wife died with cancer and then he married again they continued this practice but changed the date due to her family and his. (all seven of the kids want to be there for the fun) Some of the rhymes they had were: Pirates of the Caribbean, Disney, War Craft, Hawaiian, Star Wars, all depends upon the age group ect.....

MAKING A TRADITIONAL ORNAMENT EACH YEAR

Another fun tradition that I enjoy so much with my Grandchildren, and regret so much not doing this with my own children, and that is making ornaments with them each year and when the children leave home they have their own ornaments to take with them. It is part of their own memories from their childhood. Of coarse there are all kinds of ornaments in craft books and google, ect..... I used old CD's and DVD's and let the children paint them and we also glued their school picture on them and glued ric-rac. We used canning lids and rings and cut out festive cards an put in them and glitter to decorate. The ideas are limitless!

What better memories than those, as you look at your tree and see the years of memories. I have an ornament that was made for my dad by his aunt and it is a precious memory and tribute to my father and to me.

12 BIBLICAL NAMES GIVEN TO CHRIST

In keeping Christ in Christmas, you can take a set of 12 ornaments and on each ornament has one of the 12 names given for Jesus, and or a biblical reference on it. Starting 12 days before Christmas you can start one ornament for each day, until Christmas Day.

First read the reference on the bulb and name ending with the reading 'Luke 2' as a family. - (King of Kings, Emmanuel, The Great I Am, Savior, Lord)

BOOK ADVENT

I saw this on Pinterist, and simply fell in love with the idea!

I for one love books and have a library in my own home, it's a passion my husband and I share. Well anyway this is for the children and families to share in.

Buy 25 books, (children s Christmas Books) wrap each on individually, starting on December 1st. open one. (you could make a game out of it and let the children find the wrapped book first, it adds to the excitement). Once opened, then as a family, sit down and take the time to read the book with the child, and talk about it. This will open the door of communication, who knows, from this, what gifts you might find.

MY FAMILIES GRAB - BAG GAME

If you enjoy games, as a family, then this is a good idea as well.

My family loved playing this game each year, we each spent $5.00 or less on the gift, then wrapped it beautifully, set it on the table or designated place for the gifts. Everyone's name went into a hat (whom brought a gift)

As each name is drawn they pick a gift on the table, unwrap and show the guest's what you unwrapped. After all the gifts are opened the names will go back into the hat. Set a timer as to how long you want to play. Once again start drawing names again, as each name is drawn, you will ether keep your gift or trade with someone who's gift you like better.

One year as a trick gift someone decorated a cute little box and place a picture of a turkey in it..... well believe it-or-not, when the game ended and everyone was awing over the gifts everyone got and out comes a frozen turkey to replace the paper turkey.

LETTERS TO SANTA

Some family's traditionally write letters to Santa, my children did not but my grandchildren do; they seem to have a lot of fun with it.

You would have the children write the letters and then Mommy would mail the letters to a designated person to write a return letter to the child knowing a little about that child to make it read real. We went to Staples or Wal-mart and bought Santa printer paper with matching envelopes, we printed the letter onto the stationary and I would put into the letter a bookmark or a flat ornament with the letter and mailed it back to the child.{I purchased a stamp at the craft store that had a North Pole post mark from Santa's village, stamped on back not to mess up the mail} If you live close to the child you could simply post the front and hand the letter into the parents hands and they could deliver it to the child.

ELF ON THE SHELF

There is 'Elf on the Shelf' this tradition started about 1980-ish although quit mild then it has grown to be quit popular and increases in popularity each year. The parent needs to be quite creative with this mischievous little fellow who gets into more trouble than the children. When his job is to watch the children and report to Santa if they have been naughty or nice.

Pixies, kneehuggers, elves, gnomes or troll, what ever you choose, can make a very fun tradition, and colorful memories. Now I did find that the knee huggers went as far back as the 1940's

CHRISTMAS EVE BOX

This is such a magical tradition. When my children were small we would let them open one gift on Christmas Eve, that would be their new pajamas that I usually I made for them. Since we spent the whole day Christmas day at home and just us and grandparents, we stayed in our pajamas and laid back and played games, watched Christmas movies all day.

This is a suggestion that I received that is a cute idea. Put together in a gift box to be opened Christmas Eve by each child. Include in each gift box:

A new pair of pajamas or night gown to wear to bed for when Santa comes, A holiday book to be read to the child before bed ('The Night Before Christmas' or a story about the 'Christ Child'), Reindeer food to sprinkle in the yard and finally Santa's magic key.

LEGEND OF MAGICAL REINDEER DUST

It has once been said,
That right before you go to bed
You should sprinkle magic reindeer food,
To quickly bring Santa and his brood.
For many years the legend has been told,
To boys and girls both young and old.
Sprinkle the food throughout your yard,

Then finding your house won't be so hard.
The reindeer can smell the food for more than 100 miles.
Just do not leave it in big piles!
After doing this, you must go to sleep very fast,
So Santa and his reindeer will not pass!

RECIPE:

1 Cup Sugar - Large granular will sparkle better
1 Cup Oatmeal
1 Cup Sprinkles or 1 Cup Glitter
Mixing all very well then put into a snack size sealable bag.

SANTA'S MAGIC KEY

It's the Night Before Christmas
And we're excited as can be.
We're leaving this out for you---
It's a very special key.
You can shimmy down the chimney,
Or tip toe through the door.
Just use this key we left for you,
To find cookies, milk, and more!

(Create a tag with a fun font, and type the poem on the tag.
Tie the tag with a pretty ribbon to a skeleton key- {you can
find a key at local craft store} then hang it on the door.)

MOVIE NIGHT

I am a Christmas movie fanatic! I can watch Christmas movies 365 days a year. There was one tradition we made with our children, back in the day. Christmas day after all the gifts were opened, we would lay around in our PJ's, paying board games and watching Christmas movies all day. Now with the children grown, with children of their own, we have arranged a weekend before Christmas to have movie night with ALL of them together and feast on three to five different kinds of popcorn, lights out, pillows on the floor, laughing and having a wonderful time making memories.

DECORATING TOGETHER - HOME AND TREE

What is really fun is to make decorations with your children, for instance: paper chains, stringing cutting out old cards into ornament shapes and hang on the tree.

When I was a little girl I loved making things, I would talk my Mother out of a roll of cellophane tape so I could make paper chains to hang along the ceiling, and cut out ornaments from construction paper to tape on the windows.

I was so proud of my handy work, and what would Christmas be like without lights? We didn't have a lot when I was a kid, but with my own children we hung lights everywhere! As parents my children do the same, and they decorate their homes together and they build memories each year sing and decorating the tree and, hanging lights, ornaments or arrangements, build memories with your children.

Jazz up your home with these decorating tricks.

+ Encircle each mirror with a strings of colored lights. Their reflection will generate twice the twinkle.
+ Plant wooden snowmen and other country crafts in your flour boxes for a wintry window display.
+ Slip Holiday sheet music into your prettiest 8 x 10 inch photo frames.
  This minor touch causes a major impact.
+ Line up candlesticks of all shapes and sizes on your mantle, and alternate red and green tapers down the row.
+ Suspend garlands on hooks that have removable adhesive. With no worry about wall damage, you can fearlessly loop greenery from room to room.
+ Hole-punch Christmas cards as they arrive and use ribbon to hang on sparsely decorated branches.
+ Holiday cookie cutters do double duty--first for baking, then for tree trimming. Silver colored ones create an elegant, shimmery look when tied on with ribbon.

+ For an extra hint of glamour, wrap the trunk of the tree with several strings of white lights.
+ Place an artificial tabletop tree in the kiddies' playroom and let them adorn it with their play jewelry. Long strings of beads can serve as garland; drop earrings can hang as sparkly ornaments.

DONATING GENTLY LOVED TOYS

A tradition and a lesson: There are many needy children and we as parents need to teach our children charity. Each year in November, my children and I would go through their toys and set out what they no longer played with and would let them take the gently loved toys to the fire department or police department. Of course I had a habit of going through their toys often, we did not keep toys that were broken and God knows it was easier to teach our children respect for things, than it is today.

By allowing your child to take the toys to the needy, they learn charity and selfless giving without expecting anything back. They receive a little pride in give.

COOKIES FOR SANTA

Lots of children leave cookies and milk for Santa, maybe carrots and celery for the reindeer. But my oldest Son Roy has always had the tradition with his four children to leave a can of cola and nacho chips with spicy cheese dip. Ranie and my daughter Kate, make a special home-made sugar cookie for Santa with milk, Santa only takes a bite or two and then the next morning Ranie eats the rest of the cookie that Santa Shared with her. (because she gifted Santa with the cookie, it was kindness that Santa shared). So it matters not what you leave but that there is a lesson you can teach your children in the giving.

UGLY SWEATER PARTY

I have noticed this past year the popularity of the 'Ugly Sweater Party'.

I have a very sweet friend who has made this a traditional party, with games, food and contests, all with this theme, There are all kinds of suggestions on 'Pinterest' or you can google it.

SELECTING A LIVE TREE

Lots of families put up artificial trees, but when I was a little girl we had a real one. A lot of families put up real trees and have made it a tradition to choosing the tree and or chopping it down, and taking it home to decorate. There are some places that will serve you hot chocolate and cookies; some even offer hay-rides. They may even help you to make garlands and wreaths.

CHRISTMAS TREE CARE: The fresher the tree, the longer it lasts. Your Christmas tree should be as fresh-cut as possible and you can check this by gently tapping the trunk against the ground to see if dry needles fall. Also look with one with a fresh, fragrant odor. When you get the tree home, make a diagonal cut in the base to expose a new surface for better water penetration. Keep the base in water at all times and away from a heat sources. When you notice the tree won't absorb water any longer, it is telling you it is dried out.

WHITE ELEPHANT EXCHANGE

Times can get bad at different times in our lives, but the desire to gift and enjoy the holiday season stays the same. Instead of buying gifts, why not wrap an unwanted item to share with someone else. Everyone has an unwanted a cast off they no longer need or want. It would be fun each year to have a white elephant exchange.

COOKIE EXCHANGE

My sister has six girls and each year they bake cookies and do a cookie exchange. The seven ladies get together, and each make their favorite cookies or try new recipes they haven't had before. Then they separate each batch into seven parts and they take home an assortment of cookies for their own Christmas day celebration.

HOLIDAY COOK-OFF

What is really fun for a family is a good hearted cook-off competition with the oldest member as the judge. If you choose Chili, Pies, Decorated Cakes or Candies. I thought that it would be fun to do English Puddings, there are so many different kinds. There are so many ideas to do year after year, family's will start planning a year ahead for the next traditional bake-off.

MAKING A GINGERBREAD HOUSE

My daughter has a tradition she started herself before she ever left home basically, she started making scratch gingerbread houses and has made improvements each year, and tried different candies and recipe's to get the perfect fix for the house. She now has a daughter that will be five this year, and she helps her Mommy each year. It was so cute, Ranie's first Christmas, Kate set her in a 'bumble' seat on the table so she could watch her make the gingerbread house and Ranie has been by her mommy's side ever since. It is never to early to start these kind of traditions.

Chevanne. AGE 7

Here is a list of a few more traditions to think about:

Make a Christmas wish list.

Celebrate the lighting of candles.

Start a traditional type of Christmas dinner, Appetizers, party foods, or favorite dishes.

A special reading on Christmas Eve.

Participate in a Nativity play.

Make gingerbread ornaments to hang on the Christmas Tree.

Make a craft together each year as a family, decoration or ornament.

Go for a drive together looking at Christmas lights.

Wrap gifts together with the family.

Take children shopping for each other.

Open stockings first.

Traditional annual ornament.

Have a Birthday party for Jesus.

On Christmas eve deliver goodies for service workers such as firemen, policemen ect...

Only receive or gift three gifts to represent the three gifts from the wise men.

Cookies for breakfast

ENGLAND CHRISTMAS TRADITION

During the first week in Advent the housewives in some parts of England prepare the fruit and other ingredients for the plum puddings they will serve on Christmas day, because it means good luck, each member of the family takes a turn in stirring the pudding.

CHAPTER

History of the Christmas Card and the Christmas Stamp

In 1880 Great Britain began a nation wide Christmas card competition, thus started the Christmas card industry - Velvet Plush, Lace, Satin; crescents, stars, fold out paper-lace fans, and Victorian designs.

A Christmas card is a greeting card sent as part of a traditional celebration, of Christmas in order to convey between people, a range of sentiments related to Christmas and the holiday season. Christmas cards are usually exchanged during the weeks before Christmas day and after Thanksgiving, by many people (including non-Christians) In western society and in Asia. The traditional greeting reads "Wishing You a Merry Christmas and a Happy New Year". There is a large number of variations on this greeting.

Many cards express a more religious sentiment or containing a poem, prayer, Christmas song lyrics or Bible verse, some stay away from religion with a much simpler greeting as "Seasons Greetings".

The first Christmas cards were commissioned by Sir Henry Cole and illustrated by John Callcote Horsley in London on May 1843. His card showed three generations of family, raising a toast to the card recipient; on each side of the picture were scenes of charity, with food and clothing given to the poor. Allegedly the image of the family drinking wine together proved controversial, but the idea was shrewd: Cole had helped introduce the penny post three years earlier. Two batches totaling 2,050 cards were printed and sold that year for a shilling each.

Early English cards rarely showed winter or religious thyme's, instead favors flowers, fairies and other fanciful designs that reminded the recipient of approach of spring. Humorous and sentimental images of children and animals, were popular as were increasingly elaborate shapes, decoration and materials. At Christmas 1873 the lithograph, firm 'Pang and Mayer' began creating greeting cards for the popular market in England. The firm began selling the Christmas cards in America in 1874, thus becoming the first printer to offer cards in America. Its owner 'Louis Prang', is sometimes called the 'Father of the American Christmas Card.' By the 1900's, Prang was producing over five million cards a year by using the chrome-lithography process of print making. However, the popularity of his cards led to cheep imitations that eventually drove Prang from the market. The postcard replaced the elaborate Victorian-style cards, but by the 1920's, cards with envelopes had returned.

The production of Christmas cards went throughout the 20th century, a profitable business for many stationary manufacturer, with the design of cards continually evolving with changing tastes and printing techniques. The new widely recognized brand 'Hallmark cards' was established in 1913 by 'Joyce Hall' with the help of her brother 'Rolly Hall' to market their self produced Christmas cards. The Hall brothers capitalized on the growing desire for more personalized greeting cards, and reached critical success when the outbreak of 'world war one' increased demand for cards to send to soldiers.

The world wars brought cards with patriotic thyme's. 'Studio cards' with cartoon illustrations and sometimes risque humor, caught on tn the 1950's, nostalgic, sentimental, and religious images have continued in popularity, and in the twenty first century, reproductions of Victorian and Edwardian cards are easy to obtain. Modern Christmas cards can be bought individually, but are also sold in packs of the same varied designs. In recent decades, in technology may be responsible for the decline of the Christmas cards received by American households drop from twenty nine in 1987 to twenty in 2004. Email and telephone allow for more frequent contact and are easier for generations raised without hand written letters- especially given the availability of websites offering e-mail Christmas cards. Despite the decline, 1.9 billion cards were sent in the U.S. in 2005 alone. Now some manufacturers provide E-cards. In the U.K. Christmas cards account for half of the volume of greeting cards sales, with over 668.9 million Christmas cards sold in 2008's festive period.

Official Christmas cards started with 'Queen Victoria' in the 1840's the British Royal Family cards are usually portraits reflecting significant personal event of the year. There is a long-standing custom for the President and the First Lady to send White House Christmas cards each holiday season. The practice originated with President Calvin Coolidge, who was the first President to issue a written statement of peaceful tidings during the holidays in 1927.

President Herbert Hoover was the first President to give Christmas notes to White House staff, and President Delanor Roosevelt was the First President to utilize the card format (rather than previously used notes or written statements) that most closely resembles the cards of today.

From the beginning, Christmas cards have been avidly collected. Queen Mary amassed a large collection that is now housed in the British Museum Slades School of Fine Arts in London houses a collection of hand made Christmas cards from Alumni; and are displayed at events over the Christmas season, when members of the public can make their Christmas cards in the strong print room.

Cards from the golden age of printing (1840-1890)'s are especially prized and bring in large sums at auctions. In December 2005, one of Hersley's original cards sold for nearly $9,000. Collectors may focus on particular images, like Santa Claus, poets, or printing techniques. The Christmas cards that holds the world's records, as the most expensive ever sold was a card produced in 1843 by I.C. Horsley and commissioned by Civil Servant Sir Henry Cole. The card, One of the worlds first, was sold in 2001 by U.K. auctioneers Henry Aldridge, to an anonymous bidder for a record breaking $22,250.

Wyatt Dreyer age 6

Home-made Cards

Since the 19th century, many families and individuals have chosen to make their own Christmas cards, ether in response to monetary necessity, as an artistic endeavor, or in order to avoid the commercialism associated with Christmas Cards. With a higher preference of hand-made gifts during the 19th century over purchased or commercial items, home-made cards carry a highly sentimental value as gifts alone. A revival of interest in paper craft, particularly scrap-booking, has raised the status of the home-made card and made available an array of tools for stamping, punching and cutting.

Advances in digital photography and printing have provided, the technology for many people to design and print their own cards, using their original graphic design or photos, or those that have the computer programs or on line as clip art.

Recent concern over the environmental impact of printing, mailing and delivering cards has fueled an increase in e-cards.

CHRISTMAS STAMPS

Many countries produced official Christmas stamps, which may be brightly colored and depict some aspect of Christmas tradition or a nativity scene Mail used to be a free enterprise; the delivery was paid for by the recipient, but in 1837, an English Schoolmaster named Rawland Hill noticed that the post office lost out to much by recipients refusing delivery. He preposed pre-paid stamps in a pamphlet called 'Post Office Reform'.

THE FIRST CHRISTMAS STAMP

Canada issued a stamp with the Mercator Map Christmas "1898" inscribed.

Post offices in England and the Netherlands also issued stamps with Christmas-related thyme's. In the US, post card artist Ellen H. Clapsaddle' designed Christmas designs and Christmas thyme's for stamps. However, none were special Christmas issues. The first post stamp for Christmas was issued in 1937 in Austria: The rose and signs of the zodiac.

The first U.S. Christmas stamp was launched in 1962. This year the post office will print more than 4 billion Christmas postage stamps. They can even be bought at some ATM's, using a bank card, grocery or bank.

CHAPTER

This and That: Did You Know?

Christmas Symbols

* Evergreen Tree: Titus 1:2

Eternal Life

* Star Light: Matthew 2:9-10

Stars that told of Christ's birth

* Candy Cane: Luke 2:8-9

Staff of Shepherds who visited the Christ Child / Christ is the 'Good Shepard'

* Bells: John 10:16

Ring out to bring lost sheep back to the fold

* Holly & Berries: Titus 1:2, Luke 22:44

Green - Eternal Life Red - Blood of Christ

* Gift: Matthew 2:1, 11 John 3:16

The wise man's gifts to the Christ Child God's greatest gift to us, is the Savior

THE INNKEEPER'S KEY

This is the Christmas season, we hope you remember the real reason for the season! The symbol of the key, is to remind us: "That we, each of us is an innkeeper who decides if there is room for Jesus!"
By: Neal A Maxwell

(Find a skeleton key and place it on your key-ring to remind yourself, that you are the innkeeper and it is up to you to make room for Jesus)

MERRY CHRISTMAS IN DIFFERENT LANGUAGES

'Geseende Kersfees' (Afrikaans)

'Milad Majid' (Arabic)

'Feliz Navidad' (Argentine)

'Tchestita Koleda; Tchestito Rojdestvo Kristova' (Brazilian)

'Feliz Natal' (Brazilian)

'Gun Tso Sun Fan' Gung Haw Sun' (Cantonese - Chinese)

'Kung His Hsin Nien Bing Chu Shen Tan' (Mandarin - Chinese)

'Feliz Navidad y Prospero Ano Nuevo' (Columbia)

'Sretan Bozic' (Croation)

'Prejeme Vesele Vanoce a Stastny Novy Rok' (Czech)

'Vrolijk Kerstfeest eneen Gelukkig Nieuwjoor or Zaalig Kerstfeast (Dutch)

'juidlime pivdluarit Ukioriame Pivdluaritlo!' (Eskimo - Inupik)

'Melkin Yelidet Beaal' (Ethiopian : Amharic)

'Hyvaa joulua' (Finnish)

'Joyeux Noel' (French)

'Bo Nada' (Galician)

'Frohliche Weihnachien' (German)

'Kala Christouyenna!' Greek)

'Mele Kalikimaka' (Hawaiian)

'Mo' Adin Lesim Kha, Chena-tora' (Hebrew)

'Kelemes Karacsony; Unnepeket' (Hungarian)

'GLedileg Jol' (Icelandic)

'Salamat Hari Natel' (Indonesian)

'Nollaig Shona Dhuit or Nodliag Mhaith chunggnat' (Irish)

'Buone Feste Natalize' (Italian)

'Shinnen Onedeto Kurisumasu Omedeto' (Japanese)

'Sung Tan Chuk Ha' (Korean)

'Natale Hilare et Annum Faustum!' (Latin)

'Linksmu Kaledu' (Lithuanian)

'I L - Milied It - Tajjeb' (Maltese)

'God Iul, or Gledelig Iul' (Norwegian)

'Maligayang Pasko' (Philippines)

'Feliz Natal' (Portugeuse)

'PozdrevLyayu S prazdnikom Rozhdestva is Novim Godom' (Russian)

'Feliz Navidad' (Spanish)

'Sawadee Pee Mai' (Thai)

'Srozhdestuom Kristouym' (Ukrainian)

'Chuc Mung Giang sinh' (Vietnamese)

'Nadolig Llawen' (Welsh)

CHRISTMAS - X-MAS

P
X

    Christmas is also known as X-Mas. Some people think it is incorrect to call Christmas, X-Mas as that takes the Christ (Jesus) out of Christmas. (As Christmas comes from Christ-mass, the Church service that celebrated the birth of Christ).

But that is not quite right! In the Greek language and alphabet, the letter that looks like an X is the Greek letter for chi / X (Pronounced 'Kye - it rhymes with eye') Which is the first letter of the Greek word for Christ, Christos.

The early Church used the first two letters of Christos in the Greek alphabet 'chi' and RHO' to create a monogram (symbol) to represent the name of Jesus, this looks like an X with a small p on the top.

So X mas can also mean Christmas; but it should also be pronounced 'Christmas' rather than ex-mas!

Christmas - the name itself means literally, the mass of Christ it is inevitable that most Christmas legends are touched with Holiness.

Matthew 2

THE 12 DAYS OF CHRISTMAS

Today "The Twelve Days Of Christmas" are most known as the famous song about someone receiving lots of presents from their true love.

The original Twelve Days were started on Christmas Day and last until the evening of January 5th also known as the twelfth night. The twelve days have been celebrated in Europe since before the Middle Ages and were a time of celebration.

The twelve days each traditionally celebrate a feast day for a Saint and or have different celebrations.

Day 1 (December 25th): Christmas Day is to celebrate the birth of Jesus.

Day 2 (December 26th): (also known as boxing day): Saint Stephen's Day.

He was the first Christian martyr, It is also the the day the Christmas Carol 'Good King Wenceslas' takes place.

Day 3 (December 27th): Saint John the Apostle (one of Jesus disciples and friends).

Day 4 (December 28th): The feast of the Holy Innocents - When people remember the baby boys which King Herod killed when he was trying to find and kill the baby Jesus.

Day 5 (December 29th): St. Thomas Becket, the Archbishop of Canterbury in the 12th century and was murdered on the 29th of December 1170 for challenging the kings authority over the church.

Day 6 (December 30th): St. Egwin of Worcester.

Day 7 (December 31st): New Years Eve (known as Hogmanay in Scotland). Pope Sylvester was traditionally celebrated on this day.

He was one of the first Popes (in the 4th century) in many central and eastern European country's, New Years Eve is still known as known as 'Sylvester'. In the U.K., New Years Eve was a traditional Day for 'games' and sporting competitions. Archery was a very popular sport and during Middle Ages it was the law that it had to be practiced by all men between ages 17 to 60 on Sunday after Church! This was so the King had lots of very good archers ready in case of war.

Day 8 (January 1st): Celebration of Mary the mother of Jesus.

Day 9 (January 2nd): Saint Basil the Great and Saint Gregory Nazianzen, twoimportant 4th century Christians.

Day 10 (January 3rd): Feast of the Holy Name of Jesus. This reminds us when Jesus was officially "Named" in the Jewish Temple.

It's celebrated by different churches on a wide number of different dates.

Day 11 (January 4th): Originally it was celebration of the feast of Saint Simon Stylizes (who lives on a small platform on top of a pillar for 37 years.)

Day 12 (January 5th): Also known as Epiphany Eve.

Twelfth Night was a big time of celebration with people holding large parties. During these parties often roles were reversed in society with servants being served by the upper class. This dates back to the Medieval and Tudor times when 12th night marked the end of winter, which had started on October 31st. with All Hallows Eve (Halloween.

At the start of the 12th night, the 12th night cake was eaten. This was a rich cake made with eggs, butter, fruit, nuts and spices. The modern Italian Panettone is the cake we currently have that is not most like the 12th night cake.

A dried bean or pea was cooked into the cake. Whoever found it was the Lord or Lady of misrule for the night. The Lord of misrule leads the celebration dressed like a king, (or Queen). This celebration goes back to the Roman celebration of Saturnalia.

In later times, from about the Georgian period onward to make the 12th night, "Gentile", tokens were put into the cake, (one for a man; one for a woman) whoever found them became king or queen for the 12th night party.

In English cathedrals during the Middle Ages, there was a custom of the 'boy bishop' where a boy from the Cathedral or Monetary school was elected as Bishop on the 6th of December (St. Nicholas Day) and had the authority of a Bishop (except to preform Mass) until the 28th of December - King Henry III Banned the practice in 1545 although it came back briefly under Mary I in 1552 but Elizabeth I finally stopped it during her reign.

During 12th night it was traditional for different types of pipes to be played, especially bagpipes. Lots of games were played especially one with eggs. These included tossing an egg in between two people, moving farther and farther apart with each throw, drop it and you lose. Another is passing an egg on a spoon.

The first Monday after Christmas feast was known as "Plough Monday" this was when Farming work began again.

In many parts of the U.K. people also went "wassailing" on the 12th night.

+ During Advent, purple and sometimes blue is used in most Churches for the color of the alter cloth (in the Russian Orthodox Church), red is for Advent.

+ In medieval times blue dye and paint was more expensive that gold so it would only be worn by royalty and very rich people, Mary was often painted wearing blue to show she was very important.

+ White - is associated with purity.

+ Gold - is the color of the sun or light - both very important in the dark winter. Both red and gold are the color of fire that you need to keep you warm. Gold was also one of the gifts brought to the baby Jesus by one of the wise men and traditionally it's the color to show the star that the wise men followed.

+ Silver - is sometimes used instead of (or with) gold. But Gold is a warmer color.

+ Red - An early use of red at Christmas were the apples on the paradise tree, this represents the fall of Adam in the plays. Red is also the color of holly berries, which is said to represent the blood of Jesus when he died on the cross. Red is also the color of the Bishops robes. These would have been worn by Saint Nicholas and then also became Santa's suit.

+ Green - Evergreen plants, like holly, ivy, and mistletoe have been used for thousands of years to decorate and to brighten the home during the dark long winters. They also remind people that spring is coming and that winter would not last forever.

Most of the colors and their meanings come from the Western / Northern European traditions and customs, when Christmas is in the middle of winter, and it is dark and cold.

DID YOU KNOW?

FACT: Turkey was first brought to Europe from the America's around 1520, it's earliest known consumption in England is around 1541 and because it was inexpensive and quick to fatten, it arose in popularity as a Christmas feast food.

The war ended on 1856 but glass tree ornaments did not arrive in the U.S. until 1880 when 'F.W. Woolworth' began importing them from Germany.

In 1847 a few German Glass Blowers were making fruit and nut ornament by glass blowing into molds and soon was exported into Europe as well ans England and the U.S.

The average person in Britain sends 50 Christmas Cards each year.

There are 11 towns called 'Santa Claus' in the United States. Alaska, Arizona, Georgia, Indiana, Minnesota, Nevada, Oregon, and Utah.

there are 50 towns in the United States with 'Noel". Place names including communities named Noel in Colorado, Missouri, and Virginia, you will find Noel Lake in Spencer county, Indiana, near the community of Santa Clause.

The postmen in England were called "Robin's" because of their red uniforms.

The first Christmas stamp was released in Canada in 1898.

In the year 2004, the German Post office gave away 20 million free scented stickers, to make cards smell of fir, Christmas tree, cinnamon, gingerbread, a honey wax candle, a baked apple and an orange.

The custom called MUMMING: In the middle ages people would put on masks and act out Christmas plays. These plays are still preformed in towns and villages today.

Christmas in England began in 596 AD, when St. Augustine landed on her shores with monks who wanted to bring Christianity to the Anglo Saxon.

Boxing Day: Is on December 26th, has nothing to do with boxing as you might think today. This was the day when the family's with servants would box up food and gifts for their servants, tenants, shut-ins, and Pastor's family.

Did you know the 'cracker' was first called "Cosaques" because of the cracking whips,

Who do we have to thank for the Christmas 'crackers'?

Traditionally the credit goes to a London confectioner Tom Smith. In 1847 he was to said to have introduced England to the delight of French Bonbon's and sugared almonds wrapped in paper twisted at the ends. His competitor for the tidal of the idea was also Italian born, 'Sparagnapane', who opened his confection shop in 1846.

Did you know Crackers were used for any holiday or social gathering?

In 1904 Peter Pan was the traditional Christmas play

Did you know, It has been claimed that Jesus was born, not in December but in October. This has been claimed from astrology readings and other historical events.

The Romans would exchange evergreen branches during January as a sign of good luck.

The ancient Egyptians used to bring palm branches into their homes during Mid-winter festivals.

In many parts of Europe during the middle ages, 'Paradise' plays were performed often on Christmas Eve. They told Bible stories to people who couldn't read. The "Paradise Tree" In the garden of the play, there was normally a pine tree with red apples on it.

The most common of green, is the Christmas tree.

Did you know that most people in the Greek Orthodox Church celebrate Christmas on December 25th, but some still use the Julian calendar, and still celebrate Christmas on January 7th.

Santa Claus, Saint Nicholas, St. Nick, Father Christmas, Kris Kringle, Santy or simply Santa. He is a figure of legendary, Historical, folkloric, origins who, many western cultures is said to bring gifts to good girls and boys on the 24th of December, the night before Christmas Day.

The modern figure of Santa clause is derived from the Dutch figure (Sinterklaas) who's name is dialectal pronunciation of Saint Nicholas.

The historical Greek (Bishop) and gift-giver of (Myra).

During the (Christianization) of (Germanic European) this figure may have absorbed elements of the god (Odin) who was associated with the Germanic pagan min-winter event of yule and led the (wild hunt) ghostly procession through the sky.

1934 The song (Santa Clause Is Coming to Town) 20th century - Santa made a list, flying reindeer, categorized children according to behavior, naughty or nice - and deliver presents Christmas Eve - he uses the aid of elves - lives in the North Pole - says Ho, Ho, Ho.

Christmas was outlawed in England by Oliver Cromwell in 1645

Christmas was outlawed in Boston Massachusetts USA, from 1659 - 1681 by the Puritans because they believed Christmas to be Pagen, thus being outlawed.

Christmas was declared a federal Holiday 1870.

Coca-Cola's marketing scheme in 1931 made Christmas the "All American Holiday"

The word wassail comes from the old English 'Waes - hael' meaning to be whole, be well, it's a salutation, especially over the cup (wassail bowl) of mulled wine or ale in yuletide, Christmastide, new years and the twelfth night celebration.

Christmas was known to have been celebrated 800 years before the first carol had even been sung. Many believe the first song was "Silent night, holy night".

In the U.S., the first state to legalize Christmas as a holiday was Alabama in 1836, the last was Oklahoma (Indian territory) in 1890. Most states had done so by 1880.

Many people dread the Christmas season for many reasons. Although the season is stressful, most people don't have actual phobias connected with the holidays. But Christmas is stressful and does seem to aggravate a lot of phobias.

* Ochlophobia or Agoraphobia - Fear of Crowds

* Cherophobia - Fear of Fun

In 1531 the first retail Christmas tree lots are started in German cities.

In 1777, the tradition of the Christmas tree is brought to Colonial America by Hessian troops fighting for the Britain in the Revolutionary War.

1804, U.S. soldiers stationed at Fort Dearborn (now Chicago) bring evergreen trees into their barracks at Christmas.

1842, Charles Minnegrode introduces the custom of a decorated Christmas tree in Williamsburg, Va.

1851, Mark Carr opens a retail Christmas tree lot in New York city, the first in the U.S.

1856, Franklin Pierce, our 14th President, brings the first Christmas Tree into the White House.

1923, President Calvin Coolidge starts the National Christmas Tree lighting ceremony now held on the White House lawn.

Credit / Sources

Billy Graham
Buck Dencur 'What's in the Bible'
Country Roads Magazine 2012
Wikipedia.org
World Book Encyclopedia
santa.net
history.com
logicmgmt.com
christmas carnivals.com
allthingschristmas.com
factmonster.com
merry-christmas.com
historymedren.about.com
Joanne Forester
unlimitedrecipe.com
Better Homes and Gardens
Euro Travelogue
Museum of Science and History
food.com
Thor News
history of christmas.com
Six Sisters
Food Network
Ingrid Hoffman 2008
Kersha@nourishingjoy
Ethel Thackery Swango (1897 - 1993)
Rita Mace Watson
Howard W Hunter
Halloways Legends of Christmas
History today
People.how stuff works.com
American Lamb Council
Marian Schoeberlein - poet
Poet Corner - Chris Zamberhard
Joyce Meyer

Robin Redmon Dreyer

Hallmark
Gibson Cards / Helen Steiner Rice
unlimitedrecipes.com
paradisepraises.com Katie Hornor
Jena Redmon Wall
Carolyn Collins Redmon Carlson
Verginia Redmon Stephen
food.about.com
mrfood.com
irish foodguide.ie
Irish Central
myway.com
Reminisce.com 2014